When is it justifiable to exclude a person who wishes to enter a country? What are the acceptable moral bases for immigration policy? These questions lie at the heart of this book, the first interdisciplinary study of the fundamental normative issues underpinning immigration policy.

A distinguished group of economists, political scientists, and philosophers offer a provocative discussion of this complex topic. Among the issues addressed are the proper role of the state in supporting a particular culture, the possible destabilization of the political and social life of a country through immigration, the size and distribution of economic losses and gains, and the legitimacy of discriminating against potential immigrants in favor of members of the resident population.

The need for serious consideration of this subject is beyond question. This volume should advance discussion in an area of great practical as well as philosophical importance.

JUSTICE IN IMMIGRATION

Cambridge Studies in Philosophy and Law

GENERAL EDITOR: JULES L. COLEMAN (YALE LAW SCHOOL)

ADVISORY BOARD

Anthony Duff (University of Stirling)
Jean Hampton (University of Arizona)
David Lyons (Cornell University)
Neil MacCormick (University of Edinburgh)
Gerald Postema (University of North Carolina at Chapel Hill)
Joseph Raz (University of Oxford)
Jeremy Waldron (University of California)

This exciting new series reflects and fosters the most original research taking place in the study of law and legal theory by publishing the most adventurous monographs in the field as well as collections of essays. It is a specific aim of the series to traverse the boundaries between disciplines and to form bridges between traditional studies of law and many other areas of the human sciences. Books in the series will be of interest not only to philosophers and legal theorists but also to political scientists, sociologists, economists, psychologists, and criminologists.

Other books in the series

Jeffrie G. Murphy and Jean Hampton: *Forgiveness and mercy*
Stephen R. Munzer: *A theory of property*
R. G. Frey and Christopher W. Morris (eds.): *Liability and responsibility: Essays in law and morals*
Robert F. Schopp: *Automatism, insanity, and the psychology of criminal responsibility*
Steven J. Burton: *Judging in good faith*
Jules L. Coleman: *Risks and wrong*
Suzanne Uniacke: *Permissible killing: The self-defense justification of homicide*
Jules L. Coleman and Allen Buchanan (eds.): *In harm's way: Essays in honor of Joel Feinberg*

Justice
in immigration

Edited by
WARREN F. SCHWARTZ
Georgetown University Law Center

CAMBRIDGE
UNIVERSITY PRESS

Published by the Press Syndicate of the University of Cambridge
The Pitt Building, Trumpington Street, Cambridge CB2 1RP
40 West 20th Street, New York, NY 10011-4211, USA
10 Stamford Road, Oakleigh, Melbourne 3166, Australia

First published 1995

Printed in the United States of America

Library of Congress Cataloging-in-Publication Data
Justice in immigration / edited by Warren F. Schwartz.
p.   cm. – (Cambridge studies in philosophy and law)
ISBN 0-521-45288-0 (hardcover)
1. Emigration and immigration law – Philosophy.   2. Emigration and
immigration – Government policy.   I. Schwartz, Warren F.
II. Series.
K3275.Z9J87   1995
325'.01 – dc20   94–38247
CIP

A catalog record for this book is available from the British Library.

ISBN 0-521-45288-0 Hardback

The essays collected in this volume were presented at a conference
sponsored by the John M. Olin Program in Law and Economics of the
Georgetown University Law Center.

Contents

Contributors

JAMES M. BUCHANAN, Center for the Study of Public Choice, George Mason University

JOSEPH H. CARENS, Department of Political Science, University of Toronto

JULES L. COLEMAN, Yale Law School

GILLIAN K. HADFIELD, University of California at Berkeley Law School

JEAN HAMPTON, Department of Philosophy, University of Arizona

SARAH K. HARDING, Yale Law School

STEPHEN R. PERRY, Faculty of Law, McGill University

LOUIS MICHAEL SEIDMAN, Georgetown University Law Center

ALAN O. SYKES, University of Chicago Law School

MICHAEL J. TREBILCOCK, Faculty of Law, University of Toronto

MARK TUSHNET, Georgetown University Law Center

SUSAN B. VROMAN, Department of Economics, Georgetown University

1

Immigration, welfare, and justice

JOSEPH H. CARENS

Migration is not a new phenomenon in world history, but it has never been so extensive as it is today. Modern technologies of communication make it possible for more people than ever before to imagine living in other societies, even distant societies. Modern technologies of transportation make movement much easier; indeed, it is technically possible to get anywhere in the world in a matter of days, if not hours. And for various reasons, people are on the move. As Michael Trebilcock points out in his essay (Chapter 11), more than 100 million people live outside the states in which they hold citizenship, 18 million of them refugees. More would move if they could.

These developments take on a particular urgency for the affluent liberal democratic states of the West, since resistance to immigration seems to be growing in all of them. In traditional countries of immigration like the United States and Canada, people express anxiety about losing control of the borders and anti-immigrant rhetoric is expressed in mainstream political parties.

In Europe, the situation is even more acute. Millions of people have settled in states other than their countries of origin. Despite the fact that no European country recruits immigrants any longer, more continue to arrive: as spouses and children of those already settled, as refugee claimants, or as entrants without formal authorization. The backlash against immigrants is much greater in Europe than in North America. The United Kingdom, France, and Germany have all seen both violent attacks on immigrants and the rise of political forces that make opposition to immigrants the central focus of their rhetoric and policy proposals.

At the same time, the European Community has established a right of free movement within Europe for citizens of the member states, thus dramatically illustrating that states can open their borders without abandoning most of their claims to sovereignty. The European policy draws attention to the economic advantages of the free movement of labor, at least under some circumstances, and raises questions about the claim that preservation of *national* culture is the primary motivation for restrictive immigration policies in European countries.

While many immigrants manage to enter Western states, many more would like to come. What stops them, in no small measure, is force. Borders keep people out, ultimately because people with guns are prepared to enforce the boundaries. Are they right to do so?

I. The issues

The answer to that question depends on a number of factors. We have to consider different categories of potential immigrants, different reasons for admitting or excluding them, and different ways of admitting them. These things tend to be interconnected. One way to disaggregate the issues is to consider them under the following three headings: special claims, culture, and economics. I will try to identify some of the problems and questions that emerge under each of these headings.

A. Special claims: refugees and families

Refugees would appear to have especially strong claims to admission. In the extreme case, they are literally fleeing for their lives. In the face of such need, are we entitled even to ask whether admitting them will be good for us economically or culturally or in any other way, assuming that we are not literally overwhelmed? Yet who counts as a refugee? In deciding this, is the degree of need or the nature of the threat most crucial? The Geneva Convention defines a refugee as a person who, "owing to a well-founded fear of persecution for reasons of race, religion, nationality, membership in a particular social group or political opinion, is outside the country of his nationality and is unable or, owing to such a fear, is unwilling to avail himself of the protection of that country."[1] The definition and related practices of states draw a sharp distinction between political persecution and other threats to human well-being, privileging the former as grounds for admission to a state of which one is not a member. Yet some forms of economic or social dislocation (like famine or the breakdown of civil order) may generate more desperate needs than certain forms of persecution. Should we defend or criticize the conventional definition?

However refugees are defined, what are the responsibilities of different states for admitting them? Do these responsibilities vary according to political, economic, or cultural circumstances and, if so, how? These questions point, in part, to the issues discussed later under the headings of culture and economics.

Do states like the United States and Canada that have traditionally taken in large numbers of immigrants and thus have considerable experience with the social incorporation of people from diverse cultural backgrounds have an obligation to admit more refugees (proportionally) than a state like Japan, which has a long tradition of insularity and a very high degree of cultural homogeneity?

The problem of refugees raises questions not only about responsibilities for admission but also about responsibilities for financial support. Most refugees arrive first in a neighboring state, and since most come from the Third World, most of the states to which they flee are poor. If the refugees have any reasonable prospect of eventually returning home, it often makes sense for them to stay close to their home states and in social circumstances that are likely to be far less alien than they would be in a distant country. Yet it hardly seems fair that the states that take in the refugees should have to bear all or even most of the costs of maintaining them. They are not the cause of the refugees' plight (in most cases) and their own resources are extremely limited. How should the financial burden of caring for refugees be distributed?

However one defines fair shares with respect to admission and financial burdens, there is the further question of whether trade-offs between the two are morally permissible. Is it morally permissible for a state like Japan, seeking to preserve its homogeneous culture, to provide more financial assistance and take in fewer refugees than an initial distribution of fair shares would require?

Whether or not trade-offs are permitted, the question of our moral responsibilities for refugees will not end with the initial allocation of fair shares, because some states will not fulfill their responsibilities for admission or financial assistance or both. When they do not, should the responsible states admit more or pay more? To answer yes seems to create perverse incentives, rewarding responsibility with new burdens. To answer no seems to ignore the plight of the refugees who need a safe place as well as support. In addition, the claim that we have any responsibilities for refugees presupposes that the failures of other states (the refugee-producing ones) can create new responsibilities for us.

How should we deal with the practical problem of determining who is a refugee, whatever criteria are adopted? If immigration is otherwise highly restricted, many who do not fit the criteria are likely to claim that they do. Asylum claimants (people who arrive in a state and then assert that they are refugees) constitute the fastest-growing group of immigrants not only in Europe, where states leave few doors open otherwise, but also in North America, where immigration levels remain substantial. All Western states have adopted strategies of "humane deterrence" designed to discourage asylum claimants, strategies that inevitably keep out people with well-founded claims as well as ones with weaker cases. Are such strategies morally appropriate?

Is there any category of people besides refugees (however defined) with a distinctive and compelling moral claim to admission? People with family ties to current members might constitute such a group. It is striking that even Germany, which formally declares itself not to be a country of immigration, has felt obliged to admit immediate family members (spouses and minor children) of people residing in Germany, even when these residents are not themselves citizens and were initially admitted as temporary guest workers. Indeed, Germany has granted resident status of some sort to more (nonrefugee) aliens since the termination of its guest-worker program than it did while the program was in effect, primarily because of the principle of family reunification.

Countries of immigration like the United States and Canada place even more weight on family reunification, extending the principle to more distant family members. In both countries, immigrants with family ties to existing citizens or residents make up well more than half of the nonrefugee immigrant intake.

Should family connections play such an important role in immigration policy? Is it morally permissible for different states to place different weights on family ties in deciding whom to admit and whom to exclude? If so, what is the range of permissible variation and on what grounds may states decide? How does giving priority to family ties affect the economic well-being or cultural identity of the population in the receiving country? Is it appropriate to take such effects into account?

These last two questions lead to the two most contested issues: the proper role of economics and culture in immigration policy.

B. Culture

What should be the connection, if any, between culture and immigration? May a state decide not to admit immigrants at all (apart, perhaps, from refugees and immediate relatives of current members) for the sake of preserving existing cultural patterns as much as possible?

If a state decides to admit immigrants, may it take culture into account in the selection process, either with the goal of maintaining the cultural community (or communities) or with the aim of increasing the likelihood of successful mutual adaptation between immigrants and the existing population? If culture may be considered a factor in selection, may it be used affirmatively, to include some potential immigrants rather than others on grounds of cultural affinity, or negatively, to exclude some potential immigrants on grounds of cultural difference, or both? If culture may be used as a legitimate criterion, on what basis may cultural commitments be attributed to potential immigrants? Are some factors morally problematic as cultural markers? What about race, ethnicity, religion, national origin, language?

These are not just hypothetical questions. The United States, Canada, Australia, Israel, Germany, Japan, and many other states have used these factors in the past or are using them today in deciding whom to admit and whom to exclude. Were they and are they right or wrong in doing so? Or sometimes right and sometimes wrong?

Are all states morally required to follow the same course with respect to the connection between culture and immigration? States vary widely with respect to the cultural homogeneity of their populations and with respect to patterns of cultural difference. Some states, like Germany and Sweden, have populations that are relatively homogeneous in terms of culture. Others, like Belgium and Switzerland, contain long-standing cultural divisions that may (or may not) be related to language, territory, religion, or other factors. Still others, like the United States, have a history of receiving new members from diverse cultural backgrounds. Canada has both long-standing internal cultural divisions and a history of receiving immigrants from diverse cultural backgrounds. Are such differences relevant to the question of what immigration policy a state should adopt?

Questions about the relationship between culture and immigration are not limited to issues about numbers and criteria of selection. There is the further question of what sorts of cultural adaptation, if any, may legitimately be expected of immigrants who have managed to gain entry, either as a formal condition affecting legal status, including access to citizenship, or as an informal norm affecting social integration. To what extent and in what ways may states legitimately expect immigrants (and their children) to conform to the dominant culture of the society they have entered? To what extent and in what ways may immigrants expect the states they have entered to respect their preexisting cultural identities and commitments, as well as their responsibility to pass on these identities and commitments to their children? Again, rules and practices vary widely from one state to another, with respect to both the formal requirements for citizenship and the norms about cultural conformity. What is the range of morally acceptable variation?

These questions about the relationship between culture and immigration ultimately drive us to deeper questions about the character of culture as a human good and its relationship with other human goods, about the nature and purpose of the state, and about alternative conceptions of citizenship and membership. Liberal democratic states are committed to individual freedom and autonomy and thus to the pluralism that inevitably follows from individuals' right to pursue their own conceptions of the good within broad limits.

What does this entail with respect to a liberal state's stance toward culture? May liberal democratic states pay attention to culture at all? If so, how and under what circumstances?

Different theorists have offered different responses to these questions. Rawls and Dworkin have argued that the commitment to individual autonomy requires liberal states to be neutral with respect to different conceptions of the human good and hence with respect to different cultures.[2] Habermas has emphasized that liberal democratic institutions themselves depend upon and presuppose certain cultural commitments. At the same time, Habermas has argued that the political culture of liberalism, which a liberal democratic state may legitimately protect and reproduce, can and should be sharply distinguished from any particular historical culture.[3] By contrast, Kymlicka has argued that particular historical cultures provide the framework of choice that makes individual autonomy possible, so that if a community's culture is threatened it may be legitimate for the state to try to protect it. Kymlicka insists, however, that we should not assume an identification between the cultural community and the political community, that most modern states are culturally plural societies, that the endangered cultures are normally minority cultures, and that whatever steps are taken to preserve a particular culture must be compatible with liberalism's deep commitment to human equality.[4] Finally, Walzer has contended that the production of a rich, complex, highly particularistic culture is an integral part and inevitable outcome of the project of collective self-determination that lies at the heart of the ideal of a liberal democratic state, so that the protection and promotion of its own specific historical culture is a legitimate aspiration for such a state.[5]

These different positions seem likely to have different implications for the use of cultural criteria in immigration policy, though the implications are not all obvious and may be contested.

C. Economics

Even if one takes the position that a concern for culture should be irrelevant to immigration policy, it does not follow that states should impose no limits on immigration. In traditional countries of immigration like the United States and Canada, debate over immigration policy often focuses on its economic effects.

The conventional assumption in such debates is that states are entitled to adopt whatever immigration policy they judge to be in their economic interest (within the constraints imposed by the claims of family members and refugees). On this view, if immigration increases unemployment or drives down wages or increases the tax burden associated with social entitlement programs, states may decide to reduce or even altogether prohibit discretionary immigration (i.e., immigration of persons other than refugees and family members). By contrast, if immigration proves economically advantageous, say by increasing the national income or reducing the average tax burden, then that is generally taken to be a reason for accepting immigrants.

Even within the conventional assumption that immigration policy should be guided by the economic interests of those in the receiving country, there may be dispute over the weight to put on different interests. Immigration may create economic benefits for some current members and economic harms for others. Should we look only at the overall economic effect of immigration, or should we also consider its effects on particular subgroups or on the pattern of income distribution?

Should we focus only on the direct economic effects of immigration, or should we also try to take into account its indirect effects on policy and institutions through the participation of immigrants in politics and social life? Here the debate over the relevance of culture may reenter through the backdoor of economics. For example, if political support for social entitlement programs depends partly on feelings of identity and social solidarity that may erode with the arrival of a substantial number of people from diverse cultural origins, is that a legitimate argument for restricting immigration? How should we factor in the (inevitably) high degree of uncertainty about any such indirect effects?

Questions about selection criteria and the terms of admission and incorporation that were raised in the discussion of culture also come to the fore when the focus is on economics. Should we select immigrants on the basis of what they can contribute economically (e.g., on the basis of their education, skills, or nonhuman capital)? Should we let employers rather than government officials decide which immigrants are most likely to make a productive contribution?

What terms of admission should we impose? Every Western state provides long-term resident aliens with roughly the same range of social entitlements as citizens. (The principal exceptions are the right to vote and access to certain public jobs.) What conceptions of citizenship and membership underly this pattern? Workers present on temporary visas often do not enjoy the same sorts of entitlements (even though they are usually obliged to pay the taxes that fund these programs). Is the fact that this is a more beneficial economic arrangement from the perspective of the domestic population a sufficient argument for increasing the number of those admitted on a temporary rather than a permanent basis? Of course, the temporary workers will not come unless they find it advantageous to do so, but might there be something morally objectionable about the arrangement despite its (apparently) voluntary character? Does it respect the moral claims that the workers establish by living and working in a society? The answer to that may depend in part on how the program is organized, but it is useful to recall that European states like Germany that created guest-worker programs could not bring themselves to send the workers home when economic conditions changed.

Even if the receiving states are willing to send temporary workers home, they may not be willing to go. Overstaying a temporary work permit is only one of the many ways that people remain in a country without the formal authorization of public officials. Some call such people ''illegal immigrants,'' emphasizing that they have stayed (or come) in violation of the laws governing immigration. Others call them ''undocumented aliens'' or perhaps ''undocumented workers'' to emphasize that they lack certain papers, certain formal permissions.

Whatever we call them, what do we think of their situation from a moral perspective? Should we regard their presence as a problem at all? They come (normally) not to rob or steal or kill but to work hard in order to make better lives for themselves and their families. On the other hand, they have bypassed the immigration queue in which others are waiting patiently (if there is such a queue in a given country). Does it strengthen their moral claim to stay if the authorities make little effort to find and expel them or to otherwise prevent them from working (e.g., through severe and strictly enforced employer sanctions)? Do their moral claims to stay grow stronger over time (independent of the behavior of the authorities), simply by virtue of their living and working in the society? What about the claims of their children who are being raised within the society and who are not personally responsible for their presence?

The past few paragraphs draw attention to the potential moral claims of immigrants or potential immigrants and may lead us to reexamine the assumption with which we started this section. Should we accept or criticize the conventional assumption that immigration policy should be based upon the economic interests of current members? How should the effects of immigration policy on immigrants themselves and on their countries of origin be taken into account, if at all? Whose interests count in the moral calculus? For example, if immigration greatly benefits the immigrants themselves while leaving those already in the receiving country largely unchanged, or perhaps slightly better or worse off, should that be an important consideration in immigration policy?

These questions inevitably link the issue of immigration to the problem of international distributive justice and to questions about the moral status of states as institutions for advancing the interests of particular populations. States exclude potential immigrants because current members, or at least enough politically effective current members, fear that immigration will have a negative impact on existing economic, cultural, political, and social arrangements. But are restrictions for such reasons a legitimate way of protecting the interests and identities of current members or an illegitimate way of maintaining privilege and parochialism? Or sometimes one and sometimes the other?

Does a commitment to the moral equality of all human beings require us to open our borders to all those whose needs and aspirations would lead them to come? Why shouldn't people be free to travel and settle wherever they want as long as they are peaceful and law-abiding?

Yet one might ask whether the appeal of open borders is an illusion, an epiphenomenal by-product of much deeper forms of injustice and inequality that are not caused by closed borders and would not be cured by opening them. Perhaps trade or aid or intervention would be a more efficient way to improve the conditions of people who will be tempted to migrate if their lot remains unchanged. If so, can such policies be defended as morally legitimate alternatives to the admission of immigrants? How open should states be? What moral room is there for variation in policies among different states, especially liberal democratic states?

As this long introductory interrogatory reveals, to address the topic of immigration we must ultimately reflect upon some of the most fundamental questions of moral and political theory. To what extent and in what ways is it morally legitimate for us to pursue our own interests, and to what extent and in what ways ought we to be concerned with the interests of others? What is the moral status of states in the modern world? What are the legitimate purposes and functions of a state, especially a liberal democratic state? How should we think about membership in a liberal democratic political community? What are the duties of members to one another, and what are their duties to nonmembers, especially to people seeking to join the community? Finally, what is the range of legitimate variation among liberal democratic states with respect to all of these questions?

These are the concerns addressed by the essays in this volume. The discussions overlap, converge, and diverge in many ways, and there are many points of agreement and disagreement. The overall effect of the volume is to provide an extended conversation about immigration viewed from a normative perspective. In the rest of this introduction, I want to provide a framework for listening to that conversation by drawing attention to some differences among the normative discourses employed in the essays and noting key points of agreement and disagreement.

II. The discourses of justice and welfare

The many different arguments advanced in the essays are based in part on different kinds of normative discourse. I do not seek to advocate one kind of normative discourse over another; rather I wish to clarify the ways in which different arguments do or do not meet each other, so that it will be easier to see when differences reflect genuine disagreements and when they reflect different foci of concern.

Some of the essays focus on the question of what justice requires or permits with respect to immigration, while others, particularly those most informed by welfare economics, are concerned primarily with what immigration policy would be best or with what reasons exist for preferring one immigration policy to another. While justice and welfare are both normative considerations, there is an important difference between them, at least in the ways they are discussed here.

The language of justice is the language of ultimate moral judgement, of right and wrong. Justice establishes the morally legitimate parameters of public policy in three ways. It requires some actions, it prohibits others, and it establishes the moral permissibility of actions that are neither required nor prohibited.[6]

The language of welfare might be described as wider-ranging than the language of justice. On the one hand, it can be intimately linked with justice, as in theories that assert that justice requires the maximization of welfare (overall or on average), or the maximization of the welfare of the least well off,[7] or even the provision of some minimum level of welfare to all. On the other hand, the language of welfare can be used in a way that suggests it is only one among other normative considerations to be taken into account in assessing the desirability of alternative policies. Describing a policy as suboptimal from the perspective of economic efficiency does not convey quite the same normative urgency about the need for change as does describing it as unjust. Indeed, if an argument treats welfare as one among other relevant normative considerations, it implicitly presupposes that the range of policy options under consideration is morally permissible from the perspective of justice.

To adapt the language of some contemporary moral discussions, we might say that the right (justice) establishes the framework within which we may consider competing conceptions of the good (of which welfare is one dimension). For welfare (in the second sense) to play a normative role in the assessment of immigration policy, then, we have to assume that liberal democratic principles of justice do not settle every question with respect to immigration policy but rather establish constraints that mark out the range of morally acceptable policies. Then welfare considerations can play an important role in helping us to choose among morally acceptable policies.

Five of the essays in this volume explicitly rely primarily upon the language of justice in their assessments of immigration. Jules Coleman and Sarah Harding (Chapter 2) begin with an extended survey of contemporary practices with respect to immigration in several Western liberal democratic states and then focus on the question of what conception of justice would best defend those practices. This leads them to the question of the underlying legitimacy of states and borders. They consider the possibility of justifying states as "first approximations of optimal units for allocating and producing the world's resources" and state that, from this starting point, immigration policies can be assessed "from the point of view of whether or not they contribute to a maximal production and fair distribution of the world's resources among the world's citizens." While they find this approach illuminating in some respects, they ultimately regard it as "deeply unsatisfying" from the perspective of justice, and instead they explore the possibility of justifying current immigration policies as a way of ensuring a just distribution of the good of membership in a political community. They note that membership in a cultural community is a fundamental good for humans and that, in some states like Germany, there is a deep connection between political membership and cultural membership. They conclude that states have wide latitude to admit or exclude on the basis of collective understanding of membership, except in the case of refugees and close family members.

Jean Hampton (Chapter 4) agrees with Coleman and Harding that differences in immigration policies often reflect different types of understanding of what it means to be a member of a political community, and she proposes to assess these types of understanding from the perspective of justice. Hampton constructs an ideal-typical distinction between two types of understanding of membership: consensual and nonconsensual. She argues that nonconsensual conceptions of membership, like those of Germany and Japan, that link citizenship closely to race or ethnicity are incompatible with liberal democratic principles and hence are morally impermissible. Nonconsensual conceptions of citizenship that focus on culture rather than race or ethnicity may occasionally be defensible, she says, but only rarely and under circumstances that are not met by most contemporary states with highly restrictive citizenship and immigration policies. Ultimately Hampton uses her discussion of immigration to call into question the fundamental legitimacy of the nation-state as an ideal of political organization.

Stephen Perry (Chapter 5) explores a wide variety of questions related to immigration from the perspective of a liberal theory of justice. He argues that liberal states have much more extensive obligations to admit outsiders than are commonly recognized in practice, particularly with respect to refugees, a category that in his view should be defined much more broadly. Our obligations to potential immigrants are part of a wider set of international obligations to which we are bound by universal principles of distributive justice. Nevertheless, he insists, an adequate theory of justice will include not only universal rights and obligations but also "localized rights and obligations that apply only within particular political communities (for our purposes), states." These "robust" local rights and obligations arise out of individual and collective rights to self-determination and entail the conclusion that justice permits states significant discretion with respect to the number of immigrants they admit. This discretion does not normally extend, however, to the exclusion or selection of immigrants on cultural grounds. The very limited legitimate concerns liberal states may have with respect to the effects of immigration on culture can be met, according to Perry, by policies of gradualism and diversification of the origins of immigrants, so that discrimination and preferences are generally impermissible from a moral point of view.

Louis Michael Seidman (Chapter 6) agrees with Perry that we have both universal obligations to all human beings and special obligations to those with whom we share a particular community. Unlike Perry, he believes that there is a fundamental tension between these two concerns, which can never be entirely resolved in a theory of justice. Nevertheless, he thinks it evident that in practice we overemphasize our local attachments and underemphasize the responsibilities that justice imposes on us with respect to more distant others. We cannot directly overcome this tendency because it has deep psychological and cultural roots, so we should try instead to work around it. The key is to bring more people inside our circle of caring, which seems to be defined partly by state borders. Yet a policy of admitting more immigrants is not feasible precisely because potential immigrants are seen as outsiders, and so concern for them conflicts with our deep tendency toward an exaggerated form of bounded caring. Thus justice requires a strategy of indirection, not liberalization of immigration laws but lax enforcement of them, because once inside our borders, even illegal immigrants are able to make effective moral demands.

Mark Tushnet (Chapter 7) provides a sharp critique of Coleman and Harding's attempts to find a conception of justice compatible with current immigration policies because he regards those policies as deeply flawed from a moral point of view. Tushnet argues that from a principled liberal perspective, almost all restrictions on immigration are unjust, though he thinks that this is derivative from, and a subordinate part of, the general problem of eliminating unjust regimes and achieving international distributive justice. He argues further that no deep moral significance should be attached to existing state boundaries or to existing cultural patterns within those boundaries and that liberal states ought to be open in principle to the kinds of cultural transformations that immigrants bring.

All five of these essays thus have a common focus on the requirements of liberal democratic justice, even while disagreeing on what those requirements are. One important point of agreement among the five is that in addressing questions about the justice of immigration policy, the moral claims of outsiders must be taken seriously. In other words, all agree that we cannot simply assume the legitimacy of exclusion or assume that only current members matter morally. In effect, each essay proceeds from the assumption that all human beings should be regarded as free moral agents, worthy of equal respect, and each reaches its own conclusion about what justice permits with respect to immigration from that shared perspective.

Four of the five essays focus primarily on the task of identifying the constraints established by justice on the range of morally permissible immigration policies and not on the task of identifying the best policy among those that are morally permissible. Three of these essays – those by Coleman and Harding, Perry, and Hampton – explicitly assume that there is a significant range of morally acceptable policies. Tushnet's position on the moral permissibility of variation in immigration policy is less clear, but he explicitly endorses the general assumption ''that a range of modes of political organization can satisfy the requirements of justice in politics.'' In contrast to the other four, Seidman's essay focuses on the question of what immigration policy would be best, but best only in the sense that it would be the least unjust of politically feasible policies.

Three of the essays primarily employ the language of welfare rather than that of justice, and they do so in a way which implies that they regard it as a possibly relevant normative consideration rather than a decisive one. This suggests that they are concerned primarily with the problem of identifying the best policy among those that are morally acceptable. Thus Alan Sykes (Chapter 8) says that his analysis of the economic efficiency of immigration carries normative weight provided only that one ''assume[s] that aggregate wealth is of some interest in policy making, possibly among quite a number of other things,'' though he offers some additional reasons for supposing that it may be more important than this minimalist assumption requires. Gillian Hadfield's essay (Chapter 9) is primarily critical. Hadfield doubts the normative relevance of welfare as conventionally discussed in welfare economics, at least with respect to immigration policy. She also notes in passing that ''as a matter of practice, if not theory, empirical applications of welfare economics tend to exclude any goods that are not traded in conventional markets,'' an observation that remains relevant to the limited normativity of welfare as discussed in economics, even if her more radical critique is not accepted. Finally, Susan Vroman (Chapter 10) insists that the actual effects of immigration on income distribution are normatively relevant and not captured by the conventional criteria of welfare economics.

One crucial issue that sharply divides those who employ the language of welfare in this volume is the question of whose welfare counts. Sykes insists that he need not address the question directly, that his analysis ''simply addresses the welfare of three groups – migrants, original residents of the country of immigration, and those individuals left behind in the country of emigration. It discusses the welfare consequences of immigration from both the 'global' perspective (aggregating all three groups) and the 'national' perspective (focusing only on nonmigrants in each country)." Sykes accepts as a constraint on any conclusion about increases in welfare that there should be no systematic redistribution from the poor to the rich – presumably a constraint that applies within each of the three perspectives – but he denies that the constraint requires compensation to the particular losers or a legitimate political decision not to compensate.

Sykes argues that immigration is generally efficient from both global and national perspectives, though the picture is somewhat less clear at the national level. The major exception to this overall positive assessment of immigration is that migration motivated by differences in entitlement programs is inefficient, again from both global and national perspectives. Sykes favors specific changes in U.S. policy. He argues that the United States would gain in the aggregate from admitting more permanent immigrants, especially those with employer sponsors or with strong educational backgrounds, and would gain even more from admitting more temporary workers.

Hadfield regards Sykes's basic approach as unsatisfactory. While acknowledging that one can engage in a positive form of welfare analysis that presupposes the definition of the set whose welfare is under consideration, she insists that normative welfare economics requires a justification for its starting point and that the only starting point that does not presuppose the answer to disputed ethical questions is the assumption of a global social welfare function. In that sense, the welfare of everyone should be considered, but she notes that this does not require the welfare of everyone to count equally, since any social welfare function may give more weight to the welfare of some than of others. She goes on to argue that the absence of global political mechanisms for giving binding content to such a global social welfare function means that the conventional assumptions of welfare economics about the legitimacy of social welfare functions in the domestic context do not apply in the global context and the use of conventional criteria of economic efficiency to measure welfare is thus rendered deeply problematic.

Vroman focuses neither on global welfare nor on national welfare but on the welfare of a subset of the national population: workers who might lose their jobs or whose wages might decline as a result of competition from immigrants. She argues that the U.S. political system is unlikely to compensate them for their losses, even if the aggregate gains are sufficient in theory to provide such compensation. Thus she implicitly rejects Hadfield's assumption about the normative legitimacy of tax and transfer policies in the domestic context and explicitly rejects Sykes's assertion of the normative irrelevance of compensation to actual losers.

Again, the contrast between the discourse of justice and the discourse of welfare may be illuminating here. Vroman makes no strong claim that an immigration policy that affects blue-collar workers negatively is unjust. She might have constructed such an argument, for example, by invoking Rawls's difference principle, with its requirement that policies be to the advantage of the least well off, along with the assumption that a domestic rather than a global view of the original position is appropriate. Instead, Vroman treats the economic concerns of workers as a legitimate interest that they are entitled to try to protect through advocacy of more restrictive immigration policies.

The remaining two essays treat both justice and welfare as relevant normative considerations. James Buchanan (Chapter 3) does this implicitly and sequentially. There are two stages to Buchanan's argument. In the first, he constructs an abstract model of two countries with historically equal endowments but different rates of economic growth over time despite the absence of interactions between them or other relevant intervening variables. Though Buchanan does not emphasize the point, this model does the work of making it just (i.e., morally permissible) for the members of the more successful country to prevent immigration from the less successful one if that immigration would be economically harmful. Welfare considerations enter at the second stage of the argument. Buchanan draws attention to a potential kind of harm that he thinks may be neglected in conventional economic analyses, namely the political participation of immigrants and consequent negative transformation not just of particular policies but of the institutional structures that have made the country economically successful. Thus Buchanan focuses not on the connection between culture and identity, as Coleman and Harding and their critics generally do, but rather on a possible connection between culture and the creation of wealth. He treats this as one important (but not necessarily decisive) factor to be taken into account in determining immigration policy.

Michael Trebilcock (Chapter 11) explicitly employs both the discourse of justice and the discourse of welfare. He begins with a critical survey of justice-based arguments on immigration, noting the deep tension between those that appeal to the value of liberty and those that appeal to the value of community. He then explores the implications of these two values as well as other factors for a number of concrete questions regarding the criteria and mechanisms for selecting immigrants, assuming that some, but not all, will be admitted. Subsequently he provides an overview of the welfare effects of immigration, based partly on economic theory but primarily on empirical studies. At the level of theory, he argues that open immigration is clearly the optimal economic strategy from the perspective of global welfare, with the important qualification, as noted by Sykes, that migration for purposes of gaining access to entitlement systems does not contribute to overall economic efficiency. The empirical evidence shows that domestic populations gain modestly as a result of immigration, largely because of scale and dependency effects, and also that immigrants as a group (including refugees) compare favorably with the native population in terms of labor force participation, unemployment, and reliance on public assistance. These findings may be complicated or contested with respect to recent trends, but not sufficiently so, in Trebilcock's view, to warrant a change in policy out of concern for the welfare of the native population. He also notes that immigrants themselves gain substantially in welfare terms from migration.

Trebilcock's final discussion of what he calls "optimal immigration policies" weaves together the two kinds of normative considerations. He argues for the elimination of any constraints on the number of immigrants admitted on the basis of family ties, even relatively loose family ties, as long as the family already present can provide "a credible and enforceable commitment to accept financial responsibility" for them in case of need, thus preventing their reliance on noncontributory public assistance programs. He argues for simplification of the criteria used to judge the potential economic contribution of applicants and opposes any use of ethnic or cultural criteria. He argues for simplification of the refugee determination process, as well as standardization and coordination across states. Finally, he is highly critical of Sykes's proposal to increase the number of temporary workers as both administratively impractical and normatively undesirable (given the moral claims of the workers). In sum, Trebilcock's basic strategy is to show that considerations of justice, global welfare, and domestic welfare all converge to support much more liberal immigration policies.

Taken as a whole the various essays in this volume provide a provocative and challenging set of perspectives on a topic whose importance seems certain to increase in the years to come.

Notes

1 Article 1A(2) 189 UNTS 137.
2 John Rawls, *A Theory of Justice* (Cambridge, Mass.: Harvard University Press, 1971), and Ronald Dworkin, *A Matter of Principle* (Cambridge, Mass.: Harvard University Press, 1985).
3 Jürgen Habermas, "Citizenship and National Identity: Some Reflections on the Future of Europe," *Praxis International* 12.1 (April 1992): 1–19.
4 Will Kymlicka, *Liberalism, Community and Culture* (Oxford: Oxford University Press, 1989).
5 Michael Walzer, *Spheres of Justice* (New York: Basic Books, 1983).
6 Of course, requirements can often be recast as prohibitions, and vice versa. For the

purposes of this essay, nothing crucial hinges on this distinction, although it can play an important role in some moral theories.

7 Rawls would clearly not regard this formulation as equivalent to the difference principle, but others would dispute his claim.

2

Citizenship, the demands of justice, and the moral relevance of political borders

JULES L. COLEMAN AND SARAH K. HARDING

By what standards ought the immigration policies of nations be assessed? Answering this question requires that we draw several preliminary distinctions. In the first place, immigration is a form of access to political borders. Access, in turn, can take many forms, from travel to temporary residence, to permanent residence, and, ultimately, to citizenship. Let us refer to these as various forms of status. Different countries provide different bundles of resources to individuals depending on their status. Thus we can distinguish between status, the conditions for obtaining that status, and the bundles of resources that status entitles one to. In the first part of this essay, we explore the various forms of access to political borders individuals can obtain, the conditions that must be satisfied in order to obtain them, and the bundles of resources the status makes available. Our empirical study is restricted to eight representative nation-states.

Our approach to the normative question is to see whether important aspects of the immigration policies of the nations we consider can be defended as reflecting or consistent with alternative plausible conceptions of justice. So we look first for common elements in these practices and then ask ourselves whether these can be plausibly construed as implementing an appropriate ideal or demand of justice. In other words, before suggesting reform of existing policies, we take the view that the theorist's responsibility is to try first to make the best case for existing practices. The criticisms that stick are those that emerge after a practice has received the most sympathetic understanding and found to fall short.

To this end of internal criticism, we offer, in the second part of the essay, an architecture of various ways of thinking about a nation-state's immigration policy from the point of view of distributive justice. In the next part of the essay we explore the extent to which the various bundles of resources and immigration policies can be construed as reflecting concerns of distributive justice. Whatever other virtues and advantages they might have, political borders help to create and sustain a good apart from the goods and resources that fall within the ambit of those with authority. This is the good of "membership in the relevant political community." We wonder whether the good of membership in a political community falls outside the domain of distributive justice. If it does, then considerations other than distributive justice regulate claims to membership in a political community.

We argue, however, that membership in a political community is itself the sort of resource that can fall within the ambit of distributive justice properly conceived. Finally, we provide a framework within which the immigration policies of the nations we study can be assessed that relies on the concept of membership in a political community. The essay begins with a discussion of various ways in which individuals can have access to political borders and the goods such access typically makes available.

I. Access and membership goods

In this section we discuss the different ways a foreign national can gain access to a country's borders as provided by the immigration policies of eight countries: the United States, Canada, the United Kingdom, Germany, France, Sweden, Israel, and Japan.[1] Canada and the United States are countries of immigration.[2] They accept a large number of immigrants with the knowledge that they will stay indefinitely and eventually become citizens. Unlike these two countries, where immigration has formed "part of the national myth,"[3] the European countries we looked at have followed more restrictive policies.[4] Some European countries, particularly Germany, admitted a large number of foreign workers in the postwar years but have attempted to cut back on all immigration, including labor migration, since the mid-1970s.[5] Despite attempts by these European countries to discourage most immigration, a continual flow of family members and refugees has increased immigration in even the most unwelcoming of countries.[6] The last two countries included in our discussion, Japan and Israel, are not unlike the European countries in that they have discouraged most immigration. But unlike the other countries discussed, they more actively promote the maintenance of a homogeneous society. Japan promotes cultural homogeneity in its policies,[7] while Israel's policies tend to reinforce religious homogeneity.[8]

Although only the United States and Canada are self-professed countries of immigration, all of the countries we looked at have a significant rate of immigration and thus are suitable case studies for a project concerned with the conditions of access. Although numerous bilateral and multilateral agreements influence immigration policies in these countries, they will be mentioned only occasionally. Our intention is to provide a very broad overview of the internal immigration policies of our eight countries, noting any similarities or dissimilarities.

The following discussion is divided into two major topics: access and membership goods. In the former section, we look at the privileges and barriers encountered by various groups seeking entrance into a foreign country. In the latter section, we assess the various goods available to foreign nationals once they have been admitted. Included in our category of "membership goods" is citizenship itself.

A. Access to borders

The central division in access recognized by our eight countries is the distinction between temporary and permanent access – more broadly considered, conditional and unconditional access. This distinction is significant because it approximately reflects length of stay, which partially determines entitlement to resources.[9] But as an analytic tool for assessing access, it is not useful because in most of the eight countries permanent access is available only after one has been a temporary resident for an extended period and meets other qualifications.[10] In other words, permanent access is better characterized as a good – a right to stay – and will be discussed as such in the section on membership goods. In the following discussion we look at accessibility from the perspective of specific groups, in particular individuals who have a historical, cultural, or political connection to the country of destination, family members, refugees, and all others.

Securing some form of access as either a temporary or permanent resident presupposes at least a limited right of entry. It is not the case, however, that all individuals are acceptable applicants for admission. There are numerous grounds for excluding an individual, but most exclusions relate to health problems, criminal records, public security risks, and dependence on public assistance.[11] Not one of the countries we looked at provides an unconditional right of entry to noncitizens. All others, even refugees, must comply with a set of requirements over and above those applicable to their specific applicant pool.

Although the term "immigrant" is usually used in connection with foreign nationals who are seeking or have obtained permanent resident status, particularly in the United States, we use the term to refer to anyone seeking access to a foreign country.

1. Historical, cultural, and political connections. Each of the countries examined draws some distinction between different foreign nationals. Those individuals seeking access, whether temporary or permanent, who are from countries with a historical, cultural, or political connection are frequently exempted from entry requirements. This occurs at every level of admission. Visas are not required for travel between the United States and Canada,[12] the

United Kingdom and Ireland,[13] or New Zealand and Australia.[14] Citizens of countries belonging to the European Community (EC) are permitted to move freely within the EC,[15] and a similar arrangement exists for citizens of the Nordic countries.[16] There are a number of bilateral and multilateral agreements governing employment that allow for the free movement of workers between the signatories. Such agreements exist between New Zealand and Australia,[17] within the European Economic Community,[18] and within the Nordic Community.[19]

For most of this century, British subjects, which included citizens of all commonwealth countries, were granted the right to permanent access, but since the creation of a British citizenship in 1981, immigration to the United Kingdom has more or less halted except for family members of legal residents and refugees. None of the immigration requirements apply to nationals of other EC countries. France has continued to maintain a special relationship with Algeria since its independence in 1962, and Algerians are at present subject to separate, less restrictive immigration controls.[20] Nationals of other member nations of the EC are also exempt from immigration control.

German extraterritorial connections are of a different nature. As one author notes, "Germans . . . think of their nation not as a political unit but as a cultural, linguistic and ethnic unit."[21] Citizenship policies reflect this by making it very difficult for foreign nationals to naturalize while simultaneously providing all ethnic Germans around the world with a right to claim citizenship.

Israel follows a similar policy based on religious ties. Two documents are essential to an understanding of Israel's immigration policy. The first is the 1948 Declaration of Independence, which states that "the State of Israel is open to Jewish immigration and the ingathering of Exiles."[22] The second document is Section 13 of the Law and Government Ordinance, 1948, the first legislative act after independence, which revoked any limitations on the immigration of Jews.[23] The Law of Return, which was subsequently enacted in 1950, grants to Jews everywhere the right to immigrate and settle in Israel with only the usual health and security restrictions. The Law of Return is so fundamental that it has been characterized as the very raison d'être of Israel.[24] Former Prime Minister David Ben Gurion stated in his introduction to the Law of Return: "This Law does not provide for the State to bestow the right to settle in Israel upon the Jew living abroad; it affirms that this right is inherent in him from the very fact of being a Jew. . . . This right preceded the State; this right built the State."[25] All Jews who immigrate to Israel subsequently have a right to citizenship under Section 2 of the Nationality Law, 1952.

Japan is the most inaccessible of the countries examined in this study. Koreans are the only nationality group exempted from some of the very strict requirements for permanent access and citizenship. Koreans may claim permanent resident status as of right but only if they can prove they have been in the country since before the Second World War or are lineal descendants of such persons.[26] The vast majority of persons granted permanent resident status in Japan are Korean and Chinese.[27]

Thus, in all of the countries under consideration, immigration policies are relaxed for specific foreign individuals who remain connected, either through an ongoing cultural or religious connection or as nationals of a politically or historically connected country.

2. *Families.* A significant number of foreign nationals are permitted to enter each country on the basis of family ties. Immediate family members are usually granted some form of residence permit, either temporary or permanent, as a matter of right. For the most part only the immediate family, consisting of a spouse, dependent children, and dependent parents, are included in this category, although in some countries the definition is much broader. Remoter relations must comply with other requirements often based on economic considerations.

In Canada and the United States certain immediate family members may obtain permanent resident status upon entry. Although Canada has very recently altered its immigration policies to favor immigrants who will add to the Canadian economy rather than family members,[28] family reunification continues to be the predominant purpose of permanent immigration in the United States.[29] In the United States immediate family members of U.S. citizens are not subject to numerical limitations and quotas.[30] The remaining family visas, which are limited in number each year, go to more remote family members of citizens and the spouses and children of legalized aliens.[31] In Canada immediate family members of citizens and permanent residents have a right to permanent residence, provided that they comply with certain regulatory conditions.[32] Other dependents and more remote relations, referred to as "assisted relatives," fall within a discretionary point system,[33] which is also used to assess independent applicants, primarily those seeking entry for employment purposes.[34]

Since the creation of a British citizenship, family members have constituted the majority of immigrants to the United Kingdom. Immediate relatives of citizens and other persons who are "settled"[35] may apply for settlement.[36] An entry clearance for settlement will not be issued unless the officer is satisfied that there will be adequate accommodation and support for the applicant "without recourse to public funds."[37] In seeking entry for "settlement," these applicants must show an intention to become ordinarily resident in the United Kingdom and must wait out a twelve-month trial period, referred to as "limited leave to enter," before qualifying for settlement.[38]

The most salient feature of France's immigration policies concerning families is that distant family members may be included in the immediate family unit in situations where they were part of the family unit and/or dependent on the sponsor in their home country and where reunification is warranted for humanitarian reasons.[39] Residence permits are issued as a matter of right to immediate family members of a French national.[40] Sweden also has a more expansive approach to family immigration, permitting those who are involved in a "serious relationship" to be included in the definition of immediate family.[41]

The vast majority of nonrefugee movement into Germany has been that of family members of foreign laborers. The spouses of foreign residents are not given work permits until a period of residence has passed, a policy clearly designed to compel foreign residents to return to their home countries rather than bring their families to Germany. But immediate family members are still treated much more leniently than other individuals seeking admission.[42]

In all of the countries discussed, including Japan and Israel, the conditions for becoming a permanent resident or a citizen are relaxed for the spouse of a citizen, or one who can claim citizenship (Israel and Germany). For example, in Japan, it is necessary for someone seeking permanent residence to display upright conduct and proof of sufficient assets to support himself. These conditions are waived for the spouse or child of a Japanese national.[43] In Israel, the spouse of a Jew is entitled to the benefits of the Law of Return. In the United States and the United Kingdom, the period of residence for naturalization is reduced from five to three years for a spouse of a citizen.[44] Under French nationality law, the spouse of a French citizen can claim citizenship after merely six months of marriage,[45] and in Sweden, the spouse of a citizen may at the discretion of the relevant minister be exempted from complying with all of the naturalization requirements.[46]

Thus it is clear that family members, particularly spouses, occupy a privileged position in immigration policies. They are admitted more readily and exempted from many of the conditions of permanent residence and citizenship in even the most inaccessible of countries studied.

3. Refugees. Refugees and asylum seekers are rapidly becoming the largest group of permanent foreign settlers and represent the biggest challenge to the immigration policies of the countries under consideration. Even in those countries where there is a virtual ban on immigration, with the exception of close family members, refugees or asylum seekers are permitted to enter and settle. Many countries have openly adopted the definition of a refugee that appears in Article 1A(2) of the Geneva Convention of 1951[47] as extended by its 1967 Protocol,[48] while others, in particular France and Sweden, have actually extended the definition.[49] Most countries restrict refugee status to those who are subject to political persecution, thus rejecting the claims of economic refugees.

In Germany[50] and Canada,[51] the final determination of a claim for refugee or asylee status may take years, but during this time the claimant is entitled to stay in the country and seek employment. Consequently, both of these countries are inundated with applicants. Germany is a particularly popular destination, because the German Constitution provides a right of asylum to those who are persecuted for political reasons.[52] The German Constitution has recently been amended, and although it continues to assert a right to asylum, it also prohibits individuals who enter from a member state of the EC or from another country that is party to the European Convention for the Protection of Human Rights from invoking the right to asylum. Thus asylum seekers passing through another country on their way to Germany may be forced to return to that other country.[53]

The United Kingdom, on the other hand, does not have a particularly good record with respect to refugees. The 1951 Convention has been incorporated into the Immigration Rules,[54] but it is not directly enforceable.[55] Furthermore, the Immigration Carriers' Liability Act 1987 penalizes the carriage of asylum seekers without visas.[56] The most recent Immigration Rules do exempt asylum seekers themselves from obtaining visas before entry.[57]

Japan is one of very few countries in Asia that has acceded to the Convention and that grants permanent asylum to refugees. Japan is also part of a multilateral Asian response, the Comprehensive Plan of Action, which was established to deal with the flow of Vietnamese refugees. Most of the refugees seeking asylum in Japan are from other Asian countries.[58]

4. Workers, professionals, and others. In addition to the categories of immigrants already discussed, many foreigners are permitted entry into the countries under consideration as visitors, students, or temporary workers. Visiting and student visas are granted for a limited period of time, although many bilateral and multilateral agreements have waived the visa requirement for students and visitors traveling in designated countries. Work permits, a generic term we shall use to refer to visas for anyone seeking employment, including professionals, businesspersons, skilled and unskilled laborers, artists and academics, are invariably subject to time and purpose constraints. Furthermore, work permits are usually provided only if the applicant has already secured employment in the destination country. In fact, permits are often obtained by an employer or an organization hiring foreign workers rather than an individual applicant.[59] Regardless of who bears the responsibility for applying, the availability of work permits is very much determined by the economic and labor market needs of the receiving country. For the most part artists, writers, academics, professionals, and businesspersons, in particular those who are distinguished in their fields or are representatives of international organizations, have fewer hurdles to overcome in obtaining work permits.

Only a few countries permit those seeking access for employment purposes to apply upon entry for permanent immigrant status. Of the countries under consideration, Canada[60] and the United States[61] are the only two that grant permanent resident status upon entry to independent immigrants seeking employment. The policy of most European countries is to admit as potential permanent residents only refugees and the family members of citizens or existing permanent residents. European countries continue to provide temporary work permits, but even these are increasingly limited and the steady stream of migrant laborers into Germany and France has for the most part ceased. Many foreign nationals with temporary work permits do, however, end up adjusting their status to that of permanent resident, but only after lengthy stays.[62] Access to Japan for employment purposes is even more restricted. Unskilled workers are "categorically prohibited from entering or staying in Japan."[63] Furthermore, the activities of aliens are restricted by their residence permit indicating a specific work category.[64]

5. Conclusion. Despite the disparities in the policies of our eight countries, it is apparent that each country privileges specific foreign nationals. Germany, Japan, and Israel elevate the status of those who are culturally or religiously connected. Canada, the United States, and the European countries exempt individuals who are from countries with some established political connection, usually generated by a combination of proximity and political compatibility. And finally, the United Kingdom and France make exceptions for immigrants from countries that were once colonies, although such exceptions appear to be diminishing.

In addition, each of the eight countries discussed treats family members and refugees as exceptional categories, granting them resident permits, and (with respect to the former category) citizenship, more readily. The policies of the countries examined begin to diverge more significantly when dealing with workers, professionals, and other foreign nationals who are neither refugees nor relatives.

B. Membership goods

The preceding discussion has given us a very basic understanding of who has access to the borders of the eight countries under consideration. It appears that in each of our countries special consideration is given to family members, refugees, and those with a historical, political, or cultural connection. Whether others are permitted to enter for longer than a visit seems to depend on the peculiar needs and political climate of the receiving country. Generally, only those who have something considerable to offer to the country of destination are admitted, although Canada and the United States provide limited exceptions to this. In the following section we examine what goods foreign nationals are entitled to once they have been legally admitted. "Goods" in this context refers not only to more concrete entitlements such as employment and socioeconomic resources, but also to the right to stay and be a full member of society. Our main interest here is to determine what goods, if any, are denied to certain classes of foreign nationals.

1. Employment. Permanent residents can usually pursue any type of work, with one major exception: noncitizens are often prohibited from working in the civil service or the public sector. A common justification for this restriction is that, without citizenship, "ultimate loyalty to the state cannot be presumed."[65] The total exclusion of noncitizens from the public sector does seem, however, to be less a political precaution than a "desire to monopolize access to certain attractive and secure jobs."[66] In many places this prohibition has been loosened so that only those positions that are arguably connected to the exercise of public authority are reserved for nationals or citizens.[67] In Japan, however, the restrictions are even greater, prohibiting aliens from participating in organizations that are essential to the well-being of Japan, in addition to those public offices "related to the exercise of public authority of the State and local public bodies."[68] For example, foreign nationals cannot own mining rights, shares in the Japanese telephone and telecommunications company, or a radio license.[69]

Temporary residents are usually subject to further job restrictions. Visitors, students, and foreign government officials and their families are for the most part prohibited from obtaining employment. Professionals, businesspersons, and workers are obviously permitted to enter on the basis of their employment plans, but their work permits are typically restricted to a particular position or industry. The government is thus able to regulate and restrict the flow of persons seeking employment in areas where there is already a sufficient domestic labor force.

Illegal aliens obviously have no right to employment. But this, needless to say, does not effectively prohibit illegal aliens from entering and obtaining employment. In an effort to reduce the number of illegal aliens, some countries now penalize employers who hire undocumented aliens.[70]

2. Emergency services and socioeconomic resources. As with access to employment, the right to socioeconomic resources is determined more by the permanence of residence and the legality of status than by citzenship. The major exceptions to this are emergency services. Emergency services, particularly emergency medical care, are available to everyone within the relevant political community regardless of the length or legality of their stay. Although education is not really an emergency service, it may also be available to illegal residents.[71]

The distribution of other socioeconomic resources – for example, housing, child allowances, welfare, health care, and unemployment insurance – varies greatly depending on the status of the recipient and the country in question. Visitors and students are generally not eligible for such benefits, although students may have access to health care.[72] Temporary workers, businesspersons, and professionals maintain the right to claim the same benefits as non-foreign workers in the same industry. But since most temporary workers are admitted only on the basis of proof of employment and are forced to leave when their permits expire or their work no longer exists, such benefits as welfare and unemployment insurance are usually not available. Such resources as housing and child allowances, however, may be available to temporary residents, particularly in countries where permanent resident status is difficult to obtain.[73]

Permanent residents usually have access to the same socioeconomic resources as citizens, but often such privileges are not available until after a period of residency. When a foreign national is admitted through the sponsorship of a citizen or a permanent resident, usually in the case of a family applicant, the sponsor must prove the applicant will not become a burden on the state. This subsequently exempts the government from providing need-based support in the form of welfare or unemployment insurance for a specific number of years.[74] Similar conditions operate in Germany and Japan, where upgrading to permanent resident status is contingent on proof of adequate housing and a sufficient means of support.[75] There may be other minor exceptions, but as a general rule permanent residents enjoy a full bundle of socioeconomic resources.[76] In Japan, a constitutional right to social welfare and security was extended to foreign nationals in 1979 when Japan acceded to the International Covenant on Human Rights.[77] Sweden and other Nordic countries provide some of the most elaborate benefits to foreign nationals to assist them in integrating into Nordic society.[78] For example, foreigners are given paid leave from work to study Swedish.

Refugees are, of course, entitled to all socioeconomic benefits once their applications have been approved, but some countries deny such benefits while an application is pending.[79]

3. Political participation. Political participation remains for the most part an exclusive privilege of citizenship. Citizenship is essential to vote in any election in the United States and Canada. Both countries justify this arguably too restrictive voting policy on the basis that acquiring citizenship is encouraged and expected of most foreign nationals with permanent resident status.[80] In Japan aliens have neither the right to vote nor the right to contribute to political parties.[81]

There are, however, a growing number of minor exceptions to this apparently fundamental rule. Since 1975, noncitizens in Sweden with at least three years of residence have had the right to vote in municipal and in some cases regional elections. The same privilege has been extended to noncitizens in the Netherlands.[82] Other countries have entered bilateral agreements permitting certain foreign nationals to vote. Such an arrangement exists between the United Kingdom and Ireland.[83] The United Kingdom also permits nationals of Commonwealth countries to vote.[84]

Forms of political involvement other than voting and running for office are also available to noncitizens. The most significant of these alternative political rights is participation in industrial politics. Aliens, whether legal or illegal, can join unions and participate in factory councils and elections where appropriate.[85] This is a significant political right, given the large number of aliens who enter the industrial work force. In some countries, primarily Germany, noncitizens are also given the right to elect their own councils to act as consultants on political matters.[86] Finally, noncitizens and citizens alike have the right to freedom of expression and freedom of association in all of the countries under consideration. In practice, however, foreign nationals risk being deported for antigovernment activities if their opposition is too vocal, violent, or threatening.

4. Right to permanent access. Access to permanent resident status has been touched on briefly in some of the preceding discussions, but it is worth mentioning separately because it is here, as in citizenship, where the policies of our eight countries differ most noticeably. As already mentioned, Canada and the United States grant permanent resident status upon arrival to a few designated immigrants. But the rest of the countries under consideration insist on some period of residence before application.[87] In a few countries individuals can attain permanent resident status only by complying with qualifications similar to those for full membership.

France, the United Kingdom, and Sweden permit temporary residents to apply for permanent resident status after a relatively brief period of residence. In Sweden, access to permanent resident status is regularly granted after merely a year of residence; no other requirements need be satisfied.[88] Permanent access, in the form of a carte de resident, is accessible to all foreign nationals in France after three years of residence, provided they have sufficient funds with which to live and support their dependents and have not been imprisoned for one year or more during the five years before application.[89] Permanent resident status is actually valid for only ten years but is renewable as a matter of right. In the United Kingdom, an application for "settlement" can be made after a year for an immediate family member[90] and after four years for all others.[91]

Germany and Japan are more reluctant about granting permanent resident status. In Germany a foreign national can apply for a residence permit for an indefinite period of time after five years. After eight years, an immigrant has the right to obtain a permanent residence permit provided the applicant has adequate housing, a sufficient means of support, and a satisfactory knowledge of the German language. Permanent work permits are granted after ten years of residence.[92] Permanent resident status is available in Japan, provided that it accords with the interests of Japan and that the applicant displays upright conduct and a sufficient means of support. But the granting of permanent resident status is discretionary and very few succeed in obtaining it.[93]

Israel presents a different situation, since it virtually prohibits all non-Jewish immigration.[94] Permanent residency is not a serious concern for Jewish immigrants, as they have the right to claim citizenship under the Law of Return.

We begin to see in this brief discussion of permanent resident status the spectrum of attitudes toward foreign nationals that are evidenced in the policies of our eight countries. At one end are those countries that are very generous in granting permanent resident status and even extend such status to a select group upon arrival. At the other end are those countries – Japan, Germany, and Israel – that grant permanent resident status under only the strictest of conditions. These conditions, as we will see, are similar to those used for naturalization.

5. Immunity from expulsion. Total immunity from expulsion is a privilege of citizenship. In very rare circumstances, citizens may be denationalized and thus made vulnerable to deportation,[95] but otherwise it is one of the most important privileges of citizenship. For noncitizens, immunity may depend on numerous factors, not the least of which is duration of residence. The longer a person resides in a foreign nation, the stronger that person's claim to immunity from expulsion. In general, however, noncitizens, whether they be temporary, permanent, or illegal members of the community, can be deported. Illegal aliens are clearly the most likely to be deported.

Legally, resident foreign nationals may be deported if they violate the terms of their stay, acquire a serious criminal record while residing in the foreign country, or become a threat to the health or security of the foreign nation.[96] In those countries where citizenship is not attributed through birth in the territory, a second- or even third-generation immigrant knowing no other place of residence may be deported for any of the foregoing reasons.[97]

In some countries, immunity from expulsion is granted to those admitted under family reunification provisions. Where this is the case, a spouse, for example, cannot be deported as long as the family connection remains intact.[98]

6. Citizenship. Citizens clearly hold the greatest bundle of rights and privileges that a country has to offer. Perhaps the most important of the rights is the right to permanent access regardless of where the citizen resides.[99] Other rights and obligations may not be the same from country to country, but they invariably add up to full membership in the political community in question.

Citizenship is always attributed at birth, in some countries through birth in the territory (*jus soli*) and in others through parentage (*jus sanguinis*). It is interesting that all of the countries we looked at, regardless of which form of attribution they follow, grant citizenship to persons born in the country who would otherwise be stateless. Citizenship is never attributed to someone born outside of the country to noncitizens,[100] but it can be acquired through naturalization or registration procedures. Naturalization usually always requires some period of residence and a familiarity with the country.

Citizenship in the United States is granted to anyone born in the territory and conditionally to those born outside of the territory to a citizen.[101] In Canada citizenship is also attributed to those born within Canadian borders but *unconditionally* to the first generation of Canadian citizens born outside the borders.[102] To acquire U.S. citizenship, an applicant must have lived in the country for at least five years (three in the case of spouses), show a basic knowledge of the country, an ability to speak and write English, and proof of "good moral character."[103] Once these requirements are satisfied, an application for naturalization is granted as a matter of right. It is assumed that eligible candidates will naturalize rather than remain immigrants. In fact, it is evident from the posters that adorn the wall of an INS office that the INS actually encourages naturalization. It is worth noting that applicants for naturalization need not provide proof of integration into an American way of life but the traditional image of the "melting pot" assumes that such a process will occur.

Canada's naturalization policies require three years of residence, rather than five, an ability to speak French or English, and proof that one's record is clear of any indictable offenses for at least the three years before application.[104] Canada does not provide any exceptions, even for spouses, to its naturalization requirements.[105] The major difference between Canadian and U.S. approaches to immigration has been Canada's emphasis on multiculturalism. Canada explicitly adopted a policy that was intended to encourage immigrants to naturalize and become full members of Canadian society without abandoning their cultural identities.[106] It is perhaps because of this policy that a relatively high percentage of Canadian immigrants become citizens.[107]

It is difficult to speak of British immigration and nationality policies separately, because for most of this century the two were inextricably tied. Until the 1960s, all British subjects, which included Commonwealth citizens, could enter the United Kingdom without being subject to immigration control. This privilege slowly eroded, and by 1981 a British citizenship was created putting all others previously classified as British subjects, including Commonwealth citizens, in more or less the same class as other foreign nationals. A British citizen is defined as one who was born, adopted, registered, or naturalized in the United Kingdom and anyone who is descended from such a citizen.[108]

The attribution of British citizenship is governed by a combination of parental descent and birth in the territory. To be a citizen by birth in the territory requires that either the mother or father be a British citizen or "settled" in the United Kingdom.[109] Children born outside of the territory are British citizens if their mother or father is a British citizen by birth, adoption, registration, or naturalization but not descent.[110] British citizenship can be acquired through either registration or naturalization. Registration is a nondiscretionary process applicable to British overseas citizens, citizens of British Dependent Territories, British protected persons, and British subjects. Registration does require a period of residence.[111] Naturalization, a discretionary process, requires full age (18) and capacity, "good character," sufficient knowledge of English, Welsh or Scottish Gaelic (not necessary for a spouse), and five years of residence or three years for a spouse.[112] The United Kingdom, like the United States and Canada, does not require those seeking permanent access and citizenship to provide proof of assimilation into society beyond a language competence.

French nationality law is essentially based on parentage, so that anyone born to a French citizen outside of French territory is granted French citizenship.[113] But there are also many ways for someone born on French territory to noncitizen parents to acquire French citizenship. First, someone born of parents, one of whom was also born on French territory although not a citizen, is granted citizenship.[114] Second, a right to acquire French nationality through declaration is extended to anyone born in the territory to foreign parents, provided that she can prove habitual residence in France for five years before the declaration.[115] The requirements for the acquisition of citizenship are almost identical to those for British citizenship, except that it is necessary to show some knowledge of French customs and assimilation into the French community.[116] A spouse of a French citizen can claim citizenship after merely six months of marriage.[117]

German nationality law is based on cultural and ethnic association. Citizenship policies reflect this by making it very difficult for foreign nationals to naturalize while simultaneously providing all ethnic Germans with a right to claim citizenship regardless of their place of birth or residence. In fact, naturalization is considered rare and exceptional, granted only when "the applicant is thoroughly integrated into German society, and then only when there is a public interest in his or her naturalization."[118]

The attribution of citizenship is based solely on parentage, so that a person born of German citizens anywhere in the world is automatically granted German citizenship. But a person born on German territory to noncitizens is still a foreigner. The acquisition of citizenship is clearly discretionary, unless one can claim to be an ethnic German, in which case naturalization is granted as a right.[119] Discretionary naturalization requires ten years of residence (only five for a spouse of a German national), good moral character, and financial stability. Furthermore, it requires a "voluntary and permanent attachment to Germany" and a "basic knowledge of its political and social structures."[120] These relatively stiff requirements have resulted in a very low naturalization rate: "In 1985, there were nearly 2.6 million foreigners with ten or more years' residence; only 0.5 percent of them were naturalized through discretionary grant."[121] The discretionary nature of the naturalization process and the reluctance of many foreign nationals to cast aside their cultural identities has also contributed to this very low rate.[122]

Sweden, in contrast, has a comparatively high rate of naturalization: roughly 60 percent of first- and second-generation immigrants are naturalized.[123] Naturalization is discretionary, unlike in Canada and the United States, but the requirements are very minimal and in practice it is rarely denied. Foreign residents are granted citizenship after five years of residence and with evidence of good conduct; there are no further requirements.[124] Citizens of Finland and Norway can become Swedish citizens with only two years of residence.[125] Sweden naturalizes approximately 6.7 percent of the eligible population each year, compared with the U.S. figure of 4.9 percent. In the countries under consideration, only Canada manages to naturalize a greater percentage of its eligible foreign population.[126] Much of Sweden's success is due to the ease of the requirements, but this success can also be attributed to the fact that until very recently the vast majority of immigrants in Sweden were from other Nordic or European countries.[127] Even with respect to its refugee program, Sweden, along with the other Nordic countries, has focused on Eastern Europe and has unduly restricted the number of refugees coming from Latin America, Southeast Asia, and Africa.[128] With respect to the attribution of citizenship, Sweden has the same rules as Germany: citizenship is granted only to individuals born of Swedish parents.[129]

Israel and Japan, not unlike Germany, grant citizenship in very limited circumstances. As previously mentioned, nationality law in Israel privileges Jews. Non-Jewish residents can obtain Israeli citizenship through residence, birth, or naturalization. In accordance with 1980 amendments to the 1952

Nationality Law, a non-Jew born before the establishment of Israel can claim Israeli citizenship if he was a resident and citizen of Palestine and was registered as such.[130] A non-Jew born after the establishment of the state can claim citizenship if he was resident in Israel on the day the amendment came into force and is an offspring of someone who was a citizen and resident of Palestine at the date of the establishment of Israel. There is no distinction between the treatment of Jews and non-Jews with respect to the attribution of citizenship at birth. A child born in Israel to at least one Israeli citizen or born outside Israel to one Israeli citizen by way of birth, naturalization, residence, or return is an Israeli citizen.[131]

Naturalization is a discretionary process. The following conditions must be fulfilled before an applicant will be considered for naturalization. The applicant must be in Israel at the time and have lived in Israel for at least three of the five preceding years. In addition, an applicant must show an intention to settle, entitlement to permanent residence, and a knowledge of Hebrew. Finally, an applicant must prove that she has renounced any other citizenship or that her citizenship of another country will cease upon her becoming an Israeli citizen.[132] The spouse of a Jew is entitled to the benefits of the Law of Return, including citizenship, but the spouse of a non-Jewish citizen is subject to the stricter immigration regime and must naturalize to become a citizen.[133]

Citizenship in Japan is attributed through parentage. A child is a Japanese citizen when either his mother or father is Japanese, regardless of where he is born. If the child is not born in Japan and acquires another citizenship through birth in another territory (for example, the United States), his parents must register him shortly after the birth to preserve his Japanese citizenship.[134] The only circumstances in which an individual born in Japan to non-Japanese citizens is granted citizenship is if that individual would otherwise be stateless.[135]

The Japanese very much regard their nation as a homogeneous society and thus seriously restrict both permanent residence and naturalization. As one commentator has noted, ''It is virtually inconceivable that Japanese immigration officials would encourage someone born outside Japan to non-Japanese parents to seek citizenship.''[136] Naturalization, like the permanent residence application, is a discretionary process. Before the minister will even consider an application, it is necessary for applicants to provide proof of continuous domicile in Japan for at least five years (mere residence is not sufficient), an upright character, means of support, and the renunciation of any other citizenship. On paper, naturalization does not seem unduly inaccessible, but in practice it is a rare occurrence. The total number of naturalizations between 1952 and 1985 was 165,975, of which the vast majority were those of Koreans.[137] But many of the Koreans who have lived in Japan for an extended period of time do not want to become Japanese citizens, precisely because of the integration requirements.[138]

7. Conclusion. A few general observations can be drawn from the information set out in the preceding subsections. Political rights and immunity from expulsion are privileges reserved for citizens with some limited but notable exceptions. But socioeconomic resources, are for the most part distributed without regard to citizenship. All permanent residents have access to the same socioeconomic resources as citizens and the same rights to seek employment, with the exception of employment in the public sector. This is not the case for temporary residents, who are generally prohibited from seeking employment that was not arranged before entry. Temporary residents may also be prevented from receiving socioeconomic resources, except emergency services and those available through employment positions, particularly in those countries where permanent resident status is easily attained. Illegal aliens receive most of the same benefits as temporary residents by virtue of their presence in the territory and work in a particular industry.

Permanent residence and citizenship are the most difficult "goods" to obtain and perhaps the most coveted privileges sought by immigrants. Each country examined employs its own unique process, combining some period of residence and integration into the community. And whereas Japan, Israel, and Germany are concerned with cultural, or in the case of Israel religious, compatibility and integration, Canada, the United States, and Sweden demand little more than a reasonable period of residence and some language facility. The United Kingdom and France lie somewhere in between these two groups with respect to the ease of obtaining permanent residency and citizenship. The attribution of citizenship parallels naturalization policies in that those countries which focus on cultural integration attribute citizenship solely on the basis of parentage, typically an indication of cultural affiliation, whereas most of the other countries attribute citizenship in other circumstances.

II. Modeling the problem

Our goal here is to develop a normative framework within which the data discussed in the preceding section can be evaluated. Recall that while we may ultimately want to reform existing practices, our goal in this essay is to try to understand those practices as reflecting a plausible set of moral demands and ideals. Our goal, in other words, is to provide the best available normative interpretation or understanding of those practices. Our concern is with the principles of justice or of morality that might be reflected in the immigration policies of the nations we have discussed.

To address this concern, we need first a way of thinking about immigration policies from the point of view of justice. What kinds of principles of justice might apply to immigration policies? The natural suggestion is that because nations typically associate different bundles of resources with different statuses, principles of distributive justice will determine whether or not they do so justifiably. Articulating the ways in which considerations of distributive justice might figure in assessing a nation's immigration policies is considerably more difficult than it might at first appear to be.

Let us begin by considering two different ways of thinking about distributive justice and their potential relationship to immigration policy. In one approach to distributive justice, political borders, even if arbitrarily or conventionally set, have moral significance because they define the boundaries within which principles of distributive justice are to apply. In this view, principles of distributive justice apply to members of a political community of a certain type, loosely defined by territorial borders. Those outside the borders have no claim in distributive justice to any of the resources of the territory, while those within a territory do. The allocation of resources among members of the relevant community will be based on qualifications being satisfied. Whether someone within a territorial border is entitled to share in that community's wealth, then, will depend on whether she meets whatever additional qualifications the relevant principles of distributive justice impose. For example, in some views, citizenship might be a requirement of an individual's having access to a particular bundle of resources, whereas in other views, a term of residence within the territorial borders might suffice. We can, of course, imagine a range of views that would fall somewhere in between, in which, for example, citizenship would be a condition of access to certain goods – say, holding political office or any position in which one is called upon to act as an agent of the political authority – but in which residence of any duration would suffice for access to other goods – for example, emergency medical care.

The core of this way of thinking about distributive justice is the claim that its scope is set by political communities. The goods it distributes are those that fall within the authority of the political community to allocate. The individuals to whom it owes duties in justice are those over whom it exercises political authority. To the extent to which political communities are identified with territories and borders, principles of distributive justice apply to individuals who reside within those borders.

Whatever its ultimate force, we need to distinguish this approach to distributive justice from the very odd-sounding relativist account of distributive justice that holds that each political community has the authority to determine its own principles of distributive justice: that, in other words, there can be as many different principles of distributive justice as there are political communities to choose them. That view confuses the idea that the domain of distributive justice is a political community with the idea that the source of foundation of distributive justice is a political community. Principles of distributive justice may not be the sort of thing that gets chosen on a community-by-community basis.

The idea here is that principles of distributive justice apply to political communities, but the same principle may not apply to every political community. Instead, principles of distributive justice may apply to communities that satisfy certain conditions. So, for example, there may be a particular liberal conception of distributive justice that would apply to any and all political communities that satisfied certain initial conditions. Typically, these principles would be thought to apply to liberal democracies having a certain wealth. If the conditions are met, the principles apply whether or not the members of the community have or would have chosen them. They apply to them because they are principles of justice applicable to such communities. In the same way that there are conditions that must be satisfied before questions of distributive justice can arise – what Hume called the conditions of justice – there are other conditions that might be thought to apply before a particular conception of distributive justice governs a political community. On the other hand, there may be some set of more general constraints that a political community must satisfy before it can even claim to be a legitimate authority or to be regulated by principles of distributive justice. Among these might be the general requirement that the state not be oppressive in certain ways.[139]

In this kind of approach to distributive justice, outsiders are excluded from resources insiders can legitimately claim; therefore, whether one can have a claim to those resources will depend on whether one has access to the borders. Immigration policy determines which outsiders can become insiders; distributive justice then determines the rights of insiders. The principles of distributive justice determine particular entitlements, but do not themselves entail a particular immigration policy.

One apparent consequence of the position that principles of distributive justice apply to members of political communities is that it seems unlikely that the principles, so conceived, can provide the standard against which a community's immigration policy is to be assessed. Distributive justice assumes that the boundary question of which individuals fall within the relevant community is already resolved; they cannot provide an answer to that question. All theories of distributive justice of this sort, namely, those that take the domain of distributive justice to be set by membership in a political community, will fail to illuminate the way we should think about immigration policy, for they assume the existence of an answer to precisely the question we are asking.

Let us consider an alternative approach to immigration policies. Suppose that there are only individuals, the earth, and its resources. We do not assume the existence of political boundaries. The fundamental question is, how should the world's resources be allocated among individuals? This is naturally a question in distributive justice. The difference between this approach to distributive justice and the one previously outlined is that the latter holds that principles of distributive justice apply only within political communities, whereas the view we are currently outlining treats political communities as irrelevant to distributive justice – at least at first blush.

For very different reasons, both of the standard approaches to framing questions of distributive justice appear to shed little light on our question. The first approach assumes that the membership question to which immigration policies provide answers has been met; the second approach rejects the relevance of boundary or membership questions to which immigration policies apply. The natural conclusion is that considerations of distributive justice cannot provide the framework within which a country's immigration policy is to be assessed. The first approach makes too much of political borders; the second too little.

There is a way of understanding the second approach, however, that escapes this conclusion. Imagine a set of representatives or agents of the world's people coming together to draw up the principles by which the world's resources are to be produced and allocated. Each representative will reflect the rational desire of each person he represents to maximize the set of usable resources and his share of them. The collective problem therefore has efficiency and distributive dimensions. There will also be compliance problems. Securing an agreement on the allocation of benefits and burdens will present a significant challenge – one that, if not resolved by the parties, will lead to a failure to produce the mutually desired outcome. Moreover, once an agreement is reached, it is not obvious that each individual (whether understood as persons or nation-states) will be inclined to comply with its terms. There will always exist at least some incentive to maximize one's share, and that can sometimes be accomplished by encouraging others to comply while refusing personally to absorb the opportunity costs of compliance. These are familiar problems in certain forms of contractarian political philosophy.

Suppose that the relevant representatives settle on a particular strategy for developing and distributing the world's resources. It is likely that any strategy for optimally developing those resources will compartmentalize responsibility in some way. Perhaps, the optimal strategy would leave it to individuals to develop the resources in the geographic area in which they are located. National governments understood in the modern sense could provide relevant productive incentives and monitoring services, and might be particularly well placed to redistribute resources locally. Borders and national boundaries would serve to mark out administratively convenient units for overseeing the production and allocation of the world's resources.

Borders are conventionally or arbitrarily set. Still, they have moral significance from the point of view of distributive justice. They mark out first approximations of optimal units for allocating and producing the world's resources. We say "first approximations" to take note of the fact that whatever their virtues may be in getting the project of optimally producing and allocating the world's resources under way, the conventional setting of borders is bound to be imperfect.

The immigration policies of nation-states would then be understood as a dimension of the initial agreement to produce and distribute the world's resources according to the principles of distributive justice. Immigration policies provide a corrective to the "initial" allocation and production arrangements, responding thereby to the imperfect but administratively convenient production and distribution mechanism of nation-states. Foreign aid policies might also be evaluated from the same perspective, as rectifying distributive inequities on the global scale.

In this model, nation-states and the borders that define them are like local markets designed to create local efficient and fair equilibria when doing so at the global level is administratively too costly. Nation-states are like systems of property rights that reduce uncertainty and make efficient production and exchange possible.[140]

Though morally arbitrary of conventional in the way in which certain systems of property rights might be, political borders have moral significance because of the role they play in creating a framework within which the global demands of distributive justice – whatever they are – are satisfied. Because political borders matter morally in this way, immigration policies can be evaluated by the extent to which they contribute to satisfying the demands of distributive justice – in both its productive and allocative dimensions.

III. The claims of distributive justice

There are two ways of looking at the data we have collected from the point of view of distributive justice. The first is from the bottom up. In this kind of approach, one would ask whether the policies of various nations evidence a particular commitment to one or the other model of distributive justice. The second is from the top down. In this kind of approach, one would assess the various policies of the countries discussed from the perspective of either or both models of distributive justice. Notice that we have not developed a substantive principle or standard of distributive justice. Instead, we have focused entirely on the architecture or structure of distributive justice, on ways of thinking about distributive justice with regard to matters of immigration. We have done this for two reasons. First, we need to answer a threshold question, and that is whether the immigration policies of modern nation-states can be assessed from the point of view of distributive justice. Are immigration policies the sorts of things that fall within the ambit of distributive justice? The answer to that question depends in turn on how we think about distributive justice, less so, if at all, on any particular substantive theory of distributive justice. Second, it may be that the concerns of distributive justice that inform immigration policies are so pervasive that there will be no need in the end to settle on a particular conception of distributive justice in order to grasp their significance or impact.

With regard to the first of these concerns, thinking about immigration policies from the point of view of the second model of distributive justice might prove fruitful. If nation-states are understood as first approximations of an efficient mechanism of production and distribution, we can assess immigration policies from the point of view of whether they contribute to a maximal production and fair distribution of the world's resources among the world's citizens.

Part of the problem with such an approach, of course, is that it requires us to look at the immigration policies of all nations as a whole and ask whether the general effect of these policies contributes to a fair and efficient production and distribution of the world's resources. We cannot assess any one nation's immigration policy from this point of view.

Nevertheless, the approach suggested by the second model is not without illumination. Consider the policy of most nations to exclude others, even those with access to its borders, from political employment of one sort or another. There are several ways of looking at this policy. The first is that only citizens can be authorized to exercise political authority. Those who are not citizens, even if they are otherwise permanent residents, cannot legitimately exercise the public power. An alternative, perhaps more satisfying interpretation is that political jobs are especially secure and desirable. Thus they are to be reserved for ''insiders.'' (Moreover, there is an obvious incentive to set up an insider–outsider distinction for precisely this sort of reason.)

Suppose this interpretation is correct. Then it is possible to look at restrictive access to employment opportunities of this sort as a kind of defection or failure to comply with the initial (hypothetical) understanding, the point of which was to create an efficient and fair distribution of the world's resources among its members. Not surprisingly, some resources will be especially attractive and individuals will always be trying to renegotiate the bargain to their advantage in ways that may appear to be defections from the initial understanding.

But this is not the only way to look at such behavior. Indeed, it may be part of a sensible strategy to strengthen the nation-state in ways that are important to its stability and capacity to function as an efficient producer and distributor of the world's resources. In a similar way we might think of certain apparently selfish actions by states as ways of allowing states to secure rents as rewards for efficient production. Similar considerations might be useful in helping us to understand the nearly universal immigration policies toward family members. Allowing such individuals total access strengthens and stabilizes political units in ways that might well contribute to their overall efficiency. And so on.

In general we might apply the second approach to distributive justice to illuminate a variety of features associated with immigration policies, especially the allocation of differential bundles of resources to individuals having different statuses. In many of these cases, we can interpret differential treatment as a form of defection or as necessary to strengthen production incentives. Both are illuminating perspectives.

In this essay, we have offered only a sketch of the ways in which individuals might develop the second approach to distributive justice in its relationship to assessing or understanding the immigration policies of modern nation-states. We believe this approach to be very fruitful, but we do not intend to pursue it further here. Instead, we believe that any approach that begins by assuming that the only resources that fall within the domain of distributive justice are those that nation-states can be created to produce and distribute will be fundamentally incomplete.[141] For the state itself creates resources that are important from the point of view of distributive justice. Many of these are well known, though their impact on immigration policies is less clear. We want to focus on a particular resource that falls within the domain of distributive justice and is important for understanding and assessing immigration policies.

IV. Membership in political communities

Consider an alternative approach to evaluating a community's immigration policy. Borders establish not only a "local" framework of efficient production and distribution; borders help to make possible the creation of important resources. The good we want to focus on here is *membership in a political community.* Borders identify territories within which political communities can emerge and flourish. Political communities can extend beyond borders, but in our world they are closely associated with borders. Thus, however important they may be for the efficient production and allocation of resources, political borders play a role in creating another kind of resource: membership in a political community.

Access to borders then typically puts someone in the position, at least potentially, of obtaining membership in a political community. In a full account of immigration policies, we will have to look to access to borders both for the purposes of sharing in a community's wealth and for the purposes of sharing in a community's identity.

In this section we spell out the relationship between membership in a political community and distributive justice and explain the sense in which membership is valuable to individuals. In the final section, we show how a nation's immigration policy can be assessed from the point of view of the claims associated with membership in a political community, including the right to obtain it.

The liberal tradition emphasizes the centrality of the individual. Different conceptions of liberalism spell out the centrality of the individual in different ways. The sort of liberal theory we defend emphasizes the mixture of individual welfare or well-being and autonomy. Other than the fact that individuals have biological needs and experience pain and pleasure, the most important fact from the political point of view about individuals as we know them is that they form projects, plans, and goals and act on the basis of them. These goals provide them with reasons for acting (as do their needs). Satisfying these goals contributes to their well-being. Well-being is itself a way of assessing a life taken as a whole. Autonomy is central both to formulating these plans and to acting on the basis of them. The meaningful exercise of autonomy itself depends on the existence of a meaningful set of options and a framework within which those options can be realized. Well-being depends on autonomy; autonomy depends on options and choices.

Autonomy depends on identity as well. The set of options that appeal to a person, the range of projects and plans that seem worthwhile to her, will depend on who she is, how she conceives of herself. Membership in communities is important to individual well-being because of the way in which membership helps shape the fundamental elements of a person's identity. These communities make certain ways of life possible, while ruling out others.

The groups or communities that are important to individual well-being in this sense typically have a set of common properties.[142] In the first place, the culture and character of the group must be common to the bulk of its members. Second, the culture and character of the group must be sufficiently pervasive that those who grow up within the group acquire the characteristics of the group. Third, members must be recognized as belonging to the group. Fourth, this membership must have a high profile in the sense that it is a primary fact of one's identity. Fifth, membership is typically a matter of belonging rather than achieving. Typically, membership involves a process of assimilation that is in turn slow and not essentially voluntary. Finally, the relevant groups are typically large and anonymous, rather than small and affective. Raz and Margalit refer to these groups as "encompassing."

Raz and Margalit argue that encompassing groups are not necessarily identical with actual nation-states as we know them, yet it is encompassing groups that have a right to self-determination, that could be justifiable political authorities. We do not doubt that Raz and Margalit are right to distinguish analytically between encompassing groups and existing nation-states, but it will be especially illuminating to the general analysis if we imagine that the set of existing nation-states nearly coincides with Razian encompassing groups. Then we might ask why membership in an encompassing group is important for individuals and whether such groups have authority to restrict entrance and exit. Here we are concerned primarily with entrance requirements, but we note that constraints on exit are equally important and that (barring prohibitions against exit) whatever entrance policy a group adopts will interact with exit behavior in ways that are important for an overall account of legitimate constraints on entrance.

In many ways, the most important aspect of an encompassing group is the fact that it shares a culture, or that a culture is pervasive within it. Thus we might take some liberties and refer to encompassing groups as cultural communities. In saying that, however, we want to stress two provisos. We do not mean thereby to identify legitimate political groups with cultural groups in the narrow sense of the term. Encompassing groups require a kind of anonymity that is not present in the typical, narrowly conceived cultural group or intentional or affective community. Moreover, not every cultural community will constitute a *legitimate* encompassing group – that is, one that could have a legitimate authority to govern or rule over its members. In order for such a community to be legitimate it would have to satisfy certain constraints of justice and morality more generally. The most important of these is the requirement that the ways of life associated with it not be oppressive. In our view, this is a constraint imposed by the concept of individual autonomy. Thus, at the same time that these groups make possible the conditions of autonomy, they cannot violate the demands of autonomy.

In *Liberalism, Community and Culture*, Will Kymlicka argues that cultural communities are an integral part of the liberal tradition. In his view, membership in such communities provides a "context of choice."[143] Communities provide the framework within which individuals form identities, formulate projects, plans, and goals based on legitimate expectations regarding the behavior of others. This liberal conception of the community is significantly different from the communitarian conception. In communitarianism, communities assume a significance in and of themselves, whereas in the liberal tradition, communities are important because they provide a framework within which *individuals* formulate and execute their life plans. Communities are thus instrumentally important for the well-being of their members.

We have explained some of the ways in which membership in a political community is important for an individual, and therefore essential to liberal political theory. The question we now want to take up is whether membership in a political community is a concern of distributive justice. The first model of distributive justice we set forth earlier, in which the principles of distributive justice apply to members of political communities of certain kinds, presupposes the idea of membership in a political community. Membership is not itself a good allocated under the auspices of distributive justice so conceived; rather it sets the domain within which distributive justice is thought to apply. Thus membership is logically prior to distributive justice. And it is for precisely this reason that the model of distributive justice itself appears to provide so little guidance in thinking about immigration policy.[144]

The second model of distributive justice provides no one with any non-instrumental or noncollectivist reason for being in one nation or political community or another. One should be wherever it makes sense for one to be given the collective goal of maximally efficient and fair distribution of the world's resources. No claims are based directly on any individual's goals and the constraints those claims might impose on the actions of others. Part of the missing ingredient in the second approach to distributive justice is the failure to countenance the way in which borders can help to create resources, especially important ones from the point of view of individual well-being, namely those arising from the fact that borders help to make political communities possible.[145]

The first approach to distributive justice presupposes membership in political communities; the second approach ignores it. In fact, membership in a political community is an important resource, one, moreover, that falls within the ambit of distributive justice. Let us see if we can make this point clearer.

There are a variety of questions one can ask about distributive justice, including those pertaining to its domain. Domain questions can be of at least two sorts, those pertaining to the entities that can have claims in distributive justice and those pertaining to the objects of those claims. In the first category fall questions about animals, children, the infirm, those who might not be able to contribute to the production of wealth, and so on. Typically, questions of the second sort invite us to consider whether distributive justice allocates resources, welfare, wealth, well-being, the opportunities to secure these, or something else altogether.

In our view, the domain of distributive justice is individual well-being. The pursuit of goals is important to an individual just because it promises to contribute to his well-being. That his actions affect his welfare in this sense provides him with reasons for acting. That collective decisions can affect the welfare of others gives each of us agent-neutral reasons for acting. That some of our actions affect the well-being of others gives each of us, under certain circumstances, agent-relative reasons for acting. Opportunities and other resources are important because of the way they contribute to an individual's well-being. We do not have to reach the question of whether welfare or well-being in this sense is subjective or objective in order to realize the importance to each individual of providing a framework within which individuals can formulate and seek to execute their projects and plans.

If Kymlicka is correct, membership in a cultural community provides that framework. We should not understand Kymlicka to be claiming that this relationship between individual well-being and membership in a cultural community is in any way necessary. The world could have been other than it is. Nevertheless, the relationship, though contingent, is fundamental in our world. In another possible world, cultural communities might be freestanding, their maintenance assured by goodwill or reciprocity. In our world, this is not normally the case. In our world, the health of cultural communities is closely tied to the efforts made on their behalf by political communities. And it is therefore through access to political communities that one typically secures meaningful access to the relevant cultural community. Remember, however, that we mean by cultural community what Raz and Margalit call encompassing groups, not narrow ethnic communities or affective, intentional communities.

In the case of several of the countries we have studied, notably, Germany, Japan, and Israel, there is a virtual overlap between the political and the cultural. This is not to say that cultural diversity is absent in these countries. But the perception of a dominant culture persists and continues to be a defining feature of membership in these political communities. This is not true of the United States and is somewhat less true of Canada. In the case of the United States, at least, one thing we might want to say is that the underlying common culture is fundamentally a political culture: a liberal political culture of tolerance. This will be discussed more fully later.

For now, the key point in the argument is the centrality of membership in a political community to the particular liberal conception of distributive justice that we advance. Given these considerations, one might argue that among the "universal" principles of distributive justice, those that apply beyond the scope of political communities as such is the right to membership in a political community.

Before closing this section, we want to clarify two additional points. The first has to do with whether there is a right to membership in a political community; the second concerns liberal constraints on encompassing groups or cultural communities.

There are technical reasons for denying that individuals can have a right to membership in a political community or encompassing group. Such a right would impose a duty on an extremely large number of people to sustain such groups. Individuals do not in fact have such responsibilities; indeed, these sorts of duties seem incompatible with the idea of human freedom and autonomy. On the other hand, it is easy to see why individuals would want to have encompassing groups as well as why they would want to be members of them. So they might act to create such groups. There might be certain duties to sustain such groups based on the terms of the arrangement among the membership. But there would be no duty to sustain or create such a community just for the purposes of having a community. Moreover, though there are reasons for creating such communities, membership is typically a matter of belonging, of assimilation, not of voluntary choice or merit.

Instead of saying that individuals have a right to membership in a political community or encompassing group, we might say that membership is a *precondition* of autonomy, and ultimately of individual well-being. Without such groups, there is no meaningful autonomy, no ways of life one can choose or fundamental social practices in which one can participate. Thus, while it may be a mistake to claim that individuals have a right to membership in such groups, that such groups must be created and sustained, we should say instead that the very concept of individual autonomy that is central to the liberal ideal presupposes the existence of such groups.

Because encompassing groups are central to autonomy and individual well-being in the sense just explained, the sorts of groups that can have authority over individuals must be compatible with more abstract ideals of autonomy. At the very least, such groups cannot be oppressive; the ways of life created and sustained by them must respect personal dignity. The role of slave, for example, would be ruled out. Cultures that oppress women would also be ruled out, and so on. Autonomy requires a choice among a meaningful range of options and ways of life. Therefore, while a group need not offer all possible ways of life as options within a culture, it must offer a reasonable set of alternatives. And as we noted before, these options cannot be oppressive. We might also say that an encompassing group could have authority over individuals within its domains only if it respected human rights more generally. In other words, even though encompassing groups provide the context of choice and the preconditions of meaningful autonomy and well-being, there are independent dimensions of morality and justice as well as a more general conception of autonomy that provide constraints on the legitimate exercise of power of these groups.

In the next section we want to show how contemporary immigration policies can be understood by emphasizing the importance of membership in a political community.

V. Immigration and membership in a political community

We begin by discussing temporary immigration policies. Temporary residents are normally business travelers, workers, students, and vacationers. Most countries restrict temporary workers to those with sufficient skills to find meaningful employment. Employment is encouraged only if there is a labor market need. It turns out that this requirement is easiest to meet for professionals and other highly educated individuals. As for students and visitors, entrance to all countries will be denied if there is any indication that the applicant intends to stay indefinitely. Typically the resources a nation makes available to temporary residents are rather meager, namely, emergency services. It follows that, by and large, all who fall into this group can be thought of as net wealth producers. That is, their presence within a community's borders provides net benefits to individuals who are already members of the political community. Therefore, such policies can be understood as reflecting the responsibility of the relevant political authorities to act on behalf of the interests of its present membership. In addition, allowing temporary access of this sort may also be part of reciprocal understandings among nations. Thus permission to cross one's borders normally gives one's citizens similar access elsewhere and contributes, therefore, to their well-being indirectly.

Now let us take a look at the way in which membership in a political community figures in our assessment of other aspects of typical immigration policies, including various forms of so-called permanent residence. In the first place, if membership in a stable nonoppressive encompassing group is a precondition of autonomy and well-being, it follows that the strongest claim to immigration belongs to political refugees and other oppressed groups who have been denied a right to membership (in the relevant sense) in a legitimate political community. And it is interesting that virtually every country opens its borders to political refugees who satisfy the basic definition of political refugee set out in the Geneva Convention. Even in countries whose borders are relatively closed – for example, Japan and German – refugees are entitled to immigrate. The recognition of this right to membership is also evident in the existence of special programs designed to assist refugees in integrating into the political community in question.

Some of these claims can be stronger than others. For example, it is possible to argue that most of the Haitians seeking entry into the United States are political refugees largely as a result of U.S. foreign policy.[146] If this is correct, it would appear that the Haitian refugees would have an even stronger claim to immigrate to the United States than they would otherwise have, a claim that is nevertheless quite strong for the reasons already noted. That last claim would be equally strong against all countries. Of course, the government of the United States claims that the Haitians are escaping economic deprivation. It is significant that economic deprivation as such is not a ground for immigration under the refugee rubric, thus giving more weight to the claim that the admission of refugees is based primarily on their right to membership in a political community rather than some other recognized need.

Given the argument we have presented, another group that would have a strong claim to immigration would be those who could claim a special attachment to the destination community. Close family members fall into this category. Again, this claim is contingent. The world could be different. It could be one in which family ties were less important to an individual's sense of well-being. In fact, however, we live in a world in which family connections are strong and meaningful and directly related to individual well-being. If it is part of the role of a legitimate political community, as we claim it is, to create conditions that are conducive to the well-being of its members, then it makes perfect sense that it would encourage family reunification by admitting foreign family members.

Furthermore, some of the countries we discussed go beyond providing family members with the opportunity to immigrate for the purposes of reunification. It is not uncommon, as is the case in France, to provide family members with immunity from expulsion, as long as the family connection remains intact or, as is the case in Germany, the United Kingdom, Israel, and the United States, to reduce or eliminate some of the naturalization requirements for family members.

There is an interesting difference between the refugee case and the family member case. The argument for allowing political and other refugees follows from the responsibility of each nation to provide an opportunity for each individual to have access to the relevant communities. The beneficiary of such policies, then, would be the refugee. In contrast, the beneficiary of policies that allow immigration for family members is as likely to be the family members who are already part of the political community as it is those individuals who are seeking inclusion. It would not be worth making so much of the claims of family members and refugees to membership in the relevant political community if it were not also the case that family and refugee immigration makes up the vast majority of immigration in the countries we have studied. Even in the United States, where immigrants of all sorts are more widely accepted, family and refugee groups are not subject to the numerically limited preference system to which other immigrants are subject. A similar situation prevails in Canada.

The remaining category of individuals who have what we have identified as strong claims to membership in the relevant political community are those with historical, political, and/or cultural ties. The immigration policies of every nation we studied reveals a considerable emphasis on precisely these sorts of relationships. An obvious example is the relaxing of immigration controls in France and the United Kingdom for citizens of some of the countries that were once colonies. There are probably many ways of understanding such policies, but one way, perhaps the best way, is to see them as reflecting the sort of historical relationship that grounds a claim to immigrate. It is interesting that as time passes and the colonial relationship which provides the basis for these privileges recedes into the past, less significance is placed on the relationship and consequently fewer privileges are granted; France is trying to repatriate its Algerian population, and the only remains of the notion of a British subject, which once extended to all commonwealth citizens and provided them with privileged access to Britain, is the category of patrials. The ties that have persisted are those that are also supported by an additional cultural tie and, perhaps, geographic proximity. Nowhere is this more evident than in the relationship between Ireland and the United Kingdom, where the Irish are even granted the right to vote.

Often a weak cultural or political connection combined with assurances of reciprocal treatment suffices for the establishment of a special relationship between countries. The relationships among the various Nordic countries, the countries of the EC, and the United States and Canada have all provided the basis for agreements that relax immigration controls for members of the respective communities.

On a historical note, the quota system that prevailed in the United States and Canada until approximately thirty years ago could be viewed as a reflection of the strength of cultural ties. The quota system was designed to ensure that the majority of immigrants came from countries with cultures similar to those already prevalent in the United States and Canada: primarily European countries. Since that time, both of these countries have adopted a nondiscriminatory approach in which all immigrants, with the exception of the groups with strong claims to membership as already discussed, have at least in theory an equal opportunity to claim membership regardless of their country of origin.

If the individual in question does not have a strong claim to membership under one of the categories discussed, her claim must depend on her willingness to become a member of the relevant political community. Here there is no argument that the person is already in some fundamental way a member of the community. Instead, the person is asked to demonstrate her intention to become a member of the community. This invariably involves a period of residence in the relevant political community. Although this naturally presumes legal residence, it could be argued that extended illegal residence is an acceptable demonstration of intention. Illegal residents are often recognized as de facto members of the community as evidenced in the provisions for legalization of status during periods of amnesty.

In addition to residence it may be, as in Germany and Japan, that adjustment of status to that of permanent resident requires complying with various conditions designed to ensure that such residents have the potential to become full members of the community. The privileged status of permanent residents as potential citizens is manifested in their entitlement to all of the socioeconomic resources available in the relevant political community. Certain entitlements are reserved for citizens, primarily the right to vote and immunity from deportation, entitlements essential to one's sense of total inclusion and belonging in the community in question. Certain duties may also be required of citizens – for example, the duty to remain or to provide military service – from which noncitizens are exempt. Such duties provide evidence of the importance of maintaining the community, of ensuring that it flourishes and is conducive to the well-being of all its members. But this does not tell us anything about becoming members, about what constitutes an intention to become a member.

In Germany, Japan, and Israel, to become a member in effect means to integrate oneself into the national culture: to become German, Japanese, or Jewish. Invariably, for full citizenship, there are waiting periods and tests one has to pass, obstacles one has to overcome. The nature of the tests and the nature of the obstacles are themselves functions of the nature of the underlying political community. In Germany and Japan, the underlying political community is basically a cultural community and in Israel it is a religious community. The tests of membership reflect these conceptions of the community and are thus relatively difficult to comply with: one must learn to become German, Japanese, or Jewish.

The same is true, although not to such an extent, in the United Kingdom, France, and Sweden. The nature of the underlying political community in all three of these countries is difficult to identify. To a certain extent their policies, which are fundamentally a reflection of their particular circumstances, obfuscate the predominant character of the political community. Sweden's policies best exemplify this. Sweden's immigration and naturalization policies are in general very liberal, in many ways even more so than the policies of Canada and the United States. But Sweden is a strikingly homogeneous community. Until recently the majority of immigrants came from other Nordic countries or Northern Europe. Furthermore, Sweden has made a valiant effort to integrate its immigrants and has gone so far as to provide them with a limited right to vote. Both of these factors have allowed Sweden to pursue very liberal membership policies while simultaneously maintaining a relatively strong cultural community. To become a member of the Swedish political community is fundamentally to become Swedish.

France and the United Kingdom also continue to maintain a strong cultural base; France even requires some evidence of integration as a condition of naturalization. But again neither country can be said to be as concerned with the maintenance of the cultural community at the level of policy as Germany. This makes it difficult to identify what it is to be a member of these political communities, but at their core they are fundamentally cultural communities. It could also be argued that this is the combined effect of their respective immigration, citizenship, and naturalization policies. To become a member of the French or British political communities is to become respectively a French or British person. Perhaps the inclusion of citizens from distant countries that were once colonies has tempered the policies of these countries such that they are more receptive to diversity. But the political community in either case is still predominantly a cultural community.[147]

This is not true of the United States. We want to suggest that we look at the relevant culture of the United States as itself a political culture. It is not committed to a religion or to a way of life, but to a set of political ideals. These ideals include tolerance with respect to various ways of life, religious freedom, and the like. To be an American ultimately is to accept liberal political ideals. Unlike Germany, where the political community is based on a single predominant culture, a culture that the political community perceives as providing the context for the well-being of its members, the United States, not by accident, consists overwhelmingly of a plurality of cultures. To foster the well-being of its members, the political community cannot afford to identify with any one culture but rather must focus on ensuring the mutual toleration of the various cultural communities. It is in this way that to be part of the U.S. political community is to be part of a political culture.

This form of cultural community creates enormous tensions, for the political ideal may well be in conflict with the cultural communities it supersedes. Thus there is pressure in a large, heterogeneous society like ours to foster local cultures, to have, for example, classes in the public schools taught in what we would think of as foreign languages. There will be pressure to have such cultures represented in the public sphere, in particular in the arts and politics. And there will be outcries that the failure or unwillingness to do so reflects a commitment to Western European culture rather than the political ideal that is the culture of the United States.

This argument rests on a mistake, however. It does not follow from the fact that some cultures, including Western European ones, adopt certain values, like tolerance, liberty, and rationality, that these values are adopted in the United States because they reflect a European culture. They are adopted and defended as political ideals, as worthy of respect and support, whether or not anyone else, anywhere else, adopts them. They are not adopted to reflect in our political culture the ideals of a European culture. They are adopted because they are, one might argue, worthy of founding a nation upon.

Nevertheless, tensions of this sort will appear. Such tensions will also be reflected in our immigration policies. For on the one hand, our policies will rightly favor groups with whom we are culturally and historically tied, while on the other hand, they will ask of others who seek permanent residence here that they show commitment to political ideals above cultural ties. But that stands to reason. It is not a problem that emerges in formulating the immigration policies of largely homogeneous communities, but it is a problem at the core of heterogeneous communities.

To be part of the Canadian political community is also fundamentally to be part of a political culture, a culture similar to that which prevails in the United States. The cores of these two communities are essentially the same. But Canada has chosen to deal with the tensions inherent in such a community in a slightly different way. Canada's multiculturalism policy pushes the notion of toleration to another level in that it aims to accommodate rather than integrate diverse cultural communities. Whether or not this policy has been successful, it has been a trademark of the Canadian political community. The decision to adopt such a policy may have been influenced by the fundamental bicultural nature of Canada. But this distinction, this unique policy decision, should not obfuscate the fact that to be a Canadian is to be a member of a political culture.

Membership in each of the eight political communities we have studied entails something different. At one end of the spectrum sit the United States and Canada. In both cases, membership requires integrating oneself into what is essentially a political culture held together by political ideals. Somewhere in between reside France, the United Kingdom, and Sweden.[148] At the other end of the spectrum sit Germany, Japan, and Israel, political communities in which membership entails commitment to an ethnic association and to a particular way of life.

VI. Conclusion

Political borders are arbitrary from the moral point of view. Some might argue that no one within a political territory thus has a right in justice to exclude others. The arbitrariness of political borders entails that there is no principled ground for any immigration policy other than open borders. Yet it hardly follows from the fact that those within a political border have no rightful claim to the territory and its resources that those outside the territory do. Some might take this to mean that countries have a right in morality to close their borders to immigrants. Both of these views, however, are unacceptable. Even if borders are arbitrarily or conventionally set, it does not follow that they lack moral significance. Conventions, even arbitrary ones, can have morally significant consequences.

We have suggested that the morally significant consequences of political borders depend in part on their relationship to the idea of a political community. We have argued that the very ideas of autonomy and individual well-being that are essential to liberalism presuppose such communities. From this humble, if controversial, starting point we have argued that all refugees have a right to immigrate. Morally, all borders must remain open to political refugees. Others do not have a right to immigrate. Political communities can exclude. On the other hand, the same factors that give authorities a right to rule over a political territory give rise to a set of relevant reasons for granting access to the political community. Political communities are authorized to rule only if they contribute essentially to the well-being of their members. They can do this through policies of family reunification and those permitting access to nonmembers with cultural or historical ties. In some political communities, identified primarily with liberal political ideals – for example, Canada and the United States – the authority of the state may suggest reasons for opening borders to all persons who are prepared to demonstrate a sincere intention to become a member of that community by adopting the organizing political ideals from an internal point of view.[149]

Notes

1 These countries have been chosen partially because they exemplify different trends in immigration policies but also because we were able to find a substantial amount of accessible material on them. In particular, William R. Brubaker (ed.), *Immigration and the Politics of Citizenship in Europe and North America* (New York: University Press of America, 1989), and Richard Plender, *International Migration Law*, 2d ed. (Dordrecht: Kluwer, 1987), provided helpful information on most of the countries.

2 The United States is the leading country of immigration in the world. See Robert W. Gardner and Leon F. Bouvier, "The United States," in William J. Serow et al. (eds.), *Handbook on International Migration* (New York: Greenwood Press, 1990), 341.

3 William R. Brubaker, "Introduction," in Brubaker (ed.), *Immigration and the Politics of Citizenship*, 7–8.

4 Although France is one of the few European countries that for many years encouraged permanent immigration and settlement. See "The Loi Pasqua: 1986 Revisions to French Immigration Law," *Georgetown Immigration Law Journal* 2 (1987): 223–4.

5 Germany and France have even attempted to repatriate some foreign nationals,

particularly Turks and Algerians, some of whom originally migrated for temporary employment. See, e.g., Christian Nguyen Van Yen, *Droit de l'immigration* (Paris: Presses Universitaires de France, 1986), 203–9.

6 In Germany, for example, there has been a steady movement of foreign nationals despite its apparently restrictive immigration and naturalization policies. See Plender, *International Migration Law*, 314.

7 In 1984 there were 841,831 registered foreign nationals, 89 percent of whom were Koreans who had been there since before the Second World War. Despite this relatively large population of Koreans, only 125,945 have been naturalized since 1952. See Hosokawa Kiyoshi, "Japanese Nationality in International Perspective," in Ko Swan Sik (ed.), *Nationality and International Law in Asian Perspective* (Boston: Nijhoff, 1990), 181.

8 The apparent discrimination in Israeli immigration policy is usually justified by the argument that such policies do not so much discriminate against any racial group as privilege Jews. See David Kretzmer, *The Legal Status of the Arabs in Israel* (Boulder: Westview Press, 1989), 35.

9 Illegal access does not fit neatly into either of these divisions, and yet the legality of one's status also influences entitlement to resources. Illegal immigration is by its very nature difficult to assess. It is safe to say, however, that there are those who illegally enter foreign countries for the purpose of seeking temporary work and others who plan permanent settlement. The rising number of illegal aliens has led to an increasing concern about dealing with them in an effective and fair manner. The actual number of illegal aliens residing in the United States has been estimated to be anywhere from 1 million to 12 million. See Julian Simon, *The Economic Consequences of Immigration* (Oxford: Basil Blackwell, 1989), 279–84. In many of the countries to be discussed, illegal aliens have been able to legalize their status during periods of amnesty. See, e.g., Immigration Reform and Control Act of 1986 (hereafter IRCA) § 201 (adding Immigration and Nationality Act [hereafter INA] § 245A) (8 U.S.C. § 1255). See also Plender, *International Migration Law*, 317–18 (France).

In an attempt to reduce illegal immigration, most countries have also adopted policies imposing sanctions on employers who hire illegal aliens. See, e.g., IRCA § 101(a) (adding INA § 274(a),(f)) (8 U.S.C. § 1324). See also Plender, *International Migration Law*, 317–18 (France) and 319 (Canada); "Georgia Harvster Is Fined $1 Million in Alien Smuggling," *New York Times*, February 8, 1992.

In the 1994 election, California voters, frustrated by the ineffectiveness of employer sanctions, decided by an overwhelming majority to deny fundamental social services, including education and nonemergency health care, to illegal immigrants (State of California Proposition 187). See "Proposition 187 Backers Elated – Challenges Imminent," *Los Angeles Times*, November 9, 1994.

10 Some individuals are, however, admitted on the assumption that they will eventually adjust their status to that of permanent resident.

11 See, e.g., in the United States, Immigration Act of 1990 (hereafter IA 1990), § 601 (amending INA § 212(a)) (8 U.S.C. § 1182); and in Canada, Immigration Act, R.S.C. 1985, c.I-2, s. 19.

12 In Canada see Immigration Regulations, 1978 SOR/78-172, s. 13(1), sch. 2(5). In the United States see 8 U.S.C. § 1182 (d)(4)(B). The United States has extended this privilege of entering as a visitor without a visa to eight other countries: Japan, France, Italy, the Netherlands, Sweden, Switzerland, the United Kingdom, and Germany (IA 1990, § 201(a) amending INA, § 217 (8 U.S.C. § 1187)).

13 In the United Kingdom, Immigration Act 1971, c. 77, ss. 1(3), 11(4); and in Ireland, Aliens (Amendment) Order 1975, Art. 2(2). See Ian A. MacDonald and Nicholas J. Blake, *Immigration Law and Practice in the United Kingdom* (London: Butterworths, 1991), 122–3, 127.

14 Trans Tasman Travel Arrangement of 1973, as discussed by Ronald F. Moore, "Australia," in Serow et al. (eds.), *Handbook on International Migration Law*, 11–12.

15 European Agreement on Regulations Governing the Movement of Persons between Member States of the Council of Europe, Paris, 13 Dec. 1957, 315 U.N.T.S. 139. See Plender, *International Migration Law*, 344.

16 Agreement Concerning the Nordic Labour Market, Copenhagen, 22 May 1954, 198 U.N.T.S. 47. See Plender, *International Migration Law*, 288.

17 Moore, "Australia," 11–12.

18 Treaty of Rome, 25 March 1957, Art. 48, 298 U.N.T.S. 11. See Plender, *International Migration Law*, 193–225; and MacDonald and Blake, *Immigration Law and Practice in the United Kingdom*, 148–56.

19 Agreement Concerning the Nordic Labour Market.

20 Nguyen Van Yen, *Droit de l'immigration*, 206–9.

21 Kay Hailbronner, "Citizenship and Nationhood in Germany," in Brubaker (ed.), *Immigration and the Politics of Citizenship*, 74.

22 As quoted in Calvin Goldscheider, "Israel," in Serow et al. (eds.), *Handbook on International Migration*, 135.

23 Kretzmer, *The Legal Status of the Arabs in Israel*, 35.

24 Ibid., 36.

25 As cited in M. D. Gouldman, *Israel Nationality Law* (Jerusalem: Institute for Legislative Research and Comparative Law, 1970), 19.

26 Yuri Iwasawa, "Legal Treatment of Koreans in Japan: The Impact of International Human Rights Law on Japanese Law," *Human Rights Law Quarterly* 8 (1986): 150–2.

27 From the Second World War to 1984, 601,430 individuals had obtained permanent resident status. Of these, 577,525 were Korean and 20,825 were Chinese. Kiyoshi, "Japanese Nationality in International Perspective," 181.

28 On November 1, 1994, the immigration minister, Sergio Marchi, announced that the number of immigrants accepted each year would drop from 230,000 in 1994 to between 190,000 and 215,000 in 1995. Beginning in 1995, the percentage of family members will drop from 51% to 44% and the percentage of economic immigrants will rise from 45% to 55%. Mark Clayton, "Some Foreigners Need Not Apply Under Canada's Immigration Plan," *Christian Science Monitor*, November 3, 1994; Richard Gwyn, "Marchi Raises Flickering Torch of Canadianism," *Toronto Star*, November 2, 1994.

29 The 1992 ceiling on visas for family members in the United States was 465,000.
    IA 1990 § 101(a) (adding INA § 201(c)) (8 U.S.C. § 1151). Most of these were
    granted to immediate family members of U.S. citizens, with the remainder going
    to more remote family members of citizens and spouses and children of legalized
    aliens. IA 1990 § 101(a), 111 (amending INA § 201(b)(2), 203(a)) (8 U.S.C. §§
    1151, 1153).

30 IA 1990 § 101(a) (adding INA § 201(b)(2)) (8 U.S.C. § 1151).

31 IA 1990 § 111 (amending INA § 203(a)) (8 U.S.C. § 1153).

32 The regulations include the provision of an undertaking by the sponsor to support
    the applicant for ten years: Immigration Regulations, S.O.R./78-172, s. 6(1)(b)(i)
    and s. 2(1). Sergio Marchi has recently proposed that immigrants arriving as fam-
    ily members post bond guaranteeing that they do not resort to social assistance.
    Clayton, "Some Foreigners Need Not Apply."

33 Immigration Regulations, S.O.R./78-172, s. 10.

34 Immigration Regulations, S.O.R./78-172, ss. 8 and 9.

35 "Settled" in the United Kingdom is defined as "being ordinarily resident there
    without being subject under the immigration laws to any restrictions on the period
    for which [one] may remain." Immigration Act 1971, s. 33(2A). The phrase gen-
    erally covers those with a right of abode (for the most part British citizens) and
    those with indefinite leave to enter and who are ordinarily resident. See, generally,
    MacDonald and Blake, *Immigration Law and Practice in the United Kingdom*,
    76.

36 Immigration Rules (HC 251), paras. 50 (spouses), 53 (children), 56 (parents).

37 Immigration Rules (HC 251), paras. 50(d)(e) (spouse) and 52 (other relatives).

38 Immigration Rules (HC 251), paras. 51 (spouses) and 52.

39 Plender, *International Migration Law*, 377.

40 Ibid., 368. Although the law now requires one year of marriage as proof that the
    marriage was not one of convenience: Law of September 9, 1986, No. 86-1025,
    App. C. Pen., Etrangers, ch. II, § II, art. 15, para. 1, as cited in "The Loi Pasqua,"
    225.

41 Plender, *International Migration Law*, 378.

42 Ibid., 315.

43 Kiyoshi, "Japanese Nationality in International Perspective," 211.

44 8 U.S.C. §§ 1423, 1427. See also William R. Brubaker, "Citizenship and Natu-
    ralization: Policies and Politics," in Brubaker (ed.), *Immigration and the Politics
    of Citizenship*, 109–10. British Nationality Act 1981, s. 6(1),(2) and sch. 1(1),(3).

45 C. Nat., Art. 37-1, at 25, as cited in John Guendelsberger, "Reforming French
    Nationality Law: The Report of the Commission on Nationality," *Georgetown
    Immigration Law Journal* 3 (1988): 151, 152.

46 Brubaker, "Citizenship and Naturalization," 113.

47 The definition of a refugee found in Article 1 of the Geneva Convention is any
    person who "owing to a well-founded fear of being persecuted for reasons of
    race, religion, nationality, membership in a particular social group or political
    opinion, is outside the country of his nationality and is unable or, owing to such
    a fear, is unwilling to avail himself of the protection of that country; or who, not

having a nationality and being outside the country of his former habitual residence
. . . is unable or, owing to such a fear, is unwilling to return to it.'' Convention
Relating to the Status of Refugees, Geneva, 28 July, 1951; 189 U.N.T.S. 150. See
Plender, *International Migration Law*, 415–24.

48 Protocol relating to the Status of Refugees, New York, 31 January 1967, 606
U.N.T.S. 267.

49 See Plender, *International Migration Law*, 408 (France) and 409 (Sweden). The
Swedish Aliens Act, for example, includes de facto refugees, ''a category broader
than normally defined in municipal legislation.'' Ibid.

50 See Hilde Wander, ''Federal Republic of Germany,'' in Serow et al. (eds.), *Handbook on International Migration*, 52.

51 Immigration Act, R.S.C. 1985, c. 1-2, ss. 2(1) and 46.04; and Immigration Regulations, S.O.R./78-172, s. 40. See, generally, Lawyers Committee for Human
Rights, *Uncertain Haven* (New York: Lawyers Committee for Human Rights,
1991), 135–43.

52 Federal German Constitution of 1949 (Basic Law), Art. 16(2). The German Constitution has very recently been amended to permit the refusal of refugees who
pass through another country considered to be a safe haven on their way to Germany. The amendments replace Article 16(2) with Article 16a. It is too early to
determine the effect of this amendment on the flow of refugees into Germany, but
before this amendment, Germany received approximately 60% of Europe's asylum
seekers. See Wander, ''Federal Republic of Germany,'' 52. See also G. Stephen,
''Last Straw? Refugees Occupy Beer's Fabled Field,'' *New York Times*, March
19, 1992.

53 For a discussion of the recent constitutional changes, see Sam Blay and Andreas
Zimmerman, ''Recent Changes in German Refugee Law: A Critical Assessment,''
American Journal of International Law 88 (1994): 361.

54 Immigration Rules (HC 251), para. 21.

55 MacDonald and Blake, *Immigration Law and Practice in the United Kingdom*,
303–4.

56 Ibid., 303.

57 Immigration Rules (HC 251), paras. 21 and 75.

58 See, generally, Fernando Chang-Muy, ''International Refugee Law in Asia,'' *New
York University Journal of International Law and Policy* 24 (1992): 1171.

59 This was the method of the European recruitment programs of the 1960s and
1970s, which drew a large number of foreign migrant workers. See Plender, *International Migration Law*, 315–16.

60 Canada deals with independent (nonimmediate family) permanent immigrant applicants on a discretionary point system. Immigration Regulations, S.O.R./78-172,
ss. 8 and 9. The points granted are based on economic considerations, including
education, training, and experience, in addition to suitability factors such as age
and knowledge of either French or English. Immigration Regulations, S.O.R./78-
172, sch. 1.

61 The total number of employment-based positions was limited to 140,000 in 1992.
These openings are divided into five categories, covering everything from out-

standing professors and researchers to unskilled workers, each with its own numerical limitation. IA 1990 § 101(a) (adding INA § 201(d)) (8 U.S.C. § 1151)
(numerical limitation) and IA 1990 § 121(a) (adding INA § 203(b)) (8 U.S.C. §
1135) (preference categories).

62 The United Kingdom requires four years of residence before a foreign national,
resident for employment purposes, can apply for "indefinite leave." Immigration
Rules (HC 251), para. 139. See generally MacDonald and Blake, *Immigration
Law and Practice in the United Kingdom*, 77–8. France requires three years before
an application for a "carte de résidence" can be made. Law of July 17, 1984,
No. 84-622, App. C. Pen. Etrangers, ch. II § II, art. 14, para. 1, as cited in "The
Loi Pasqua," 225. See also Plender, *International Migration Law*, 160. Permanent
work permits are not granted in Germany until after ten years of residence. See
Plender, *International Migration Law*, 314–15. In Sweden, access to permanent
residence is available to foreign nationals after only a year of residence. William
Brubaker, "Membership without Citizenship: The Economic and Social Rights
of Noncitizens," in Brubaker (ed.), *Immigration and the Politics of Citizenship*,
150–1.

63 Kiyoshi, "Japanese Nationality in International Perspective," 223.

64 Ibid. Germany has a similar restriction: it provides nonspecific work permits only
to those who have been in residence for more than five years. Spouses and refugees are automatically granted nonspecific work permits. See Plender, *International Migration Law*, 314–15.

65 Brubaker, "Membership without Citizenship," 152.

66 Ibid., 153.

67 See, e.g., *Sugarman v. Dougall*, 413 U.S. 634 (1973) (New York law restricting
competitive class civil service jobs to citizens was held to be unconstitutional),
and *Hampton v. Mow Sun Wong*, 426 U.S. 88 (1976) (federal law restricting
competitive class civil service jobs was held to be unconstitutional). See also
Iwasawa, "Legal Treatment of Koreans in Japan," 131.

68 Kiyoshi, "Japanese Nationality in International Perspective," 217.

69 Ibid., 214–15, 221–23.

70 See, e.g., IRCA § 101(a) and Plender, *International Migration Law*, 317–18
(France) and 319 (Canada).

71 In the U.S. see *Plyer v. Doe*, 457 U.S. 202 (1982). But see State of California
Proposition 187.

72 Firsthand experience has taught me that foreign students in England are entitled
to the benefits of the national health care system.

73 See, e.g., Kiyoshi, "Japanese Nationality in International Perspective," 213–15,
221–2 (for a discussion of socioeconomic rights available to aliens in Japan); and
Brubaker, "Membership without Citizenship," 156–7 (for a brief discussion of
the socioeconomic rights available to aliens in Germany).

74 Brubaker, "Membership without Citzenship," 158–9. Brubaker cites policies in
Canada and to a limited extent the United States for support. In England, an entry
clearance for settlement will not be issued unless the officer is satisfied that there
will be adequate accommodation and support for the applicant "without recourse

to public funds." Immigration Rules (HC 251), paras. 50(d)(e) (spouse) and 52 (other relatives).

75 Plender, *International Migration Law*, 314–15 (Germany); Kiyoshi, "Japanese Nationality in International Perspective," 211.

76 See Brubaker, "Membership without Citizenship," 156 (Germany), and 157 (Sweden).

77 Kiyoshi, "Japanese Nationality in International Perspective," 189, 213–14; Iwasawa, "Legal Treatment of Koreans in Japan," 166–7.

78 Goran Melander, "Nordic Refugee Law and Policy," *Michigan Yearbook of International Legal Studies* (Ann Arbor: University of Michigan Press, 1982), 229.

79 Brubaker, "Membership without Citizenship," 157.

80 Mark Miller, "Political Participation and Representation of Noncitizens," in Brubaker (ed.), *Immigration and the Politics of Citizenship*, 130. Of course, this does not explain why voting rights are restricted in countries where citizenship is more elusive.

81 Kiyoshi, "Japanese Nationality in International Perspective," 215.

82 Miller, "Political Participation and Representation of Noncitizens," 129, 131.

83 Ibid., 130.

84 Ibid., 129–30.

85 Ibid., 138–9.

86 Ibid., at 137–8.

87 For example, Germany requires eight years, Sweden one year, France three years, and Britain four years. Brubaker, "Membership without Citizenship," 149–52.

88 Ibid., 150–1.

89 Law of July 17, 1984, No. 84-622, App. C. Pen. Etrangers, ch. II § II, art. 14, para. 1, as cited in "The Loi Pasqua," 225. See also Plender, *International Migration Law*, 160.

90 Immigration Rules (HC 251), paras. 51.

91 Immigration Rules (HC 251), para. 139. See, generally, MacDonald and Blake, *Immigration Law and Practice in the United Kingdom*, 77–8.

92 Plender, *International Migration Law*, 314–15.

93 Kiyoshi, "Japanese Nationality in International Perspective," 211.

94 Regulation of non-Jewish immigration is covered under the Entrance to Israel Law, 1952, as cited in Kretzmer, *The Legal Status of Arabs in Israel*, 36, n. 6. See also Goldscheider, "Israel," 135.

95 For a discussion of denationalization, see T. Alexander Aleinikoff, "Theories of Loss of Citizenship," *Michigan Law Review* 84 (1986): 1471.

96 Plender, *International Migration Law*, 462–8.

97 For a discussion of this problem, see Henry Schermers, "The Second Generation of Immigrants," *Michigan Law Review* 81 (1984): 1415.

98 Plender, *International Migration Law*, 377–8.

99 One exception to this can be found in British nationality law. For most of this century Britain was trying to sort out the immigrant status of various categories of citizens and subjects until a more limited British citizenship was created in

1981. See, generally, Laurie Fransman, *Fransman's British Nationality Law* (London: Fourmat, 1989).

100 Although in some countries, primarily Israel, the right to claim citizenship may be extended to certain groups – in the case of Israel, Jews – regardless of their parentage or place of birth.

101 8 U.S.C. § 1401. See also William Brubaker, "Citizenship and Naturalization," 104–5.

102 Brubaker, "Citizenship and Naturalization," 105.

103 8 U.S.C. §§ 1423, 1427. See also Brubaker, "Citizenship and Naturalization," 109–10.

104 Brubaker, "Citizenship and Naturalization," 109–10.

105 Ibid., 113–14.

106 Ibid., 110.

107 Ibid., 117–18. Brubaker points out that 12.7% of the eligible population in Canada is naturalized each year. With respect to cumulative naturalizations, 78% of all eligible persons have been naturalized (119). Compare this with the U.S. statistics: the cumulative percentage is 60% and only 4.9% of the eligible population is naturalized each year (119).

108 See, generally, British Nationality Act 1981, ss. 1-6 and 11; and Fransman, *Fransman's British Nationality Law*, 140–5. Descendants who can claim citizenship are called "patrials." Patrials include those who emigrated from the United Kingdom or had a parent or grandparent who emigrated from the United Kingdom. Ibid., 116–19.

109 British Nationality Act 1981, s.1 (1).

110 British Nationality Act 1981, s.2 (1).

111 See, generally, Fransman, *Fransman's British Nationality Law*, 171, 178–9, 182–3.

112 British Nationality Act 1981, s. 6(1),(2) and sch. 1(1),(3).

113 John Guendelsberger, "Reforming French Nationality Law: The Report of the Commission on Nationality," *Georgetown Immigration Law Journal* 3 (1989): 151–2. See also Brubaker, "Citizenship and Naturalization," 106, and Plender, *International Migration Law*, 35.

114 C. Nat., Art. 23, at 24, as cited in Guendelsberger, "Reforming French Nationality Law," 152.

115 Ibid., Art. 44, at 25–6, as cited in Guendelsberger, "Reforming French Nationality Law," 152. See also Brubaker, "Citizenship and Naturalization," 106, and Plender, *International Migration Law*, 36.

116 Ibid., Arts. 59–71, 27–28, as cited in Guendelsberger, "Reforming French Nationality Law," 152; Brubaker, "Citizenship and Naturalization," 111. See also Nguyen Van Yen, *Droit de l'immigration*, 327.

117 Ibid., Art. 37-1, at 25, as cited in Guendelsberger, "Reforming French Nationality Law," 152.

118 Hailbronner, "Citizenship and Nationhood in Germany," 67.

119 Ibid., 67–8, 73. (Ethnic Germans are referred to as "Germans without German citizenship," 73.)

120 Ibid., 68.

121 Ibid., 70. Brubaker notes that only 0.45% of the eligible population is naturalized each year. Brubaker, "Citizenship and Naturalization," 120.

122 Ibid., 76. Hailbronner comments that most foreigners have no intention of getting German citizenship. In 1985 only 7.5% of Turks, 6.9% of Yugoslavs, and 4.4% of Italians expressed an interest in getting German citizenship.

123 Brubaker, "Citizenship and Naturalization," 122.

124 Ibid., 110.

125 Ibid., 114.

126 Ibid., 118–19.

127 Brubaker, "Introduction," 10.

128 Melander, "Nordic Refugee Law and Policy," 245. Melander states that the Nordic countries base their refugee selection "more on political than on humanitarian grounds."

129 Brubaker, "Citizenship and Naturalization," 105.

130 Nationality Law, 1952, s. 3A, as cited in Kretzmer, *The Legal Status of Arabs in Israel*, 38.

131 Nationality Law, 1952 s. 4(a)(1),(2).

132 Nationality Law, 1952 s. 5.

133 Kretzmer, *The Legal Status of Arabs in Israel*, 40, n. 17.

134 Kiyoshi, "Japanese Nationality in International Perspective," 191–4.

135 Ibid., 206–7.

136 Daniel H. Foote, "Japan's 'Foreign Workers' Policy: A View from the United States," *Georgetown Immigration Law Journal* 7 (1993): 707.

137 Kiyoshi, "Japanese Nationality in International Perspective," 194–8.

138 In the past, it was recommended that applicants take Japanese names at the time of naturalization. Iwasawa, "The Legal Treatment of Koreans in Japan," 149.

139 One can read the post–*Theory of Justice* Rawls as advocating the view that principles of distributive justice are relative to particular political communities in the way we have just outlined. Political communities are connected to actual borders, though there is no reason to think that Rawls himself is committed to the view that borders define in any strong sense the boundaries of the relevant sorts of political communities within which principles of justice apply. There is also no reason to impose any particular theory on Rawls about the principles that ought to apply in deciding upon a defensible immigration policy.

140 In any such scheme, there will be problems of production, distribution, and defection. Immigration as well as foreign aid policies might then be understood as correctives to production inefficiencies and distributive inequities that remain in the system of nation-states. As the distributive dimension of the problem increases in significance, defection incentives likewise increase. This problem is reflected in tensions that exist in modern immigration and foreign aid policies, in efforts to protect our family members, our jobs, and restrictions on immigration to "peoples" most like ourselves.

141 However interesting or illuminating this approach appears to be, we want to suggest that it would remain deeply unsatisfying in two ways. The first problem

is that the world's resources strike us as very unfairly distributed. And if they are, there is something quite disingenuous about reconstructing existing policies in the light of how they contribute to a just distribution. From some not implausible perspective, there exists no just distribution to which current immigration policies can be seen as contributing.

Of course, one could deny that we are far away from a just distribution. But such a critic will have in mind a very different account of what it is that makes a distribution of holdings just. It will not be part of her view that a just distribution conforms to the principles drawn up among free and equal persons of roughly equal initial bargaining position. Her view might be that a just distribution can result from a bargain struck among differentially endowed individuals, or that justice depends on initial acquisition or the like, in which case simple good fortune can dictate the parameters of justice.

Even if we are wrong and the current distribution of the world's resources is just or approximates the demands of justice, a deeper problem would remain with assessing immigration policies from only the distributive justice perspectives we have outlined. The real problem with the second approach is that all claims that particular individuals have to immigrate are fundamentally instrumental or goal driven. Whether someone should be allowed to immigrate depends on whether doing so is likely to have desirable incentive and allocation consequences. By the same token, if the best consequences would result from requiring individuals to immigrate, individuals might have a positive duty to do so. This seems counterintuitive. Moreover, in this view, individuals have no real or fundamental claim to the resources they control. Their relationship to all resources is mediated by the relevant principles of efficient production and fair distribution. The relationship between individuals, territory, and resources, one might argue, is in this approach too tenuous to reflect adequately the normative dimensions of standard claims to immigrate or to immigration policies.

Moreover, all the claims in distributive justice that someone has are claims to a share of the world's resources. Those are the goods that are to be produced and distributed. Whatever those claims may be, they can, if legitimate, be satisfied by some form of wealth transfer. On a larger scale, this sort of wealth transfer is what we might think of as foreign aid. Satisfying these claims hardly requires that we reach issues of immigration. Again, immigration surfaces only to the extent that it may be a better (cheaper, more efficient, or more effective) way than wealth transfers of satisfying the demands of justice.

142　The characteristics that are included here may be too inclusive. Membership in a community that does not have all of the following characteristics may still be important in the relevant sense already discussed. The characteristics included, which come from Joseph Raz and Avishai Margalit, "National Self-Determination," *Journal of Philosophy* 88 (1990): 439, have been chosen because they identify the relevant characteristics of a group that in addition to being essential to the identity and well-being of its members can also legitimately claim the right to self-government. This makes the characteristics identified particularly relevant to our discussion of political communities.

143 Will Kymlicka, *Liberalism, Community and Culture* (Oxford: Oxford University Press, 1991), 162–81.

144 But this model is not necessarily inconsistent with our emphasis on the significance of a claim in justice to membership in a political community. In fact, the essence of this model, that resources are distributed within a political community in accordance with principles of distributive justice, supports the special emphasis we have placed on membership in a political community as far as the distribution of conventional resources is concerned. The legitimacy of a political community is assessed on the basis of its ability to contribute to the well-being of its members, and essential to this is ensuring that members receive adequate conventional resources. This would help explain two aspects of the immigration policies discussed: first, that resources are distributed in accordance with permanence of residence and that a few significant resources which are most essential to a sense of belonging to a political community, voting, for example, are reserved for citizens; second, that all of the countries discussed, regardless of the differences in their admission policies, adopt a similar approach to the distribution of conventional resources. Thus the essential characters of the political communities discussed may be very different but their purposes are fundamentally the same.

145 The claim is not that a political community necessarily requires borders or territory. A political community requires community and political authority, not territory. However, in our world, political authorities are typically associated with territories, and therefore in our world, boundaries facilitate political communities.

146 See, generally, Thomas David Jones, ''The Haitian Refugee Crisis: A Quest for Human Rights,'' *Michigan Journal of International Law* 15 (1993): 77; Andrew I. Schoenholtz, ''Aiding and Abetting Persecutors: The Seisure and Return of Haitian Refugees in Violation of the United Nations Refugees Convention and Protocol,'' *Georgetown Immigration Law Journal* 7 (1993): 67.

147 France, Sweden, and the United Kingdom may be moving toward being political communities held together by political ideals rather than cultural traditions. For more on this see note 149.

148 These three political communities are not easy to characterize, and it may be that they are in a state of flux, slowly transforming from fundamentally cultural communities to communities bonded by a political ideal. We have characterized these political communities on the basis of our own observations of membership in each community and a brief analysis of their immigration, citizenship, and naturalization policies. A more in-depth analysis taking account of historical as well as political changes and the growing significance of the EC as a dominant political and economic force might, we accept, lead to a different characterization.

149 Of course, this responsibility of a state to open its borders will be constrained by its responsibilities to those already within its borders. But it is not obviously true that the claims of those within the borders have an absolute priority over the claims of others.

3

A two-country parable

JAMES M. BUCHANAN

Consider a conceptual experiment. There are two physically separated locational units (call them "countries") that are descriptively identical and also are inhabited initially by equal numbers of humans, who are possessed of identical potential capacities. Throughout the historical period to be considered, there is no economic relationship between inhabitants of the two countries that extend across boundaries. Each unit exists in autarky.

Over some period of time, one of the two countries, call it A, either through an evolutionary process not well understood or through deliberative design and construction of constitutional constraints, comes to be organized in such a fashion that facilitates the production (and potential consumption) of a relatively high level of economic value (as determined by the preferences of inhabitants) and also facilitates relatively high increases in this level of value through time. By comparison, the other country, call it B, although initially equally endowed, does not experience a similar evolution and/or does not undergo a process of successful design and construction of constitutional parameters, effective as measured by the potential for facilitating the generation and growth of economic value. As a result of these disparate histories, the economy of country B produces a relatively low level of value, as measured by the preferences of its inhabitants, and this level increases relatively slowly through time, if at all.

In simpler terms, no matter where he or she is situated positionally within a country, the life of an inhabitant differs substantially between the two separated countries. Persons are relatively "rich" in one setting, A, and relatively "poor" in the other, B. In this situation, many of the inhabitants of country B will desire to migrate to country A if given any opportunity to do so. The question at issue here is: Do those who find themselves to be inhabitants (citizens) of A have any obligation, grounded in principles of justice, to allow those who seek entry to become members?

I suggest that the conceptual experiment constructed here offers the appropriate framework for addressing the issues. It seems inappropriate to postulate the existence of some "glob" of potential economic value in the world, a "glob" that emerges independently of productive effort on the part of persons and, in particular, emerges independently of organizational-institutional constraints within which persons act to produce value.

To separate the issues from those that might be based on measured economic interests, I postulate that in-migration, within reasonable limits, will neither increase nor decrease the economic well-being of those persons who initially inhabit the "rich" polity. We may think of a situation in which the effect of increasing returns from an expanded network of production and exchange (which allows for an extended division and specialization of labor) is precisely offset by the decreasing returns that arise from congestibility of fixed environmental parameters, including physical space itself. Possible economic effects on those inhabitants who might remain in the "poor" country after others have emigrated may also be made irrelevant by assuming that the two forces mentioned offset each other in directions that run counter to those in the "rich" country.

Under these highly abstracted conditions, immigrants do not impose either costs or benefits on previously existing inhabitants of the country A or on those inhabitants of country B who might remain after emigrants have departed. The situation, as described, would seem to offer the most favorable set of circumstances under which potential immigrants might advance claims for relocation based on principles of justice.

I suggest, however, that even in this idealized setting, no such claim can be supported. Let me attempt to justify my argument by examining more carefully just what immigration involves. The entry of an immigrant into an ongoing social-political-legal-economic order, with a defined membership, an experienced history, and a set of informal conventions, necessarily modifies the structure of "the game" itself, the complex and ill-understood set of interpersonal and intergroup relationships that generates the pattern of results that are observed by participants. I have postulated that there is no net effect on other persons that results from the addition of a person to the economic network. But this economic assumption is not itself sufficient to ensure an absence of effects from the addition of a full member to the existing group of inhabitants. Membership involves more than a joining of the economic interchange network. Membership carries with it power and authority, even if small, to modify the political-legal-constitutional parameters within which the ongoing economic game is played. The logic of partial derivation, which may be helpful in evaluating the measured economic effects of changes in the size of the interacting network, loses explanatory power to the extent that we allow persons to exercise genuine choices in their participation as ultimate sovereigns in the choices among the rules within which they carry out their relationships, one with another.

The argument here suggests that there is a direct relationship between the "democratization" of the parametric structure for sociopolitical interaction and the tolerance for immigration. An order that is described by constitutional stability that is based on continuing consensus that is, in turn, based on a genuine understanding of the difference between choice within rules and choice among rules may be much more tolerant toward entry of new members than an order that is described by continuous constitutional change emerging from shifting political coalitions. As my colleague Jennifer Roback has argued in connection with secession and territorial expansion, the coalitional politics of modern democracies make for major shifts in the evaluation of any alternatives that involve shifts in membership size.[1]

The argument is not intended to imply that immigration barriers should be established in any and all polities unless there are dominating, strictly economic reasons for allowing the entry of new members. The argument is intended to suggest, instead, that the effects of adding new members extend well beyond those that might be measured in economic terms and that they become especially important in modern democratic states. The institutional parameters that have made some of these states relatively "rich" are often not understood, and the fragility of these parameters in the face of noninformed politicization must be incorporated in any calculus of evaluation. Action toward potential immigrants that may seem motivated by considerations of justice or compassion may generate results that are directionally reversed from those initially anticipated.

Finally, my argument does not carry with it any putative claim that those who happen to be current inhabitants of "rich" countries have other than purely existential rights to the positions they occupy. These persons may have had little or no part in the selection and maintenance of the institutional-constitutional structure that has allowed for the creation of relatively high levels of value. But in all such discussions, it is necessary to recognize that the starting point is the here and now. That which might have been will never be.

The argument that I have advanced suggests that there is a logical basis for differentiation between the entry of full members in an ongoing political community and the entry of persons into relationships that exclude direct political participation. Under the abstract conditions postulated for the example, persons from B might be allowed entry into A as "guest workers," since they impose no net economic harms on other persons in A or B, while themselves securing major benefits. Compassion alone might dictate this result. And, of course, an even stronger argument might be made for opening up markets in A, which may serve as a substitute for immigration.

Notes

This essay is a commentary on Chapter 2 of this volume, by Coleman and Harding. It has proved the most difficult I have ever tried to write. The argument presented here is the third in a series of efforts. My only consolation is that the authors of the main essay seem to have had comparable difficulties.

1 Jennifer Roback, "Expansion, Secession and Lawlessness: A Contractarian Constitutional Approach" (George Mason University: Center for Study of Public Choice, March 18, 1992), paper presented at a meeting of the American Philosophical Association, Portland, Oregon.

4

Immigration, identity, and justice

JEAN HAMPTON

In general, political philosophers have not been terribly interested in the topic of immigration, although there are a few exceptions. In the early part of this century, a philosopher named Horace Kallen wrote a number of articles on the topic and even coined the term "cultural pluralism" to describe what he took to be the type of society that would result from the United States' generous immigration policy if Americans sustained their commitment to tolerance and freedom.[1] More recently, the articles of John Rawls discussing the kind of liberalism appropriate for a pluralist society such as our own have been indirectly motivated by the way in which the large-scale immigration of people from all over the world has made the United States one of the most heterogeneous of all liberal societies and, for that reason, a country that might become increasingly difficult to govern unless mutually acceptable and unifying terms of association can be sustained.

However, by and large, the focus of political philosophy has been on defining distributive justice within, and sometimes between, political societies. Yet how a state responds to outsiders who want to live within its borders raises questions of distributive justice. And more basically, a state's policy on immigration is connected to its sense of itself and its own identity. In this essay, I wish to pursue the connections between citizens' sense of societal identity, the immigration policy pursued by that society's government, and social justice.

To do so, I will discuss citizenship, an issue that raises questions about the nature of a society's identity. Even if a country puts out a big welcome mat for immigrants (e.g., for economic reasons, repudiating trade barriers with respect to labor), it may nonetheless be chary of granting such people full citizenship and may thus set up criteria for obtaining citizenship that are difficult, and perhaps even impossible, for any foreign-born person to meet. Other countries might be more strict about admission, but decidedly less strict about granting citizenship once a person has been admitted. As we shall see, such differences reflect different views not only about the economic impact of large-scale immigration, but also about the extent to which allowing the foreign-born to belong to a society affects the culture and identity of that political society. I shall argue that some views are more defensible on moral grounds than are others and will reject most citizenship policies driven by a strong sense of nationalist identity.[2]

I. Two conceptions of belonging

In Chapter 2 of this volume, Coleman and Harding nicely detail the way in which countries define different forms of (what I will call) "political status" connected with different bundles of rights, from guest worker to full citizen. But I want to argue that countries can differ in what they take citizenship to *mean,* even if they bestow upon those whom they call citizens roughly the same bundle of rights. Citizenship and immigration policies are often driven by a society's conception of what it means to say that one is a member of it. Specifically I will argue that in our world there are two prominent and competing conceptions of citizenship. I do not mean to suggest that these are the only such conceptions that exist, or could exist; but I do believe they are particularly prominent and important. First, there is the conception of citizenship as analogous to being a (voluntary) member of a club; second, there is the conception of citizenship as analogous to being one among many organs in a kind of (social) body. As we shall see, it is much easier to gain citizenship rights in a country that conceives of citizenship in the first way than in a country that conceives of it in the second way.

Consider the following fact about citizenship rights: until 1981, Great Britain, while granting its citizens the right to leave the country, maintained that (with a few exceptions) they could not lose their British citizenship. For example, a person could not do so simply by renouncing her British identity in the course of taking an oath required to assume, for example, U.S. citizenship. Despite this oath, the British government would still regard that person as a British subject, with not only the rights but also the responsibilities of a citizen – including being subject to a draft in time of war.[3] As a result of changes in the 1981 immigration law, the government will not allow someone to renounce his citizenship, but it requires that he do so by explicit declaration to the secretary of state, who can "deny" the renunciation in certain circumstances (e.g., in time of war).[4] So until quite recently, British citizenship was regarded by the government as a kind of inalienable feature of anyone born British. The 1981 law doesn't really abandon this conception so much as modify it; that is, it grants that citizenship can be alienated, *but only with the state's permission* (which it will refuse in certain circumstances), so that, whereas before 1981 a British citizen was permanently "owned" by her state, now she is owned until the state decides to set her free.

I suspect (although I am not a medieval scholar) that this way of conceiving of citizenship is derived from the idea that a ruling lord "owns" his serfs and vassals, and it fits well with the claim by many early modern thinkers (e.g., Hobbes in his *Leviathan*) that sovereigns of a nation-state are the "owners" of their people. But what, precisely, is this concept of social "ownership"? In today's world, it certainly does not mean that the government or head of government has what we would normally call a property right in the citizenry. Instead, it seems to involve the idea that there is a special kind of bond between the individual and her society, a bond that is not voluntarily assumed and cannot be unilaterally relinquished by the individual. By virtue of this bond, the individual holds certain entitlements, but will also be required to assume certain responsibilities toward the social group for as long as that group considers her to be a part of it.

Call this an example of a *nonconsensual conception of social membership*. In the end, as I will discuss later, Britain is not a good example of a society united by this conception of membership. Its liberal tradition, the large number of immigrants recently absorbed into it, and the political agitation of some of its Irish, Scottish, and Welsh population have been pushing it toward a more voluntaristic conception of social membership, the outlines of which I will present later. Instead, I want to suggest that this nonconsensual conception of membership is better realized in countries such as Germany and Japan, which explains why it is very difficult to "become" a German or Japanese citizen if one emigrates to one of these countries.

Officially, Germany refuses admission to all immigrants who wish to live within its borders, but in fact access to Germany has, until recently, been very easy, since it granted admission to any outsider who considered himself a political refugee.[5] Germany's liberality in this regard was connected to the fact that many anti-Nazis survived World War II because other European countries allowed them permission to stay as refugees of political terror.[6] However, the requirements for citizenship in Germany are remarkably stringent and detailed. To review those requirements:

The attribution of citizenship is based solely on parentage, so that a person born of German citizens anywhere in the world is automatically granted German citizenship. But a person born on German territory to noncitizens is still a foreigner. The acquisition of citizenship is clearly discretionary, unless one can claim to be an ethnic German, in which case naturalization is granted as a right. Discretionary naturalization requires ten years of residence (only five for a spouse of a German national), good moral character, and financial stability. Furthermore, it requires a "voluntary and permanent attachment to Germany" and a "basic knowledge of its political and social structures." These relatively stiff requirements have resulted in a very low naturalization rate. . . . The discretionary nature of the naturalization process and the reluctance of many foreign nationals to cast aside their cultural identities has also contributed to this very low rate.[7]

Moreover, like Britain, Germany makes the renunciation of citizenship difficult and presumes that it is something the state must grant, not something the citizen can insist on as her right.

So the German government essentially requires that, to be a German citizen, one must have the national identity of a German. This involves, among other things, having a mastery of the language, history, social practices, and beliefs of the German culture. To be a member of this social group normally means being accurately described by predicates that apply to anyone who has been reared in this culture. But even more important than the cultural requirement is having German "blood." No matter where a person is born, and no matter what culture he is reared in, that person has a right to German citizenship if either one of his parents, or one of his grandparents, is German. Moreover, even if his parents or grandparents previously renounced their German citizenship in order to become citizens of another state, the child can apply for and be granted German citizenship, solely on the basis of the German nationality of his parents or grandparents.[8] Note that insofar as someone can be accorded German citizenship on the basis of her "blood," apart from where she was born or the consensual political affiliation of her parents, we have here an exception to the rule, articulated by Coleman and Harding in Chapter 2, this volume, that no country grants citizenship to the child of a noncitizen born outside of that country's borders.

Because Germany regards ethnicity as a more important criterion of membership than culture, German rules on citizenship do not grant citizenship automatically to people born in Germany to non-German parents (unless they would otherwise be stateless). While the rules allow that those of foreign parentage born in Germany may eventually be granted citizenship if they show evidence of "assimilation," in practice that evidence is hard to furnish if their racial and cultural background is perceived to be substantially different from that of the traditional German.[9] As one German descendant in the United States has noted about German citizenship rules:

This writer, who speaks no German, has never lived there, and whose only connection with Germany is that his paternal grandparents left Baden for the United States a century ago, has a better legal claim on German citizenship than the child of a Turkish worker in Germany, born in Germany, educated there, culturally German, and speaking no other language than German.[10]

So in Germany a certain genetic background is more important than culture for the granting of citizenship. In the end, to be a citizen of this country is to be a member of an ethnic nationality.

Hence Germany is an example of a country that conceives of itself as a nation-state and justifies its citizenship policies by reference to what is necessary to preserve the nation politically. I will define a *nation-state* as a state that is run by and for members of a particular nation.[11] And I will define a *nation* as, first, comprising a group that is typically large and anonymous; second, having a common character and a common culture; third, possessing a system of socializing children so that they share and participate in this culture; fourth, having a conception of membership that makes membership important for each member's self-identity and is a matter of belonging rather than of achievement; and fifth, possessing a shared genetic connection, such that most members take themselves to be genetically similar and/or related (sometimes very distantly) to most other members of the group.[12] This last characteristic is one that recent defenders of nation-states, including Raz and Margalit, Coleman and Harding,[13] do not admit in their definitions of groups, whose preservation is, in their view, protected by right. Following Raz, I will call those groups with only the first four characteristics "encompassing groups,"[14] whereas I will call those with all five "nations." Being "English" or "Canadian" is belonging to an encompassing group. However, in the eyes of the German state, being "German" is belonging to a nation, insofar as one must possess the fifth characteristic, a certain ethnic background. As we shall see, this distinction is very important in evaluating the legitimacy of nonconsensual citizenship policies.

One can see the ethnicity-driven conception of membership influencing the policies of nation-states in Eastern Europe, many of which were (essentially) colonized by Russia in the twentieth century, or else held under its control by military might. Countries such as Lithuania and Latvia have attempted in the past few years to define citizenship so as to exclude "the Russians," hoping thereby to ensure both that their state has a certain ethnic identity and that those who will henceforth play a role in running it are not of the same ethnic background as their former imperialist masters.

Another country that exhibits a conception of social membership connected with ethnicity is Japan. Like Germany, Japan grants citizenship on the basis of parentage rather than place of birth: one is automatically granted citizenship if one is a child of Japanese parents, no matter where one is born, whereas a child of non-Japanese parents born in Japan is not automatically a citizen and can become one only through naturalization procedures. The requirements for earning naturalized citizenship seem relatively lenient – at least on paper:[15] for example, the would-be citizen must be continuously domiciled in Japan as a permanent resident for five years, must exhibit upright conduct, and must have sufficient assets not to be a burden on the state. However, the rules also require that making someone a citizen must "accord with the interests of Japan," and that phrase essentially makes the granting of citizenship a largely discretionary matter and, in practice, makes citizenship remarkably difficult to obtain. Moreover, it turns out that even permanent resident status, which is a necessary condition for citizenship, is granted only at the discretion of the government and is difficult to obtain.[16] To become a permanent resident, one must fulfill a vaguely stated assimilation requirement, which has been interpreted to involve, among other things, the taking of a Japanese name. (This last provision, among others, has offended many of those who are of Korean descent in Japan and has proved to be a serious impediment to their becoming citizens.) Its interpretation by the Japanese government has been so strict that from 1952 to 1984 only 600,143 people were granted permanent residence, and among those 577,525 were Korean and 20,000 were Chinese.

So not merely the rules, but more important the practice, of the Japanese government indicate that to be "one of us" in Japan is not only to have a certain kind of cultural identity, which it would be very difficult for anyone to assume unless he had been raised by parents who were thoroughly part of this culture themselves, but also to have (almost always) a certain kind of genetic connection to others in the group – to have a certain "bloodline." And as in Germany, the cultural requirements are not as important as the genetic background since, no matter where a person is born (and subsequently raised), the Japanese government will grant a right of citizenship to a child born of Japanese parents.[17] Japan is therefore another country with a nationalist conception of citizenship.

In contrast to this conception of social membership is the *consensual conception of social membership* held in countries such as the United States and Canada (and, to an increasing degree, Great Britain), which makes membership largely *voluntary* for the citizen. The idea that membership in a society rests on consent was a common theme of social contract theorists such as Locke, Rousseau, and Kant,[18] and it has received much criticism over the years. One of the most famous of these criticisms came from Hume, who dismissed the idea that consent rather than birth is the basis of the rights of citizenship.[19] But while Hume's nonconsensual conception correctly characterizes the foundations of citizenship in countries such as his native Britain in the eighteenth century, in fact it does not characterize the foundations of citizenship in countries such as the United States and Canada.[20] If someone is born within these states and/or is born to parents at least one of whom is a citizen, the state will grant that person citizenship, but such a grant is always made with the understanding that this person has the right to renounce it *unilaterally*, if she so chooses, after reaching the age of majority. It is important that such membership is always understood to be something that a person can voluntarily renounce. Hence it is assumed that if she does not voluntarily and unilaterally renounce it after the age of majority, she has tacitly consented to the responsibilities and rights of citizenship. Henceforth, I shall understand a citizen to have tacitly consented to membership when she is born into a society that accepts her unilateral right to renounce her membership in it and when she does not exercise that right after the age of majority. Moreover, for those who want to become citizens who have not been born within these countries or born to parents who are already citizens, the primary and most important (albeit not the only) requirement for doing so is the performance of a voluntary and *explicit* act of consent and commitment.

So in societies such as the United States and Canada, to be a citizen is not to exhibit certain fundamental social or genetic characteristics, nor even to be born within the state's boundaries, but rather to choose to become a member of the state if given an opportunity to do so, by giving consent, either tacitly (as just defined) or explicitly, to membership. This conception of consent may still not be sufficient to *legitimate* a government or justify its authority over its citizens; all that I am claiming is that, in these societies, it is a necessary condition of *membership*.[21]

Consent by the individual to a regime is not, however, a sufficient condition of membership. That consent must be solicited and accepted by the political society. A country such as the United States or Canada grants all who are born within its borders the right to join it if they choose, and outsiders are granted the right to do so as long as certain conditions are met, which include acceptance of certain political beliefs. This is, in part, because these countries understand the basis of the unity of their society in a political way. They take it that it is because the citizens of these countries have consented to the same political ideals and institutions that they are part of one political society, even if they have different genetic backgrounds, religions, lifestyles, languages, and social customs. Note that one can choose one's political views in a way that one cannot choose the culture in which one has been raised or the genetics of one's family. So in these societies, it is possible to voluntarily assume the defining identity of the society simply by embracing its ruling political conceptions (which one will choose to do as long as one's own ideas are in accord with its institutions and ideals). Hence, in these countries, becoming a citizen is a voluntary act based upon giving the political society one's consent to be part of it.

Moreover, because the country itself plays a consensual role in this process, citizenship in these countries depends to a very real extent on the *mutual* consent of both the would-be member and the rest of the political community, which has to decide whether or not to admit him. So the voluntary consent of the would-be member results in membership only if the rest of the community chooses to accept him. This means that such a society rests upon an ongoing social contract between that community and each of its members.[22]

In contrast, a political society such as Germany does not consent to someone's being a member; instead, it *recognizes* the fact of someone's Germanness after evaluating and tallying up the kind and number of an applicant's
characteristics to determine whether they are sufficient for German nationality.

In those societies that embrace the nonconsensual, nationalist understanding of citizenship, the nation, understood as I defined it earlier, is conceptually prior both to the individual and to any political community. Indeed,
this idea was embodied by a 1913 German law (relied upon by West Germany after World War II to establish its laws on citizenship), which states
that the German nation should not be understood, at bottom, as a political
entity, but as an ethnic identity, so that German citizenship could not be
understood as a purely political matter, but was rather an issue that be-
longed to "the German people." So in Germany, the ethnic or national society is understood to be that which defines and authorizes the political
society. In contrast, in countries in which political membership is consensually based, the citizenry's genetic backgrounds and cultural identities in
matters of custom, dress, religion, or recreation are entirely a function of
those who have chosen to constitute it. Hence, in social (and nonpolitical)
matters, the individual member of this type of political society is understood to be conceptually prior to the society itself (so that, in general, these
countries are multicultural). If I am a member of such a society, my citizenship does not depend upon whether I have displayed the cultural and
genetic characteristics common to the rest of the country's members; instead, the cultural and genetic identity of the country depends upon which
individuals (such as myself) have decided to join it. Although membership
in these latter societies does depend upon individuals' choosing to embrace
the political identity of the group, which is understood to be a permanent,
unifying, and defining feature of these societies, this is the sort of thing
that individuals *can* voluntarily choose. Thus, given the opportunity to be a
citizen, actually doing what is necessary to become one is within the rational control of the individual.

But what about states organized around religious beliefs? We can imagine
states dedicated to preserving a certain religious group that would welcome
members of any ethnic group or cultural community as long as they accepted
the religious beliefs of that group or community. Do these states understand
citizenship consensually or nonconsensually? Consider Israel, which is not
really a nation as I have defined it, not only because non-Jews born in Israel
can be citizens but also because anyone can become a citizen of Israel as
long as she is a Jew, and Judaism is a religion that can be chosen no matter
what one's race, sex, or ethnic origin (although what counts as conversion is
a controversial subject in Israel). Compare fundamentalist Christian plans for
a future America defined as a Christian commonwealth: advocates of this

vision would presumably insist that they are conceiving of this new America not as a nation-state, but as a kind of voluntary association, albeit a unireligious one, to which all human beings are invited, whatever their ethnic or cultural heritage. Critics might maintain that religion is so deeply connected with our identity, which is in turn so deeply connected with our membership in groups to which we have not chosen to belong, that it is stretching the truth unduly to say that religious affiliation is subject to our consent. On the other hand, it is possible to choose to be Jewish or Christian in a way that it is not possible to choose to be, say, an ethnic German. I leave aside how to categorize these sorts of political societies in this essay, but let me note that if religious affiliation is equated with affiliations one cannot choose, some (but not all) of the arguments I make against granting citizenship on the basis of whether or not a person is a member of a certain nation will work against "nations" defined along religious, rather than ethnic, lines.

In an important sense, the histories of political societies explain how each of them has come to embrace one of these two very different conceptions of membership. I once had a conversation with a Chinese citizen whose ancestors had been Chinese for literally hundreds of generations and who could not conceive of what it was like for me to be a U.S. citizen by virtue of my very recent forbears having turned up here (in one case, to escape incarceration for felonies). A nation made up of immigrants cannot have the same strong sense of homogeneous cultural identity as a nation with a long cultural tradition and a long tradition of warding off outsiders. Hence an immigrant nation's sense of citizenship as a voluntary affair is as inevitable a consequence of its history as is another country's perception of citizenship as a nonconsensual, nonvoluntary fact of social identity.

It is also likely that the concept of citizenship developed in countries such as the United States and Canada was influenced by the social contract tradition. Contra Hume, the idea that a contract exists between citizens and their state is, in a certain sense, literally true in these societies, insofar as membership is a function of an agreement between member and state (either explicit, through the naturalization process, or implicit, insofar as the state agrees to the citizenship of the native-born, who have the right of unilateral renunciation and are assumed to consent to these regimes if they do not exercise that right). So these states' emphasis on individual consent as a necessary condition of membership, and their assumption that the state exists to serve the individual rather than some kind of national community, fit the contractarian account of the nature of political membership to a remarkable degree. I would therefore propose that the contractarian argument has had a powerful effect on the historical development of political societies over the past four centuries – encouraging the creation of a type of political society (unknown in Hume's day) united by consent rather than by ethnicity, culture, or conquest. Moreover, as the contractarians would wish, that consent is supposed to reflect what its members see as mutually advantageous and morally important reasons for working together and a sense that the terms of cooperation (at least as they are ideally stated, albeit perhaps not always as they are implemented) are fair.[23]

The consent-based conception of citizenship in the United States also affects how this type of society understands to whom it should grant the right to vote. In the United States only a citizen may vote because only the citizen has repudiated a previous political affiliation and *by so doing* has implicitly accepted a cornerstone of the concept of citizenship that this country embraces as the basis of its union. So in a society that insists it is the common commitment to a political culture that defines its identity, the act of voting is not only a political act, but also an act indicating one's commitment to the nation's defining political identity. Hence the act of voting becomes one of the most important rights withheld until the society is clear that the person seeking membership is genuinely choosing to belong to and participate in the political culture of that society. In contrast, a country such as Britain, which understands its identity partially in a nonpolitical, cultural way, believes it can afford to grant noncitizens the right to vote on the grounds that the action of voting is not an indication of whether or not one can now be considered to have a British identity.

The consensual attitude toward citizenship also shows up in the U.S. policy toward dual citizenship. The Supreme Court has ruled that it is proper for the U.S. government to demand of those who wish to become citizens of this country that they renounce their prior citizenship; as I have noted, such a renunciation assumes that becoming a citizen is a voluntary decision on the part of each individual. However, there are circumstances in which the Court will permit dual citizenship, and the way in which it allows this shows that it accepts that there are circumstances in which a person can belong to more than one political society. For example, it allows someone to choose to be both an Israeli and a U.S. citizen.[24] The fact that the United States should even think that this makes sense shows the extent to which it separates a person's religious, cultural, and ethnic identity from his American identity – which is defined in a largely political way. A person can also have dual citizenship if he is born in this country and the child of a foreign national: he is automatically granted U.S. citizenship (subject to his consent to it at the age of majority) by virtue of his birth, and he may also be entitled to citizenship by that foreign country by virtue of the child's parentage. If the parents, on the child's behalf, request such foreign citizenship, the child will enjoy citizenship rights in both countries, and the Supreme Court has ruled that the U.S. government cannot, consistent with the Constitution, do anything to make the child renounce that foreign citizenship or make continued U.S. citizenship dependent upon such a renunciation. Hence, the ruling means that belonging to the United States involves something like the following: "You can belong if you are born here and implicitly consent to being a citizen by not rejecting U.S. citizenship at the age of majority, or if you choose it over your previous political affiliation after having renounced that previous affiliation; but if the former is true, then if some other political society also gives you citizenship rights, that can be no affair of ours. Your citizenship is therefore a function of your consensual relationship between this political community and you, and cannot be affected by the independent decisions of a third party." Hence "being American" does *not* mean manifesting characteristics that are difficult or impossible to assume voluntarily and that mark one as a lifelong member of a nation; instead, "being American" means belonging to a political "club" (which is perhaps not the only club of which one is a member) after having tacitly or explicitly consented to do so.

II. Nationalism and social identity

Are both of the consensual and nonconsensual conceptions of citizenship morally acceptable? Are there moral reasons for rejecting or modifying either of them?

In order to answer these questions, let us first consider an argument against a nonconsensual conception of political membership. This argument begins by claiming that a nonconsensual basis for citizenship is inconsistent with the basic tenets of democratic societies. If that is correct, and if (as many of us believe) all political societies ought to be democratic in order to instantiate justice, the argument's conclusion is that, to be just, all societies ought to embrace a consent-based conception of political membership.

On this argument, to take the attitude that only immigrants of a certain race or religion or culture will be allowed to immigrate and become citizens of the country is to represent the country as something other than a community defined by democratic political ideals. Such a country conceives of itself as united as much by racial, genetic, and cultural characteristics as by ideals such as tolerance and respect for individual rights. In deciding who will become members, it will therefore behave intolerantly toward those people whose skin color or culture are perceived to be substantially "different" – and more than likely, by virtue of that difference, inferior. Such attitudes, on this view, represent a betrayal of the ideal that all human beings are equal and that all human beings have the same basic bundle of fundamental rights. Therefore, this argument concludes that we are rightly critical of a country representing itself as a democratic society but doing its best to refuse citizenship to those people whose ethnic and cultural background is distant from that of the current citizens.

The argument grants that a democratic society can reasonably put restrictions on immigration and citizenship. After all, the arrival of newcomers places costs upon those who are already there (e.g., economic costs, possible overcrowding of schools, high demand for housing, pressure on health care); too many newcomers can make these costs extremely high, which constitutes a legitimate basis for restricting the number of those allowed to enter. But the argument also insists that even while such restrictions are permitted, they must be formulated in a way that avoids racial or cultural bias, and that citizenship standards should rest, in the main, on the immigrant's willingness to consent and remain committed to the democratic ideals of freedom and equality in the nation.

The problem with this argument, however, is that a society such as Germany, which espouses democratic political beliefs but which also insists on a person's meeting strict requirements for membership in the German nation in order to become a citizen of the German political society, will maintain that it does not want to be simply a democratic society, but rather an ethnic/cultural society operating according to democratic principles. While those Germans who espouse this point of view will admit that the ideals of freedom and equality are important, they will also maintain that the social cohesion they value and aim to protect is created not (as in the United States and Canada) by the acceptance of those universal ideals but by the bonds of ethnicity and culture. "We want to live under these ideals," members might say, "but we don't want to give everyone the prima facie right to live under those ideals *here*. We value our Germanic heritage, and wish to see that heritage preserved and sustained. We can only do this by putting strict requirements on successful citizenship applications."

So to determine the legitimacy of a nonconsensual conception of state membership, we must confront the issue of the legitimacy of the nation-state, since it is the claim of the moral importance of nations that is the foundation for an argument justifying the nonconsensual conception. Coleman and Harding, in Chapter 2 of this volume, defend nonconsensual citizenship policies on the grounds that what they call "encompassing groups" have a right to be preserved. Recall that encompassing groups are just like nations, except that they do not define themselves using ethnic criteria. Yet as we have seen (and as Coleman and Harding's review of the various immigration policies shows) it is the very hallmark of citizenship policies in states with a nonconsensual conception of membership that ethnicity is the primary prerequisite for membership. So Coleman and Harding ask the wrong question when they evaluate the citizenship policies of nation-states such as Germany: they should ask *not* whether those policies are legitimate insofar as they enable an encompassing group to protect itself, but whether they are legitimate insofar as they enable a nation (defined in part as an ethnic entity) to protect itself. After considering how to answer this second question in the rest of this section, I will go on to consider the relationship between (mere) encompassing groups and nonconsensual citizenship policies in the next section.

The argument that the nonconsensual policies of nation-states are legitimate goes as follows. If nations have a right to political self-determination in certain circumstances (when they are prepared to govern justly, when the territory occupied by the nation is viable as a state, etc.),[25] then according to this argument, nonconsensual citizenship policies are permitted (and appropriate) once the nation-state is created, insofar as such policies protect the nation – whose state this is.

There are two ways to mount this kind of argument; the first I will call *communitarian*. This argument fits most naturally with the rhetoric of Germany's laws – particularly the 1913 law expressing the idea that the state exists to serve the German nation. It starts from the assertion that nations (as earlier defined) have a right to self-determination (appropriately qualified), and when nations exercise this right, they are nation-states. Note that, on this argument, this right is held by a *group*, in this case the nation, and not by individuals in the group. On the basis of this right, the argument goes, nation-states can legimately limit citizenship to those who are members of the nation. Otherwise, the state will no longer be for, and under the control of, the nation. In other words, it will no longer be the *nation's state*. This is particularly true when the state is organized along democratic lines, since allowing people who are not members of the nation into the state will affect legislation, democratically determined. (A communitarian may want to argue that nation-states are obligated, for reasons of justice, to construct a democratic form of government; but even if she does not wish to argue for this conclusion, she can maintain that a large number of non-national citizens can affect the policies, influence the legislation, and in general take at least some political control out of the hands of the nationals. Note that this is true only with respect to citizens; it may not be true if the non-nationals are mere residents rather than citizens, with only limited rights.)

The second, or *liberal*, argument for the same conclusion also grants a nation the right to self-determination, but attributes this right to the *individuals* of the nation, not to the group. On this liberal argument, groups do not have rights; only individuals have rights. Nonetheless, the liberal can maintain that groups are instrumentally valuable to individuals because they are vital to individuals' well-being and because they are central to defining individuals' identities.[26] As Will Kymlicka has argued,[27] membership in groups has been an important component of the liberal tradition, providing a "context of choice" in which individuals form identities and formulate projects, plans, and goals based on legitimate expectations regarding the behavior of others.[28] So whereas the communitarian maintains that these groups are intrinsically valuable, Kymlicka argues that, for the liberal, these groups are instrumentally valuable insofar as they are important to the well-being of their members.

On this basis, the liberal argument grants individuals the right to the flourishing of the groups in which they are a part (assuming, of course, that the groups are not abusive or disruptive of justice), groups that include nations. The argument continues that nations flourish when they are organized in states. So individuals have a right to the statehood of their nations by virtue of the fact that such political standing will ensure the flourishing of these groups. Having established the right to self-determination by nations, the liberal argument concludes in the same way as the communitarian argument: as long as nation-states are legitimate, it is morally permissible for them to limit citizenship to those who are members of the nation. Otherwise, the state will no longer be for, and under the control of, the nation. That is, it will no longer be the "nation's state."

Thus we see that the defenders of a nonconsensual conception of citizenship can employ the terminology of liberalism to justify that conception by saying that this conception's legitimacy ultimately rests on the individual's right to live in a group that he believes is closely connected to his own welfare and personal identity. So understood, it is a right held by each individual by virtue of the instrumental importance of groups to the individual's identity and welfare, and is not in any way held by, or attributable to, a group. Whatever other rights liberals recognize, the argument would insist that liberals must also recognize this right and thus tolerate the restrictions that a society would find necessary to preserve its identity. And note that those restrictions may involve ethnicity and race insofar as the nation's identity is intimately connected to a certain genetic inheritance.

Differences between communitarians and liberals with respect to the issue of citizenship in nation-states seem, therefore, irrelevant. Although they disagree about where the right protecting the integrity of nations comes from and who holds it, both arguments use this right to establish that it is morally legitimate for "a nation to own a state" and that because the criteria for being a member of a nation are nonconsensual, criteria for being a member of a nation-state must also be nonconsensual. Now, I will admit to having grave reservations about the existence of the right relied upon by both arguments, and even more serious reservations (which I will discuss later) about the assumption underlying this right that our identity and well-being are or must be connected with a *single* culture. But for now I will grant its existence and consider the soundness of these two arguments.

On the basis of this right, Coleman and Harding refrain from criticizing the citizenship policies of a country such as Germany, and accept the idea that immigration and citizenship can be restricted to people who are culturally or ethnically similar to those who are already citizens. As this paper is being written, essentially this position is being espoused by members of Germany's right-wing parties, who have gained recent electoral victories after promising to reform the immigration policies of the country. As I noted earlier, Germany has taken seriously the position that political refugees have a right to be admitted to another state in order to seek asylum, and they have liberally granted to anyone declaring him- or herself a political refugee the automatic right to reside in the country – albeit not as a citizen.[29] So the stringency of the citizenship requirements in Germany has been matched by Germany's astonishing leniency in one area of immigration policy. Not surprisingly, the country has incurred considerable costs as a result of such a lenient policy, costs that are now resented greatly by the nonimmigrant population. But the lesson learned by a number of Germans is not that the liberal admission policy should be tightened, and the tight citizenship policy liberalized, but rather that all access to Germany by any outsider should be radically curtailed, whether she wishes to be a citizen or merely to reside in the country. Ironically, efforts to limit the number of immigrants admitted to the country have been of only limited success, in part because many Germans believe that to reform the policy would simultaneously involve admitting that theirs was "an immigration country" rather than a "racially pure country."[30]

On reflection, however, neither the liberal nor the communitarian defense of maintaining the purity of a nation-state is satisfactory. Both arguments are built around a right to preserve the identity of a nation. But even assuming such a right exists, it cannot be sufficiently powerful to trump all other rights held by outsiders. The right to the preservation of a group identity is only one among many in a society, and thus one that must be appropriately balanced against other claims that individuals or groups outside the dominant cultural community might make against it.

Thus consider, first of all, the claim that everyone has a right to citizenship in *some* political society.[31] Not only would liberals tend to agree with this claim; more strikingly, in granting citizenship to children born within its territories to, respectively, non-German or non-Japanese parents who would otherwise be stateless, Germany and Japan recognize that these children's right to citizenship in some political society trumps other citizens' rights to preserve their group's identity. This right is reasonably understood to be stronger than individuals' right to preserve their group's culture. And thus the latter right could not be used to exclude membership to individuals born within the society, who nonetheless are from an ethnic and cultural group other than that of the dominant group (e.g., Koreans in Japan, Russians in Lithuania, Turks in Germany) and who do not have citizenship in the country of their ethnic origin. Depending upon how large an ethnic minority is, the effect of acknowledging the power of these childrens' rights to citizenship could result in the state becoming a multiethnic society, whether the majority liked it or not. A nation cannot own a state when too many non-nationals born within its territory require political affiliation and only that state can give it to them. (I take it as obvious that it is not morally acceptable for an advocate to reply to this argument that the way to solve the problem of these non-nationals is to engage in some kind of ''ethnic cleansing.'')

Second, a nation cannot prohibit non-nationals from gaining citizenship when a substantial number of non-nationals have lived a long, productive life within the territory of the state and require citizenship in order to live on an equal basis with other nationals. If a country persisted in denying rights of citizenship to these non-nationals, it would be allowing a system of different classes of residents in that society, with non-nationals having to accept unequal treatment and second-class status. The ideals of liberalism would certainly rule out such a policy. So even if liberalism grants that an individual has a right to preserve his group's identity, liberalism also recognizes the right of any long-standing, productive, and law-abiding resident of a country to gain eventual citizenship if he so chooses, even if he cannot meet all of the genetic and cultural requirements that would mark him as a member of the nationality of the dominant group in that country. And this latter right is grounded in the liberal and democratic requirement that all people in a political society be treated equally and fairly, no matter how much any of them might differ from the majority. Indeed, in nationalist countries, such as Germany, that have actually, in years past, *solicited* foreign immigrants to augment their own labor force, their subsequent refusal to grant these people citizenship, no matter how law-abiding or productive they have been, on the grounds that they are not (and cannot be) members of the nationality defining the political society, violates the right to equal treatment required by liberalism. Such a refusal essentially permits a hierarchy among the society's residents that is not only unjust but also destablizing by virtue of the fact that such a policy engenders anger and resentment among those denied the rights of full citizenship. Communitarians might resist the idea that justice requires this kind of equality (e.g., if the nation's culture sanctioned racist or sexist views); if so, I would maintain that it is a further argument against their position that equality is morally required whatever the cultural views of the nation.

Third, rights associated with distributive justice can also trump rights to group preservation. Consider that not only individuals who are refugees from political terror but also individuals from countries that are desperately poor might be thought to have some kind of right to enter a nearby wealthy society (albeit perhaps only in reasonable numbers, given the costs of their immigration). If this wealthy country had a nonconsensual conception of its identity and refused citizenship rights to all the poor of other societies on the grounds that they did not display the genetic and cultural characteristics that would mark them as members of this society, then depending upon the circumstances of those who wished to enter the society, and on how wholeheartedly such a country forbade their entry, we might consider their policies on immigration and citizenship callous and even cruel. Perhaps if such a society gave a large proportion of its wealth to poor countries in foreign aid, its generosity might be thought to offset the stinginess of its immigration policy. Indeed, Germany's Helmut Kohl has suggested foreign aid as a way of curtailing access to Germany by the poor from former Eastern Bloc countries: "If we don't want them to come to us," he has said, "we have to help them so they can have better lives at home."[32] But while Kohl's call for economic aid to these countries is commendable, giving a certain amount of foreign aid to the countries of the desperately poor seems analogous to members of an exclusive country club giving handouts to the poor whom they wish to help but not associate with. Moreover, given the preceding argument, a wealthy country cannot defensibly admit a reasonable number of poor non-nationals but deny them any chance of eventual citizenship by virtue of the fact that they exhibit the wrong race, or the wrong culture, or both; the right to preserve a national identity cannot be outweighed by the rights associated with equal treatment under the law.

On the basis of these three arguments, it would seem that even the right to preserve a group identity cannot reasonably be thought to preclude citizenship to *all* who do not meet the nonconsensual cultural or genetic requirements of citizenship in all circumstances. Hence the preceding arguments establish that no society appropriately animated by individual rights can have an *exclusively* nonconsensual policy of citizenship.

Nonetheless it also seems to establish that some kind of nonconsensual policy of citizenship is allowable, on both communitarian and liberal conceptions of the state. Using one of the arguments just presented, it would seem that a (relatively) homogeneous society could justify the general practice of limiting immigration and citizenship to those who met the nationality test of the dominant group, making certain exceptions to accommodate the rights of (at least some) political refugees, long-term and productive immigrant (non-national) residents, and (at least some of) the economically destitute. To put it succinctly, the argument concludes that even if the *pure* nation-state is not morally defensible, a state that is nonetheless animated by the principle of preserving a nation is morally legitimate, as long as it makes some exceptions (connected to certain rights of individuals and demands of distributive justice) that grant citizenship to certain individuals who are not members of a nationality.[33] Is this argument sound? In the next section, I will argue that it is not.

III. Liberalism and community

There are two important components of both the liberal and the communitarian arguments:

1. It is morally required to preserve groups that give their members identity and contribute in a substantial way to their well-being. (The communitarian argument grants these groups an intrinsic right to exist; the liberal argument places the right in the hands of the individual members who receive the benefit of group membership.)
2. A nation-state is an effective vehicle for preserving those groups, including ''nations'' and ''encompassing groups,'' that are important to their members' identity and well-being.

In what follows, I will not challenge the first assumption.[34] I will, however, present a series of arguments against the second.

The first argument challenges the claim that *nations*, as I have defined them, are worth preserving, even granting that it is morally required to preserve groups (on either liberal or communitarian grounds) that are central to an individual's identity and well-being. The problem with nations is that they are defined, in part, by reference to race and ethnicity. As I have already noted, philosophers who defend nation-states are happy to talk about preservation of *culture*, but omit the fact that in most of the world the concept of nationality is intimately connected to the ethnicity or race (narrowly defined) of the members of that society. And there is no reason to think that preserving cultural groups vital to an individual's identity and well-being demands that a government forbid anyone to join the group unless that person is of the same ethnicity or race. To claim that one can be a real member of a culture only if one has a certain genetic background is to assert something false about the role that a genetic background plays in a person's acculturation. And such a falsehood is most likely just a cover for the racism of a group, which holds its members superior by blood to certain other types of human beings. In any case, because it is simply untrue that someone's mere race or ethnicity is vital to the preservation of a group's identity, and because this idea usually goes hand in hand with racist attitudes, it is indefensible as a foundation for immigration and citizenship policy, and indefensible as an argument on behalf of the nation-state. So even if we grant that maintaining a group's identity is instrumentally valuable to individual members' well-being, we have good reason to reject that this identity can be maintained only for as long as the group is ''ethnically pure'' and thus good reason to reject citizenship policies in any society that restrict citizenship to those of a particular ethnic group.[35]

Suppose that we reconstruct the liberal and communitarian arguments so that they allow the preservation of groups that are defined solely in terms of culture, not of race, whose nonconsensual citizenship policies do not discriminate on the basis of race or ethnicity, and that recognize the rights of non-nationals to citizenship in certain instances. We might call them "encompassing groups," using Raz's term; for convenience, however, I will henceforth use the term "nation-state" to refer to political societies that are controlled by, and for the benefit of, a single encompassing group. This would involve us in reinterpreting tenet 2 above, so that it now reads as follows:

2. A state organized on nonconsensual grounds is an effective vehicle for preserving those "encompassing groups" that are important to their members' identity and well-being.

Note that this reconstructed argument would disallow most of the nonconsensual citizenship policies (including those of Germany and Japan)[36] around the world and would thus be an ineffective defense for nationalistic citizenship policies as we know them today. At best, the argument would support citizenship policies that did not restrict (or automatically give) citizenship to people of a certain ethnicity, that required strict tests of cultural assimilation, and that put restrictions on the rate at which those of other cultures could enter the community. Arguably, such citizenship policies would be more like consent-based policies than non-consent-based policies, insofar as joining the state would be a function of a person's decision to do what was required to meet the criteria for membership as well as the state's consent to have any person as a member. In any case, does the claim that encompassing groups have a right to be preserved establish that these groups have a right to political self-determination, and thus a right to these kinds of citizenship policies?

No, it does not. Consider that the preceding argument assumes that a unicultural state is the best vehicle for the protection of an encompassing group's identity, and therefore of individual well-being. Is this true? Countries that have formed around a certain group's culture, ethnicity, and history, such as Estonia, Croatia, and Armenia, have been convinced that it is. Indeed, the experience of the people in countries such as these has been that not only their group identity, but indeed their very lives, were threatened for as long as they were part of a society *not* composed, in the main, of people from their culture. So their longing for a nation-state has been based on a desire to achieve the preservation not only of their culture but also of their people. It is certainly understandable that members of minorities badly persecuted in states dominated by other groups would hold this belief. To be in control of their political destiny would seem to be the cure for the persecution they have suffered at the hands of a government controlled by other groups hostile to them.

But the history of the twentieth century does not show that a unicultural state is a highly successful vehicle for the protection of groups of people who are, for various reasons, at risk. I want to propose that Raz and Margalit, Coleman and Harding, and Kymlicka are in the grip of a nineteenth-century solution to the problems of conflict among different groups proximate to one another, and there is good reason to conclude, at the close of the twentieth century, that this solution has generally failed to deliver the protection it was supposed to provide.

In Western Europe, many consider the nation-state to have been a primary *source* of conflict, not a cure for it. Despite the fact that many European states were built upon liberal ideals, strong ethnic and cultural identifications in many of those states have played a role in generating vicious wars, politically sponsored attempts at genocide, and economically damaging trade wars. Group identity is not well-preserved by the nation-state when the groups, which had previously sought to damage one another inside a state, now do it in wars between states. As this essay is being written, the former Yugoslavia is rent by war, as factions that coexisted within a single state now battle with one another as separate states. The creation of nation-states to "protect" these ethnic groups has been completely unsuccessful. When people want to kill one another, rearranging political boundaries can make things no better, and sometimes worse.

Moreover, the nation-state itself can encourage pride-driven aggression and pride-driven reprisals. The behavior of Nazi Germany is instructive and needs no review. So too is the history of Sri Lanka: a peaceful society composed of two distinct communities, one Sinhalese-speaking and Buddhist, the other Tamil-speaking and Hindu, was thrown into internecine conflict as a result of a prime minister's edict, in 1956, that made the religion and language of the Sinhalese majority the official state religion and the official state language. This attempt to harness the state machinery on behalf of the Sri Lankan majority represented an attempt to turn Sri Lanka into a nation-state. That aroused the fury of the Tamil minority, resulting in the murder of two prime ministers, communal riots, civil warfare, and the military involvement of another country (India, whose own prime minister, Rajiv Ghandi, was most likely murdered by a Tamil militant). Whatever value the nation-state has had in preserving certain groups, it has also encouraged others to behave in ways that have threatened the rights of members of minority groups living among them.

Indeed, the example of Sri Lanka shows that the nation-state can actually be a self-defeating strategy for preserving group identity and culture. When a certain nation is only one of the groups residing in a territory, its insistence that the state controlling that territory become its nation-state will inevitably worry and anger members of minority nation(s), who fear they will end up residing in a political society that is officially organized for the benefit of a group other than their own. Not only will their rights as individuals be under threat, but, worse, their group's right to be preserved and to flourish within this territory will be under threat. Hence they will understandably want to fight for the preservation of that group against the majority, provoking dissension and possibly war, which can be damaging to all the groups in the territory. The ethnic fighting in the former Yugoslavia offers the most striking and tragic confirmation of this point. Therefore, recent history would seem to show that the nation-state is one of the *worst* vehicles for preserving a group in situations where a substantial number of people who belong to other groups also reside in the same territory – and that includes most areas of the world today.

The European Community's attempt to weaken national ties and foster political and economic interdependence has been a way of forestalling conflict and encouraging peace among nations emboldened to wage war with one another despite, and even because of, the fact that some of them became, or wanted to become, nation-states. Ironically, in contrast to many Americans fearful of the disruptive nature of a highly pluralist society, Europeans have come to perceive homogeneity as a threat to peace rather than a state of affairs that precludes it. (And it is interesting to speculate about how a closer union of European states by the end of this decade will affect what will eventually have to become a common immigration policy.)

The lesson to be learned from such conflict is that groups may flourish and be best preserved not in separate (and often hostile) nation-states, but in other kinds of polities that foster the preservation of cultural identity, protect the members of different cultural groups, and promote a network of economic and political interaction and interdependence, making war and economic competition unacceptable ways of resolving disputes.

In the end, both the communitarian and the liberal arguments for nation-states, and thus for the conception of citizenship that links citizenship to national background, are consequentialist: both claim that nation-states are a vehicle for the preservation of nations. So the fact that the consequences are often otherwise is important. Of course, there may be situations where the nation-state *is* an effective vehicle for the preservation of a group. But history shows not only that such a political arrangement often does *not* secure the well-being of the group, but also that the idea of the nation-state has been an incitement to political actions that have encouraged conflict severely damaging cultural communities.

So if we agree that cultural communities are important for the well-being of the individual, and thus worthy of protection, we need to consider how such protection can be genuinely secured. My argument against nation-states is *not* an argument against the importance of a cultural community, but it is an argument against the idea that cultural and political communities should always – or even usually – overlap. What kind of political community should one construct to secure this protection?

I take that to be one of the most open, and interesting, political questions today. The European Community is attempting to construct one answer to this question; and if it can resist the lure of establishing a nation-state, Quebec may well provide another answer by filling out the concept of "sovereignty association" (although to do so, it will also have to come to grips with the rights of subcultures within it – most notably native populations such as the Mohawks – to the preservation of their culture). Finally, the possibility of different groups getting along even while maintaining (more or less) their distinctive identities has been demonstrated by the history of immigrant nations such as the United States and Canada. So the key to peaceful coexistence may be not separation and exclusivity, but interdependence and tolerance of diversity. The peace-securing values of liberalism may be best employed in the service of group identity in political societies that are not traditional nation-states, and in the next century several types of such societies may emerge.

Because both the communitarian and liberal arguments for nation-states are consequentialist, there is a Humean assumption about the nature of human polities in both arguments: namely, that political arrangements are merely conventions, justified to the extent that they are instrumentally valuable to the individuals and/or groups affected by them. There is no "natural" moral boundary between states, and the traditional notion of the state along with its link to nations need not be a permanent feature of our political landscape if there are better, more peace-producing vehicles for political order. But those like Coleman and Harding who would defend nonconsensual citizenship policies, and the conception of the nation-state that undergirds them, need to consider the extent to which they have *not* been instrumentally valuable either for the protection of individuals' rights and well-being or for the creation of efficient and productive uses of the world's resources, especially when race and ethnicity have animated the conception of nationality. Particularly for liberals, who are ultimately concerned to protect and secure the rights and well-being of individuals, they can justify only those states organized along cultural rather than racial lines, and only when such arrangements are genuinely peace-producing. Given the history of the twentieth century, it simply will not do to assume that these arrangements are successful.

The third challenge to the liberal and communitarian defenses of nation-states has to do with a hidden assumption in the argument: namely, that the culture of a nation is best preserved by keeping out anyone who was raised a member of another group. But consider that groups giving us identity can be preserved in a state that is *multicultural*; indeed, as Coleman and Harding point out, this has been one of the animating principles of Canada. Moreover, Kymlicka, Margalit and Raz, and Coleman and Harding surely cannot believe that only a unicultural background will secure our identity and well-being as persons, particularly since all of them live in multicultural societies. Defenders of consent-based states such as the United States and Canada would insist not only that the various groups defining the cultural identities of the members of these states enjoy considerable protection, but also that members of these groups are enriched by the presence of people with different cultural backgrounds. Nor do I see any compelling argument that the economic order of the world will be most effectively promoted only if each cultural community has its own state; it is arguable that economic growth is fostered better in a multicultural environment.

Hence supporters of the liberal argument for nation-states may be making a substantial mistake about what kind of society is genuinely good for us. Perhaps the best reason to support a consent-based policy of citizenship grounded upon liberal ideals is that such a policy encourages a multicultural society that is more interesting, more conducive to peace, more economically productive, and more nourishing to the individuals who live within it than societies with only a single cultural tradition. And if this is so, both ethnic nation-states and ''encompassing society states'' can be bad for us: not only might they foster, rather than cure, conflict among groups, but they might also inhibit the economic development and the diversity of social practices, ideas, and lifestyles that enable us to flourish as individuals.

IV. Conclusion

Let me end by making explicit what my arguments have, and have not, established. First, in attacking the nation-state, I have not wished to attack the idea or the importance of groups that contribute to our identities as persons. Indeed, my attack has been largely motivated by the way in which such polities threaten, rather than preserve, group identity.

Second, I have not been attacking the idea that a political society can place limits on who can become a citizen. Instead, I have been attacking a particular conception of what citizenship involves – namely, the nonconsensual, nationalist conception. Moreover, I have noted that in political societies in which membership derives from consent, that consent must come not only from the would-be member, but also from the political society itself, which may have a variety of morally acceptable reasons for being chary of giving it (e.g., because of environmental concerns or concerns about its present members' health or economic well-being). I have not given any kind of exhaustive specification of the grounds upon which a state could justifiably withhold its consent to grant someone citizenship. Instead, I have argued that, in general, a state is not justified in viewing citizenship as a function of nationality rather than the mutual consent of state and immigrant. So it is a particular conception of citizenship, and thus a particular model of political society, that has been my target.

Finally, I have not argued that a nonconsensual policy of citizenship is *never* justified: I have allowed that, in some circumstances, a community, one defined along cultural rather than racial lines, may be able to protect itself only by establishing itself as a (nonethnic) nation-state and thus may be justified in limiting citizenship to those who are members of that community. But most of the nation-states that exist today cannot defend their citizenship policies along these lines, either because their policies are racially driven or because they cannot credibly claim that non-nationals who are presently denied membership would threaten their cultural community if admitted (e.g., the Turks in Germany or the Koreans in Japan). Many of the members of these states are participating in political movements (such as the European Community) that, if they succeed, will weaken and even destroy the nation-states in which they now live. So if my arguments are right, the conception of citizenship that is usually justified is the consensual conception.[37]

However, it is an implication of my argument for this conception that a consent-based political society would, in order to be just, have to require that, in order to be a citizen, an applicant must commit herself to respecting and tolerating the operation and continued existence of the other groups in the society (who would themselves already be under the obligation to respect hers). However, it is important to note that this very liberal idea is itself something that members of certain cultures might find difficult to accept, demonstrating that, at least for members of these cultures, entry into a consent-based political culture will involve *changing* either the beliefs or the cultural traditions of their group. Some might argue that such change already constitutes a threat to the integrity of such a culture; I would argue that such change would be a way of morally improving it. In any case, there is a certain sense in which my position does indeed constitute a partial (and I would argue justified) attack on some cultural traditions. To respect the right to a group's integrity cannot mean respecting its intolerance and aggressive attitudes toward other groups.

Notes

I am indebted to Julia Annas, Jules Coleman, Sarah Harding, Christopher Morris, and Joseph Raz for their comments on this essay, which have improved it substantially (albeit, I fear, not to the point where any of these people would agree with all its major theses).
1 Horace Kallen, ''Democracy versus the Melting Pot,'' in his *Culture and Democ-*

racy in the United States (New York: Boni & Liveright, 1924); article reprinted from *The Nation*, February 18 and 25, 1915.

2 In this essay I have relied on information about citizenship policies in various countries supplied by Sarah Harding. I owe Harding a great deal of thanks for her work on my behalf.

3 This particular British notion was partly responsible for the War of 1812, when British ships seized U.S. sailors on U.S. ships to fight in the Napoleonic Wars, arguing that these Americans were really British citizens and thus obliged to fight for "their country."

4 See Section 12 of the 1981 Immigration Act. For more on the 1981 law, see Ian MacDonald and Nicholas Blake, *Immigration Law and Practice in the United Kingdom*, 3d ed. (Boston: Butterworths, 1991).

5 Federal German Constitution of 1949 (Basic Law), Art. 16 (2).

6 William Pfaff, "Neo-Nazi Backlash: Immigration Difficulties Cause Germany to Turn Rightward," *Arizona Daily Star*, April 10, 1992, 19. (Article copyrighted, 1992, Los Angeles Times Syndicate.)

7 From Coleman and Harding, Chapter 2, this volume.

8 To state the rules precisely, all people born outside of Germany to German parents or grandparents must accept only German citizenship if they apply for it (and thus renounce any other citizenship they might have at the time of application). Moreover, although such people will be considered "naturalized citizens," they are in the category of citizens "naturalized by right" as opposed to citizens (born of non-German parents) who are "naturalized by discretion" of the German government. For further discussion, see Kay Hailbronner, "Citizenship and Nationhood in Germany" in William R. Brubaker (ed.), *Immigration and the Politics of Citizenship in Europe and North America* (New York: University Press of America, 1989), 67–8, 73–4. Cited by Coleman and Harding in Chapter 2, this volume.

9 Moreover, these immigrants often perceive the assimilation requirement as involving changes in their way of life that are disrespectful of their heritage, and thus refuse to make them. A very large percentage of German residents of Turkish descent refuse to apply for citizenship because they believe that by doing so they will lose all of their Turkish identity. Only 7 percent have applied to be naturalized.

10 William Pfaff, "Neo-Nazi Backlash," 19.

11 To be a nation-state, the state need not include all members of the nation. Hungary is a nation-state, but does not include Hungarians living in Croatia. But the members it does include must, almost exclusively, be members of the nation.

12 This list of characteristics is based on those defined by Avishai Margalit and Joseph Raz, "National Self-Determination," *Journal of Philosophy* 87, no. 9 (September 1990): 443–7. My fifth characteristic is not, however, one that they recognize, despite the fact that it is the animating principle of such nations as Germany, Japan, and Serbia. I include it because of its importance in understanding the citizenship policies of such nations.

13 See ibid. and Chapter 2 by Coleman and Harding, this volume.

14 See Margalit and Raz, "National Self-Determination." This phrase is also used by Coleman and Harding, Chapter 2, this volume.

15 These requirements are set out in the 1946 Japanese Constitution.

16 See the Permanent Resident Act of 1951.

17 The parents must, however, request this within three months of the child's birth.

18 See, e.g., John Locke's *Two Treatises of Government*, Rousseau's *The Social Contract*, and Immanuel Kant's *Metaphysical Elements of Justice*.

19 E.g., in "Of the Original Contract."

20 Coleman and Harding provide an excellent review of these countries' citizenship policies in Chapter 2, this volume.

21 In a way, Hume's criticisms work better against theories that rely on tacit or explicit consent to *legitimate* governmental authority over its citizens. In "Of the Original Contract" Hume asks: "Should it be said, that, by living under the dominion of a prince, which one might leave, every individual has given a *tacit* consent to his authority, and promised him obedience; it may be answered that such an implied consent can only have place, where a man imagines that the matter depends upon his choice. . . . We may as well assert that a Man, by remaining in a vessel, freely consents to the dominion of the master; though he was carried on board while asleep, and must leap into the ocean and perish, the moment he leaves her" (263, in *Hume's Ethical Writings*, ed. A. MacIntyre [New York: Collier, 1965]). But while tacit consent, as I have defined it, may not justify the legitimacy of an individual's domination by a government, in countries such as the United States and Canada, it explains why the political society takes people to be members of it.

22 Peter Schuck argues that U.S. citizenship is based on "mutual consent" in his *Citizenship Without Consent: Illegal Aliens in American Polity* (New Haven, Conn.: Yale University Press, 1985).

23 Still, it is unlikely, as I noted in note 17 above, that this consent is *sufficient* to legitimate a government's authority over its citizens in these sorts of countries.

24 Great Britain also allows joint British and Israeli citizenship.

25 On conditions necessary for the exercise of a national right to self-determination, see Margalit and Raz, "National Self-Determination," esp. 459–61.

26 Ibid., 449.

27 Will Kymlicka, *Liberalism, Community and Culture*, 2d ed. (Oxford: Oxford University Press, 1991), 162–81.

28 See the discussion of this point by Coleman and Harding, Chapter 2, this volume.

29 See Pfaff, "Neo-Nazi Backlash."

30 "Anti-Immigration Policies Rattle Bonn," *New York Times*, April 7, 1992. Among those supporting the halting of immigration is a party whose dominant member is a former Nazi SS member. The movement is regarded as ominous by Jewish leaders.

31 Coleman and Harding maintain that "individuals everywhere have a right to be a member of a political community."

32 "Anti-Immigration Policies."

33 I believe that this is the argument that Coleman and Harding are implicitly putting forward in Chapter 2, this volume.

34 It is, however, challenged by Stephen Perry in Chapter 5, this volume.

35 How might one argue otherwise? Might one maintain that ethnic groups deserve preservation in the same way that breeds of dog or horse (e.g., golden retrievers, thoroughbreds) deserve preservation? The idea is hard to take seriously, although at times the rhetoric of defenders or ethnicity suggests it.

36 But arguably the citizenship policies of Israel survive this argument. Not only can non-Jews acquire citizenship in Israel, but citizenship for Jews is (at least officially) defined along lines of religious affiliation rather than race or ethnicity. On the other hand, the nature of citizenship for Jews differs from that for non-Jews, Palestinian residents of the West Bank live in a legal limbo, and the question "Who is a Jew?" is a highly charged political issue. The importance of this question is obvious: the answer determines the definition of the nation that Israel was created to protect.

37 This does not necessarily mean that an individualistic justification of political societies is vindicated. Even though consensual states such as the United States and Canada conceive of the individual as conceptually prior to the state and the cultural community with the state, it is possible for the consensual conception to be justified by communitarian arguments, e.g. because it is the best policy for preserving a state committed to the flourishing of all cultural groups within it.

5

Immigration, justice, and culture

STEPHEN R. PERRY

The question of whether an individual has, as a matter of justice, a right to enter, permanently reside in, or become a citizen of a state to which she currently stands as an outsider is unavoidably bound up with questions of whether and to what extent there exist rights in justice to certain kinds of goods. The relationship between borders and goods is complex, but as a first approximation we can distinguish between two categories of goods access to which is affected by restrictions on entry to states. The first consists of land and other natural resources that are located within a state's territory. The second comprises goods that depend for their existence on the activities and ways of life of people living in the state. One good in the second category is the social surplus or national wealth that results from economic activity. Others are various kinds of public goods, that is, goods that are relatively nonrival in consumption and that are not easily subject, as far as the distribution of their benefits is concerned, to centralized control. The existence or at least the general character of some of the public goods in this category is intimately connected with the nature of the legal and political systems in individual states; public security and markets are examples that come to mind. Other public goods, such as the good of cultural community, exist more or less independently of the state but are capable of being protected or nurtured by it.

In Section I of this essay I consider, in a general and schematic way, how a liberal theory of justice should deal with questions of immigration. My general conclusion is that liberal states have extensive but not unlimited obligations to admit outsiders. They are not in principle obliged to adopt completely open immigration policies, as some writers have claimed. On the other hand, they are almost certainly not living up to the obligations they do have, particularly in the case of refugees. More specifically, I argue that, in principle, a single criterion of distributive justice should apply globally to the goods in the first of the two categories just distinguished (land and natural resources). This requirement of justice can often be satisfied only by permitting immigration. Outsiders also have certain rights in justice to goods in the second category, but their claims tend to be weaker than those of insiders. The reason is that an adequate liberal theory of justice will recognize, in addition to universal rights and obligations that apply globally, localized rights and obligations that apply only within a given political community. In the case of second-category claims by outsiders that can be met by drawing on a country's social surplus, the states with the corresponding responsibility may have a discretion either to permit immigration or to make direct transfers of wealth (foreign aid). But many goods in the second category are public goods, which are essentially nonexportable. The most important of these is public security. Outsiders who have rights with respect to this good are typically refugees whose claims can, for the most part, be satisfied only if they are permitted to take up residence in a well-ordered state.

Discussions of justice in immigration often bring in another important good in the second category, namely, the good of cultural community. Section II of this essay is concerned primarily with this good. Accepting arguments that massive cultural disruptions can affect political stability and interfere with the conditions for attaining individual autonomy, I ask whether the value of cultural community might help to justify states in excluding some immigrants, or giving preference to others, on cultural grounds. I conclude that, in a liberal state, such actions are generally impermissible. Some restrictions on immigration, the precise scope of which will depend on prevailing circumstances, might nonetheless be justified in order to avoid excessive cultural disruption. In this section I also consider the bearing that the value of cultural community might have on a right of inclusion, that is, a right on the part of potential immigrants to be admitted as permanent residents to a state on the ground of a shared culture. I conclude that, at least in a liberal state, cultural affinity with some or all of the state's current residents does not give rise either to a right to be admitted or, except in very limited circumstances, to a right to preferential treatment in the immigration process.

For the most part my concern in this essay is with the justice of claims to be admitted to a state as a permanent resident. I make occasional mention of citizenship, but for the most part I simply assume, following a number of powerful arguments that have been advanced in the literature, that persons who have been admitted as permanent residents have a right, after they have met fairly minimal conditions of qualification, to be granted citizenship.[1]

I. Immigration and justice

A. *Two conceptions of justice*

It will be helpful to begin by considering two different benefits that can reasonably be thought to flow from membership in a political community, either of which might give an outsider a reason for wishing to be admitted to a particular state. These benefits are, first, the provision of a framework for mutually advantageous cooperation among individuals and, second, the provision of an efficacious mechanism for protecting basic rights and serving basic needs. Both benefits fall into the second of the two categories of goods distinguished earlier, which means their existence depends on the activities and ways of life of people living in the state. Both subsume more specific benefits, some of which are public goods and some of which are not.

Of course, I do not mean to claim that there are no advantages to political community other than those associated with these two benefits, or to suggest that the benefits in question do not in large measure overlap; the public enforcement of prohibitions on violence and theft can plausibly be regarded, for example, as an aspect of both. But it is nonetheless important to distinguish between these benefits, since each corresponds to a quite different conception of justice. These two conceptions in turn generate different justifications for treating compatriots differently from other persons in the world. The question of whether and under what circumstances it is permissible to exclude outsiders from joining a political community is just one aspect of the larger issue of whether and to what extent the differential treatment of compatriots is justified. The two conceptions of justice have different things to say about this more specific issue as well.

The first conception of justice can be called, following Allen Buchanan, *justice as reciprocity.* It corresponds to the benefit of providing a framework for mutually advantageous cooperation. The essential idea is that "distributive justice (if not the whole of justice, or even of morality) is founded solely on reciprocity, or, more precisely, that an individual has a right to a share of social resources (or moral rights of any kind) *only* if that individual contributes or at least can contribute to the cooperative surplus."[2] There are two versions of justice as reciprocity, namely, justice as self-interested reciprocity and justice as fair reciprocity. According to the former, which is best exemplified in the work of David Gauthier,[3] justice is grounded entirely in rational self-interest; an individual has reason to adhere to principles of justice only if it is to his advantage to do so. Justice as fair reciprocity, by contrast, holds that as a matter of fairness, rather than rational self-interest, every participant in a cooperative enterprise who benefits from the contributions of other participants owes something to those persons, but only to the extent that they do or can contribute to the cooperative surplus.

The second of the two conceptions of justice, which corresponds to the benefit of providing an efficacious mechanism for protecting basic human rights and needs, can be called, again following Buchanan, *subject-centered justice.* It holds that "basic rights to resources are grounded not in the individual's strategic capacities but rather in other features of the individual herself – her needs or nonstrategic capacities."[4] Different versions of subject-centered justice ascribe rights or moral status on the basis of different characteristics of persons. At the heart of this conception, however, lies the idea that rights and perhaps morality are generally grounded in the fundamental moral equality of persons and in the respect and concern for persons that is thereby due to them.

Buchanan offers a persuasive series of objections to the conception of justice as reciprocity, most of which need not be mentioned here. The most important objection for our purposes, although not the most telling from a broader perspective, is that justice as reciprocity is committed, in both its individual-rationality and fairness versions, to the intuitively unacceptable thesis that those who do not or cannot contribute to a mutually beneficial cooperative scheme have no rights in justice, and perhaps no moral standing at all. The difficulty, in other words, is a problem of exclusion,[5] and although Buchanan emphasizes the exclusion of those who are initially already within a society, such as the severely handicapped, there will clearly be implications for what justice requires vis-à-vis those who are at present outsiders but would like to become insiders (i.e., would-be immigrants). Before we consider these implications, however, it should be made clear that Buchanan is not saying that special rights *cannot* be generated by mutually beneficial cooperative schemes. His point is, rather, that justice as reciprocity is wrong to claim that it is *only* in this way that justice and rights can be grounded. A more limited thesis, to the effect that such schemes are one source of rights but not the only one, is consistent with the existence of rights that have their source in a subject-centered understanding of justice – for example, a general right to a minimal share of social resources.[6]

Distinctions that roughly correspond to the one between justice as reciprocity and subject-centered justice have figured prominently in the philosophical literature dealing with the complementary questions of whether there are obligations of justice across borders, and whether and to what extent differential treatment of compatriots is justified. Robert Goodin's discussion of these issues is a good example.[7] Goodin makes the point that in domestic and international law the different status accorded to compatriots sometimes requires that they be treated more favorably than others, but it also sometimes requires that they be treated less favorably; compatriots can be subjected to duties and asked to make sacrifices that are not appropriately applied to or demanded of outsiders.[8] He suggests that one way to make sense of these facts is to conceptualize states as ''ongoing mutual-benefit societies.'' To the extent that such a conceptualization is underpinned by an account of justice, it will clearly be justice as reciprocity. Goodin observes that ''the entry ticket to a mutual-benefit society should, logically, just be conferring net benefits on the society.''[9] In other words, whether an outsider has a right to enter a political community based on justice as reciprocity is a matter to be determined by the community itself, in accordance with its assessment of the social contribution the outsider is capable of making. The obvious corollary is that many people may be left without a right to join any political community at all.[10]

Goodin argues that the special duties we have toward compatriots can be explained and justified by a different understanding of justice. He begins with the assumption that there are ultimately no distinct special duties but only general ones, of both a positive and negative character, which all persons owe to all other persons. He begins, in other words, with a universalistic approach to justice and morality that is clearly comprehended by the subject-centered conception. Goodin refers to this understanding as the *assigned-responsibility model*. The general duties that constitute its starting point will for various reasons, which include but are not limited to the advantages of specialization and a division of labor, be subdivided: special responsibility for particular portions of the larger task will accordingly be assigned to particular persons or institutions. He argues that the boundaries of states function in just this way: "National boundaries simply visit upon . . . particular state agents special responsibility for discharging those general obligations vis-à-vis those individuals who happen to be their own citizens."[11] In the first instance we as individuals all owe duties to every other individual, but these agent-neutral general duties come to be mediated by the intervening institution of the state.[12] One could then add (although Goodin does not) that the desirability of having relatively local mediating institutions is one factor in the justification of a system of sovereign states, as opposed to, say, a world government of some kind.[13]

Goodin states that the assigned-responsibility model differs from the mutual-benefit society model in two ways, both of which have implications for immigration policy.[14] The first difference concerns the treatment of the "useless," such as the severely handicapped, and the helpless, such as refugees and stateless persons. On the mutual-benefit society model, states have essentially no duties toward the former group, and will have reason to assist the latter only if admitting them would provide a net benefit to the state. On the assigned-responsibility model, however, states have unavoidable obligations toward both groups. Refugees and the stateless become the residual responsibility of all states, which taken together have a duty, admittedly imperfect as against any one of them, to give such persons refuge.

The second difference concerns the international distribution of resources. On the mutual-benefit society model, transfers across borders need not be made, and would ordinarily occur only if they constituted mutually beneficial exchanges. Similarly, modifications of borders can be justified only by a positive cost–benefit analysis. The assigned-responsibility model, by contrast, calls for a roughly equitable allocation of resources to states, taking account of the number of persons within each state. If there is a misallocation, then redistribution is in order. Goodin does not say what form this redistribution should take, but it is obvious that there are three possibilities: first, the re-drawing of borders; second, wealth transfers, in the form of, for example, foreign aid; and third, immigration from states that are, taking account of the proportional availability of natural resources, relatively overpopulated to those that are relatively underpopulated.[15]

An understanding of state responsibilities similar to Goodin's offers a good starting point for determining what criteria should be employed in the moral evaluation of immigration policies in a liberal state. But Goodin's assigned-responsibility model is in at least two respects too simplistic. For one thing, it is implausible to think that localized obligations of justice within a state can be explained solely in terms of a prima facie division of labor. For another, the model does not distinguish very clearly among the different kinds of goods that might be subject to claims in justice. Dealing with these points in a fully adequate way would require the formulation and defense of a complete theory of justice, which is clearly not possible here. Instead, I shall propose some relevant constraints that liberal theories of justice must meet and sketch how these constraints would bear on the formulation and assess-ment of morally acceptable immigration policy. Of necessity the result will not be a detailed blueprint, but more in the nature of a series of guidelines.

B. Universal and localized obligations

To begin, I would like to suggest that any adequate theory of justice must make room both for rights and obligations whose scope is universal and for localized rights and obligations that apply only within particular political communities (for our purposes, states). Goodin's model contains rights and obligations of the former kind, but none of the latter. Localized obligations of the type I have in mind are more robust than those Goodin's model yields, since they represent something more than a prima facie division of a universal responsibility owed to all persons. It seems very plausible to think, for ex-ample, that a citizen of one state can have a moral obligation to pay higher taxes than a citizen of a neighboring state because the first state made a democratic decision to implement a more comprehensive social welfare scheme.[16] Without a more robust conception of localized obligations than Goodin's it is difficult to account for his own enumeration of the many complex ways in which compatriots are, and apparently can justifiably be, treated differently from other persons.

Such differential rights and obligations *might* be justified by reference to a conception of justice as reciprocity[17] – the Hart–Rawls principle of fair play is an obvious possibility here – but it is also quite conceivable that they could be justified by reference to principles of subject-centered justice. The latter would be universal in the sense that they applied to all persons and all communities, but the reciprocal rights and obligations the principles generated would nonetheless be localized because the scope of the obligation owed by a given individual would be limited to the other members of her community. Moreover, the content of such localized rights and obligations might, within limits, permissibly vary from community to community. Thus the content and scope of the obligation must be distinguished from the content and scope of the underlying principle that justifies it.

One route to justifying localized rights and obligations within subject-centered justice might be Rawls's natural duty of justice, which "requires us to support and comply with just institutions that exist and apply to us."[18] Jeremy Waldron has offered a persuasive argument, based on the Kantian claim that persons should enter into a form of society with those immediately adjacent to them in order to avoid arbitrariness, violence, and conflicts over resource use, that shows, in effect, how the Rawlsian natural duty could give rise to what I have called robust localized obligations.[19] It will not, however, be necessary for the purposes of this essay to decide whether localized obligations have their roots in subject-centered justice or in justice as reciprocity. I shall simply assume that, one way or the other (and possibly by means of a combination of both conceptions of justice), the preference that states show to their own citizens and residents is, at least up to a point, justified. As for the universal obligations of justice, these, it should be clear, will always be grounded in subject-centered justice.

What are the universal obligations of justice? What, in other words, are the obligations of justice that are owed across borders, to all persons regardless of where they live? This question, unsurprisingly, admits of no straightforward, uncontroversial answers. Some writers who make the explicit or implicit assumption that Rawls's theory gives rise only to universal obligations have argued, for example, that the difference principle should apply internationally, without regard for borders.[20] Others argue that only the principle of mutual aid, which requires that assistance be rendered to persons in urgent need by those able to do so with little cost or risk to themselves, should apply across borders.[21] It will not be possible to settle all such controversies here. But the following four constraints on a theory of universal justice (as I shall call that part of a comprehensive theory of justice that deals with universal obligations) seem plausible.

1. It is reasonable to think that the basic principle of justice in holdings, which might be the difference principle, a principle of equality in holdings, or something else, should apply across borders to the totality of land and natural resources in the world, without distinguishing between the residents and nonresidents of particular states. To put the point another way, it is

reasonable to think that ultimate entitlements to natural resources cannot be determined, at either the group or individual level, by a principle of initial acquisition (or first occupancy).[22] A principle of initial acquisition, say of a Lockean character, is the natural complement to a pure reciprocity-based theory of justice (although neither in fact entails the other). A subject-centered theory of justice, on the other hand, is likely (although, again, not bound) to regard natural resources as subject to what has been called a general-right-based argument for property.[23] This is an argument that takes an individual interest to be sufficiently important to justify holding others to be under duties to respect private property, where the importance of the interest is due to its qualitative character and not some contingent event (such as an act of initial acquisition). On such a view property ought to be distributed to groups and ultimately to individuals on some appropriately equitable (but not necessarily equal) basis. For present purposes I shall assume that some version of a general-right-based argument is the morally appropriate way of dealing with natural resources.[24]

The bare statement of this thesis calls immediately for a host of qualifications and caveats, and it will not be possible to present even these in an adequate fashion here. But let me state, necessarily without proper argument, three of the more relevant points. First, a general-right-based view does not presuppose a static, completely determinate conception of patterned distributive justice that has no room for markets or other forms of interchange.[25] Second, such a thesis need not claim that all natural resources have a neutrally determined, transcultural value that is independent of particular social forms; hence it need not claim that there is a hard and fast division between natural resources, on the one hand, and social or cultural resources, on the other. Finally, a thesis of this kind does not presuppose a central distributing authority, nor need it claim that questions of global distributive justice must be settled all together, once and for all, at one time.

2. An adequate theory of universal justice will accept a version of the principle of mutual aid (also known as the principle of rescue or principle of humanity) that applies not just to individuals, but also to states (regarded, ultimately, as the agents or representatives of individuals). The essence of such a principle is, to repeat, that those who are able to render assistance to persons in urgent need at little cost or inconvenience to themselves should do so.[26] What constitutes minimal inconvenience to a state will be relative to its total national wealth, and not just to the value of the natural resources within its borders. The principle may, in other words, require a country to draw on the accumulated social surplus that economic activity has produced within it. Thus a rich country like Japan will not escape the application of the principle on the ground that it is relatively resource poor.

3. An adequate theory of universal justice will also recognize, I shall as-

sume, a right on the part of all persons to a minimum need-based share of material resources. The precise level of resources to which an individual is entitled will be determined by the specific theory one defends, but it will presumably be at least sufficient for subsistence. The basic idea is that it is wrong to let people starve or die for lack of shelter or basic medical care, wherever they may live in the world, if there are sufficient resources elsewhere to prevent this. This right could be respected either by direct transfers of, say, food or by helping a society to develop its agricultural, industrial, or market infrastructures. The principle at stake here resembles constraint 1 and differs from constraint 2 in that the demands it places on states may be more than minimally inconvenient. It resembles constraint 2 and differs from constraint 1 in that it may require states to draw against their accumulated social surplus and not just the value of their natural resources. Two further points should be noted. First, the share of a given country's social surplus to which outsiders might be entitled on the basis of constraints 1 and 2 together might well be less, and ordinarily will be less, than the entitlement of an insider, as determined by localized rights and obligations of justice. Second, the lower the minimum level of resources to which persons are entitled – the closer, in other words, that that level approaches the bare minimum required for subsistence – the more likely it is that constraint 3 will supplant constraint 2, or at least render it redundant.

4. I shall assume, finally, that an adequate theory of universal justice will recognize an instrumentally justified right of permanent residence within some appropriately constituted and reasonably well-ordered state. The case for such a right depends on, among other factors, the fact that our world is divided almost in its entirety into sovereign states, so that individuals do not have the choice of opting out of the system, and the fact that a well-ordered state gives rise to certain nonexportable public goods, including in particular the good of public security, that are extremely important to the well-being of all persons.[27] Individual states will owe the corresponding obligation to, in the first instance, those who already have a moral and legal right of permanent residence within their borders, but they may come to owe it to others as well, on an imperfect basis; in particular, they may come to owe it to persons who become stateless or whose current state is no longer capable of offering them an appropriate degree of protection.

C. Justice in immigration

Let me now try to outline how the considerations adduced in the preceding section would apply to immigration. To begin, states are properly regarded, in the manner of Goodin's assigned-responsibility model, as mediating institutions that bear the initial responsibility of universal justice toward their own citizens and inhabitants. (This does not, of course, preclude the possibility of robust localized rights and obligations of justice of the kind discussed earlier.) Because the obligations in question are universal, other states (as the agents of their populations) are not thereby relieved of all responsibility toward noncitizens or nonresidents. To the extent that a state is unable to secure its inhabitants' basic universal rights, other states will have a collective duty to assist (assuming they are able to do so without jeopardizing their own citizens' rights). This duty will be imperfect as against any one of them, but the determination of who will do what for whom does not absolutely demand a single central authority; if necessary, these matters can be worked out on an ad hoc, give-and-take basis.[28]

Many states in the world are in fact unable or unwilling to honor the basic rights in universal justice of their own citizens and inhabitants, either because they are governed by ineffective or repressive regimes or because of an imbalance in the global distribution of material resources. How do the four constraints just enumerated affect the international obligations of other states, particularly as regards immigration? The first three constraints apply to material resources and wealth. As was noted earlier, there are three main methods by which transfers of resources might be effected: redrawing of borders, direct transfers in the form of foreign aid, and immigration. The redrawing of borders will often be impracticable, the scope of assistance it permits will be limited, and for a variety of other reasons, such as the possible effect on the stability of states, it is generally undesirable. This leaves foreign aid and immigration. It is reasonable to think that, in a great many cases, states will have a discretion to rely on one or the other technique, or on a combination of the two. Many factors will enter into the determination of which policy option is preferable, including a country's ability to absorb immigrants and the desirability of not breaking up cultural communities abroad. For example, in the case of a functioning state that is governed by leaders of goodwill but is temporarily incapable of meeting its inhabitants' basic needs (due to, say, a famine), foreign aid would probably be the best option.

There are, however, some strong arguments that tend to favor immigration over foreign aid, such as that immigration avoids the administrative inefficiency and corruption that may exist in the beneficiaries' home countries and that it is economically more efficient than foreign aid.[29] Moreover, in some cases immigration may be the only possible way of satisfying a state's obligations under universal justice. This is especially likely to be true with respect to constraint 1, which applies to land and other natural resources, since land, at least, cannot be exported. Thus consider the case of a country with vast territories that are unpopulated, or barely populated. Henry Sidgwick wrote, very plausibly, that "an absolute claim to exclude alien settlers adequately civilized, orderly, and self-dependent, from a territory greatly under-peopled, cannot be justified on the principle of mutual non-interference."[30] Michael Walzer has more recently accepted this claim as well.[31] Even in today's crowded world this is an argument for immigration that, in the case of some countries at least, is still likely to carry force.[32]

It is with respect to constraint 4, however, which recognizes a right to permanent residence within a reasonably well-ordered state, that immigration really comes into its own, since the goods to which the right ensures access are nonexportable, public goods. This right will typically be claimed by persons who are persecuted by their own government or whose basic rights are unprotected due to the collapse or complete ineffectiveness of political authority in their home country. It may sometimes be possible to honor this right by helping to create the relevant public goods abroad, either by enabling an existing but ineffective state to become functional again[33] or by assisting a persecuted group to exercise its collective right to national self-determination (assuming it possesses this right).[34] In a great many cases, however, the provision of refuge in the assisting state's own territory is the only practicable means of honoring the right to permanent residence within a well-ordered state. This is particularly true of persecuted individuals who happen to be outside their home countries, these being the persons who fall under the definition of "refugee" in current refugee conventions.[35] But it may also be true of individuals who have not been able to leave their homelands, some of whom may not actually be persecuted but simply live in conditions of anarchy. There is a very strong case to be made that refugee status is currently defined too narrowly as regards both alienage and persecution.[36] On the approach advocated here, refuge should be granted much more liberally to persons who do not have effective political protection of their basic rights within their home countries, whether or not they are outside that territory and whether or not they are actually persecuted.

I have merely sketched the basic obligations of universal justice that are owed across borders rather than attempted to characterize their substance in detail. Enough has been said, however, to suggest that wealthy Western states are not doing nearly enough to fulfill their obligations and that they should almost certainly be taking in more refugees and, probably, more economic immigrants as well. The universal obligations I have discussed are, taken together, potentially quite onerous. (Only the principle of mutual aid is restricted to actions that are minimally inconvenient.) But these obligations are not without limit. Once a society has completely met these obligations – and I emphasize that no Western state currently appears to have done so – there is, I wish to suggest, a discretion concerning whether to take in more immigrants. There are, as we shall see later, restrictions on the exercise of this discretion – discrimination on the basis of race is prohibited, for example – but liberal states are nonetheless not obliged to open their borders completely.

Why are there limits to universal justice of a kind that would justify a discretion rather than an obligation to take in further immigrants? There are two related reasons. First, any liberal, nonutilitarian theory of justice must acknowledge the value of autonomy by granting to individuals a certain measure of moral space in which to live their own lives and pursue their own interests. There is thus an upper limit on the self-sacrifice that liberal states can demand of their citizens, and once the obligations of universal justice have been met this limit will apply to the treatment of outsiders.[37] Second, justice is, at least to some extent, a matter of determining the rights and obligations of persons who are actually interacting and cooperating with one another within an existing society that contains common institutions and shared social practices. It is, of course, justice thus conceived that gives rise to the localized rights and obligations discussed earlier. It is also this view of justice that animates theories of justice as reciprocity. Whether or not justice as reciprocity in the strict sense characterized by Buchanan is the ultimate source of localized rights and obligations, *some* notion of reciprocity is clearly at work here. As will become clear in Section II, however, this notion of reciprocity must not be confused with the value of community.

I am assuming that the substantive requirements of justice, as these apply to ongoing societies with existing practices of cooperation, are sufficiently open and flexible to permit individual states to adopt possibly quite different regimes of distribution and redistribution. To revert to an earlier example, I assume that states can legitimately adopt, within limits, more (or less) extensive systems of social welfare. Part of the point of this flexibility – and hence part of the point of recognizing the possibility of localized rights and obligations in justice – is to ensure that societies have some degree of self-determination, thereby permitting their members to express a commitment to one another in the form of shared political undertakings. We can see here a link between the two reasons for acknowledging limits to universal justice, since an element of self-determination is common to both. One aspect of self-determination at the political level is self-definition. Thus liberal states have, within fairly circumscribed limits, a discretion to decide whether to permit outsiders to enter. The limits, however, are crucial. These are of two kinds, both of which have already been mentioned but which it will be helpful to summarize here. First, the universal obligations of justice can often be satisfied only by permitting immigration, and this is particularly true with respect to refugees; in these cases, the discretion to exclude does not apply. Second, states' discretion to permit or prohibit immigration beyond that required by universal justice is fettered; in exercising that discretion states cannot give expresson to racial preferences or, except in very restricted circumstances, to preferences based on culture. The justification for these constraints is taken up in Section II.

D. Should borders be completely open?

Contrary to what has just been argued, some writers have maintained that liberal states have an obligation grounded in justice to adopt a policy of completely open borders. Joseph Carens is a prominent example.[38] I cannot address here all the points Carens raises, but he advances one particularly powerful line of argument that should be discussed. Carens recognizes the force of the argument that "there is considerable room for legitimate collective self-determination even within the context of a commitment to the welfare state."[39] Thus one state might permissibly provide free higher education, whereas another might subsidize only those in particular need. Carens acknowledges that the capacity for collective self-determination might be undermined if current inhabitants of the latter state were allowed to travel freely across the border to take advantage of free education in the former. Although he does not put the point in quite this way, I think he also acknowledges that in cases where one state is simply not living up to its internal obligations of justice but is capable of doing so, there is something unfair about permitting it, in effect, to rely on policies of open immigration to export its failures in justice elsewhere; the claim of redress that can be made by an individual affected by such a failure lies, at least in the first instance, against his own state and not against other states. But despite recognizing the force of these considerations, Carens concludes that they are outweighed by an argument grounded in a liberal right of free movement that applies as much across borders as within. This is the argument I want to discuss.

Carens argues that a liberal right of free movement across borders can be grounded in a global application of Rawls's original position. He holds that the parties behind the veil of ignorance would insist on a right of free movement between countries because this might prove essential to their plans of life. Since Rawls insists that liberty can be restricted only for the sake of liberty, this right could be limited only by a real risk of a breakdown in public order; it could not be limited with a view, for example, to protecting the economic well-being of current inhabitants.[40] Carens buttresses this argument by pointing to the right of free movement that exists within states, and in particular to the right to move freely between the subunits of federations. He maintains that "the right of free movement within a state is widely regarded as an important personal liberty and not just a necessary component of national citizenship."[41] The same attitude should prevail, he suggests, at the international level.

In responding to this argument, it is important to emphasize that Rawls's original position is not readily subject to a globalizing interpretation. Like some other writers who make this move, Carens implicitly assumes that the Rawlsian approach to justice can generate only universal obligations, along the lines of Goodin's assigned-responsibility model.[42] While it seems reasonable to conclude that Rawls's theory is *subject-centered*,[43] it does not follow that only universal obligations flow from it. As was explained earlier, localized rights and obligations, limited to particular societies with ongoing cooperative arrangements, can arise within a theory of subject-centered justice that is itself based on universal principles. Rawls's own account of reasoning within the original position leads him to recognize certain universal duties, such as the natural duty of mutual aid.[44] But his insistence that the primary subject of justice is the basic structure of society,[45] together with his definition of a society as "a cooperative venture for mutual advantage,"[46] suggests that his primary concern is with localized rights and obligations. Rawls's own view of the matter is hardly determinative, of course, but there is surely an onus on someone who advocates globalizing the original position to show why Rawls's assumptions about its role in a theory of justice are wrong. Carens makes no attempt to do this.

It thus cannot be taken for granted that the rights and obligations arising from the principles of justice Rawls defends would apply between societies and not just within them.[47] The original position is not appropriately employed to create as radically uncertain a situation as possible, in which, for example, the parties all live in different countries or societies and do not know which one is theirs. Rather the character of the original position, and more specifically the scope of the veil of ignorance, must be related to certain initial assumptions about the nature of justice. Rawls's own assumptions, as he has clarified them in his later work, are based on "a certain conception of the person together with a companion conception of social cooperation."[48] The conception of the person is characterized by two moral powers: a capacity for a sense of right and justice and a capacity for a conception of the good. The former capacity Rawls also describes as a "capacity to honor fair terms of cooperation."[49] The social conditions necessary for the full development and exercise of the two powers can be achieved, according to Rawls, only within an institutional framework of cooperation based on appropriate principles of justice.[50] It is for this reason that the scope of the original position is limited to persons within a single society. This understanding of justice is quite consistent with the two reasons noted earlier for recognizing limits on universal justice. It is also compatible with Waldron's argument for the natural duty to support just institutions that was sketched in Section I, B. As Waldron explains it, entering into cooperative arrangements with others living within the same territory is not just a matter of self-interest or convenience but is itself a requirement of justice.

As has already been mentioned, Rawls assumes that deliberation in the original position will produce universal natural duties as well as localized rights and obligations. The reason for this, presumably, is that in the original position even parties who know that they all belong to the same society will find it in their interest to accept, for example, a universal principle of mutual aid. From *our* point of view, outside the original position, the justification for such a principle will presumably have to do with the mutual respect that equal moral persons owe one another, whether they live in the same society or not. There is, of course, room for disagreement concerning which obligations will be universal and which localized within the Rawlsian schema. I have already argued that the basic criterion of distributive justice, the content of which has been left open but which might well be the difference principle, should apply globally to land and natural resources. This may involve a departure from Rawls's own views, and the manner in which his general theory should accordingly be modified is perhaps not immediately evident. But the justification for the departure is clear enough, and it is consistent with Rawls's basic premises: groups are no more entitled to acquire absolute property rights by means of unilateral acts such as first occupancy than Rawls assumes individuals are.[51]

What, then, are we to say about the right of free movement? Rawls's general justification of the basic liberties proceeds by reference to the two moral powers associated with the conception of the person. The equal political liberties are intended to secure the effective exercise of citizens' sense of justice, while liberty of conscience and freedom of association are intended to ensure that citizens are effectively able to form and pursue a conception of the good.[52] The other basic liberties, including freedom of movement, "can be connected to [these] two fundamental cases by noting that they are necessary if the preceding basic liberties are to be properly guaranteed."[53] Given Rawls's assumptions about the connection between justice and social cooperation, the upshot of this argument is clearly that freedom of movement is a localized, not a universal, right. Are there any independent reasons to reject this conclusion?

Refusing to recognize a universal right to take up permanent residence anywhere on the planet – as opposed to a right to *visit*, which raises different concerns – does not seem to be fundamentally illiberal. The two reasons canvassed earlier for recognizing limits to universal justice are powerful arguments for rejecting such a right, as Carens's own discussion of how open borders might undermine collective self-determination shows. As for the analogy with the right to free movement within national subunits of states, Carens rightly acknowledges that this right could conceivably be the consequence of political choice rather than a morally fundamental matter.[54] It seems reasonable to think that *some* version of the right to free movement within states is morally fundamental, but any such right will inevitably be subject to important limits. Thus I cannot, in Canada, take up permanent residence wherever I like in the country, for example, on someone else's private property or on a Native reserve. It should be noted, finally, that Carens's argument for a universal right of free movement depends on an international application of the Rawlsian stricture that liberty can be restricted only for the sake of liberty. Our previous arguments about the status of the basic liberties within the Rawlsian schema suggest that this move to the international level is unjustified, but even if we leave that point aside, the fact remains that this stricture is independently subject to serious difficulties.[55]

There is, however, the following kernel of truth in Carens's argument. A liberal theory of justice must ultimately be grounded in a universal respect for the autonomy of all persons. This will generate certain minimal universal responsibilities, and also certain special responsibilities, in the form of localized rights and obligations that apply within particular states. I have argued that there is no universal *right* of freedom of movement. Even so, however, it seems appropriate to think that a liberal state should, in exercising its discretion with respect to nonmandatory immigration, bear in mind the underlying value of autonomy and make an attempt to respect all persons' choices concerning where to live, to the extent that it is possible to do so. This would mean, among other things, generous admission quotas and standards for admission that are not overly exclusionary. States may demand that discretionary immigrants not be a burden on society, and even that they be capable of making a positive contribution. But it is not appropriate to demand that they be capable of making an extraordinary contribution.

Finally, it is worth remarking that Peter Schuck has drawn attention, within the context of a discussion of immigration law and citizenship, to a supposed tension within liberal thought.[56] He notes that liberalism has traditionally emphasized, first, the importance of consent, by which he means not just the consent of the individual to the government of the state but also the consent of the state to the inclusion of the individual within the community;[57] and second, the "somewhat contradictory theme" of the universality of certain natural rights. Like Carens, Schuck takes liberal universalism to imply completely open borders, such as prevailed in the United States up until the 1880s,[58] but the preceding discussion suggests that this move may be too quick. That discussion also suggests that the tension Schuck perceives within liberalism can be dissolved by the recognition that universal and localized obligations can peacefully coexist within liberal theory.

As for the right of the state to consent to the membership of the individual, this could mean either of two things: first, that as things are in the world, it is the state that has the final authority to decide who is entitled to reside within its territory or become a citizen; and second, that the state has in addition a strong substantive discretion to determine the grounds upon which persons will be *morally* entitled to reside within its territory or become a citizen. The first interpretation is consistent with the position on justice and immigration taken in this essay, since in the absence of appropriate international institutions, states must of necessity have the final authority to decide who gains entry. The second interpretation is also consistent with my argument, if the substantive discretion is constrained in the two ways described earlier. If states' discretion is not so constrained, then the second interpretation is most consistent with a pure theory of justice as reciprocity, which regards political communities as morally entitled to exclude *all* outsiders who are incapable of making a positive social contribution. But it is difficult to see how a pure reciprocity theory could be reconciled with the universalism that Schuck thinks is also inherent in liberalism.

II. Immigration and the good of cultural community

I argued in Section I that modern liberal states have fairly extensive but not unlimited obligations to permit immigration; once these obligations have been satisfied, states have a discretion concerning whether to admit further immigrants. The question then arises as to whether this discretion is fettered. In particular, can states legitimately exclude immigrants whom there is a discretion to admit on the ground that they do not share the prevailing culture (or one of a number of predominant cultures) within the state? Can states show a preference to would-be immigrants who share cultural affinities with current inhabitants? For that matter, given that the universal obligations of justice as these pertain to immigration are imperfect and that states will in effect have something like obligatory quotas to fill rather than obligations owed to particular individuals, can they fill these quotas by systematically giving preference to some cultural groups over others? If immigration policies based directly on cultural affinity (or lack thereof) are prohibited, might any other restrictions related to culture be permissible? In this section, I attempt to provide answers to these questions.

The value and significance of the good of cultural community are illuminatingly captured by Joseph Raz and Avishai Margalit in their characterization of so-called encompassing groups.[59] Raz and Margalit describe such groups in terms of six features, the most important of which for our purposes are the following three. First, the group in question has a common culture that is pervasive, in the sense of encompassing many varied and important aspects of human life, and that determines, at least in part, the identity of its members. Second, membership is determined not by formal institutions but by mutual recognition. Third, membership is a matter of belonging rather than of achievement and is usually determined by nonvoluntary criteria; one can come to belong to such a group, but only through the unavoidably slow process of adopting its culture. Raz and Margalit make the claim that membership within encompassing groups – or, as I shall call them, cultural communities – is of great importance to individual well-being. This is, I think, clearly correct. Will Kymlicka makes the further claim that membership in cultural communities is also of concern to liberal political theory, because the range of options available to a person in life is determined by her cultural heritage; that heritage provides, in Kymlicka's phrase, the appropriate "context of choice."[60] This too is plausible, although the precise relationship between liberalism and membership in cultural communities is a matter of some controversy.

A. *Three arguments for exclusion*

At least three arguments might be advanced to defend the claim that outsiders can be excluded from a state because they do not share the cultural heritage of some or all of its inhabitants. All three would also support a right on the part of a state to accord preferential treatment in immigration matters to persons who *do* share its cultural heritage. The first argument begins with the premise that one of the purposes of the state is simply to serve and protect the shared culture, which would be regarded as a valuable way of life in itself and, possibly, as the *only* valuable way of life. This kind of communitarian (or perhaps perfectionist) entrenchment of a particular culture within the political framework of a state is contrary to liberal thought. Even a perfectionist liberal like Raz does not argue that particular cultures are entitled to political support. Raz's perfectionism is pluralistic in form and grows out of a concern for fostering the conditions in which individual autonomy can flourish. Individual autonomy requires a range of options, and Raz argues that governments can noncoercively support those options that are independently morally valuable (whence his perfectionism).[61] But this is quite different from saying that an entire culture can be given political support.[62]

It is evident that there are nonliberal states in the world today in which a communitarian or perfectionist preference for a particular culture prevails, and, not surprisingly, they tend to discourage or prohibit immigration by persons who do not share the dominant culture. In this essay I say nothing about either the moral legitimacy of such states or the extent to which they are justified in limiting immigration on this basis. This is due in part to my uncertainty concerning what ought to be said about these matters, but also in part to the fact that our primary concern must be with the formulation of a just immigration policy for liberal societies like our own. Accordingly, I will not consider the first argument further, although I shall have something to say later about related issues in the context of minority rights.

The second and third arguments for justifying the exclusion of outsiders who do not have cultural affinities with the state's inhabitants are both developments of the idea that states are entitled to control immigration so as to prevent themselves from being "swamped" by foreign influences. Both arguments are potentially relevant to liberal as well as to nonliberal societies. The basic idea underlying the second argument is that cultural homogeneity is necessary for preserving social stability and cohesiveness, which are in turn necessary for securing political stability. The perfectionist (or communitarian) argument just considered could perhaps be summed up, necessarily somewhat crudely, by saying that the purpose of immigration policies limiting access to a country by those who do not share its dominant culture is to protect and preserve that culture. The argument now being considered could then be summed up, again somewhat crudely, by saying that the purpose of such policies is to protect and preserve not a dominant culture as such, but rather the state. I shall refer to this as the argument from stability. A variation on the argument holds that while true cultural homogeneity is not ordinarily necessary for this purpose, a certain degree of cultural stability is. According to another variation, it is not so much the state itself that is in need of protection as it is liberal and/or democratic institutions within the state.[63]

The third argument for excluding foreigners on the basis of cultural differences draws on the idea that the possession of a determinate cultural background is an important element of well-being and, more particularly, is a prerequisite for attaining individual autonomy; in Kymlicka's terms, it provides the necessary context for choice. The basic argument is that the existing culture or cultures must be prevented from being overwhelmed by foreign influences, not in order to preserve social cohesiveness or social institutions as such, but rather to ensure the individual well-being of current citizens. If excessive immigration from alien cultures were permitted, the argument runs, the original culture or cultures would be effectively displaced in public life and the persons who were raised in those cultures left rootless and alienated. The social forms that could contribute to their well-being and permit them to achieve autonomy would be pushed aside or destroyed. I shall refer to this as the argument from autonomy.

B. The argument from stability

There is a tendency among modern liberals of a Rawlsian stripe, who advocate a strict neutrality principle, to regard any political sustenance of cultural communities as impermissible; membership in such communities is to be treated as a private matter, constituting a particular conception of the good.[64] Will Kymlicka has recently pointed out, however, that the idea that the state should adopt an attitude of neutrality toward different cultural groups has not always figured so prominently in liberal thought. Cultural homogeneity within any one state was at one time thought to be important, but not because the culture was necessarily valued for its own sake. Rather, homogeneity was believed to be necessary for the preservation of political stability. For liberals like J. S. Mill and T. H. Green, liberal democracy could be achieved only if people felt bound to the state by "ties derived from a common dwelling place with its associations, from common memories, traditions and customs, and from the common ways of feeling and thinking which a common language and still more a common literature embodies."[65] This would mean, among other things, that states should ideally coincide with nations and that national minorities might have to be dealt with by either forced assimilation or redrawing boundaries. Another consequence is that liberal states would be entitled, and perhaps obligated, to prohibit immigration except by those who shared the prevailing culture, or at least were certain to be assimilated. On the less strict version of the argument described earlier, which holds that only cultural stability, not homogeneity, need be protected, states would still be entitled to impose culturally related restrictions on immigration in order to achieve that end.

The argument from stability in its strictest form insists that social and political stability depends on cultural homogeneity. This is, empirically, an implausible claim. The true nation-state, in which a homogeneous cultural community coincides fairly closely with the associated political community, is the exception rather than the rule in the modern world. Most states are either multinational – that is, they contain more than one nation or people, each of which shares a language and a traditional homeland within the state's territory – or polyethnic – that is, they contain immigrant cultures that have maintained their cultural particularity. It is of course true that, particularly in the case of multinational states, the presence of more than one culture has often led to serious tensions and conflict, as recent events in the former Eastern Bloc countries and in the Balkans attest. On the other hand, there are enough examples of liberal, well-governed, and relatively harmonious multicultural states to make it difficult to maintain that cultural homogeneity is a prerequisite for either political stability or the preservation of liberal/ democratic institutions. There is thus no reason to think that the strict version of the argument from stability, which insists on cultural homogeneity, is generally true. Of course, it cannot be denied that there are relatively homogeneous, intolerant societies in the world that have difficulty coexisting with other cultures. I shall suggest later that at least in cases where the associated states profess to accept liberal political values, such societies should take it upon themselves to encourage more liberal social attitudes as well.

This leaves us with the looser version of the argument from stability, which maintains that a certain degree of cultural stability and cohesiveness is necessary to preserve either general social and political stability or the liberal/

democratic character of existing political institutions; the conclusion is that immigration may be restricted accordingly. There is undeniably some sense to this argument, but it is important to take note of two points.

First, the core issue here appears to be the rate of cultural change, not the preservation of an existing culture or cultural mix. What is at stake is cultural continuity rather than the substance of the dominant culture or cultures. A demand for cultural continuity is perfectly compatible with pluralism, and it does not mean that one or more cultures are being elevated to a special status within the state. All it means is that cultural change, whether in the form of cultural diversification or transformation within a dominant culture, must be sufficiently gradual as to ensure social and political stability. A demand for cultural continuity thus understood is compatible with liberal political theory, which I earlier assumed forbids the political entrenchment of dominant cultures (other than, of course, the political culture of liberalism itself). The general principles of liberalism emphasize tolerance, openness, and the moral equality of persons, as well as at least some degree of neutrality among cultural groups.[66] Restrictions on immigration that are intended to preserve cultural stability should therefore generally do so not by favoring certain cultures or discriminating against others, but rather by limiting the overall number of immigrants so as to ensure that cultural change within the state is not too rapid and present social forms are not simply overwhelmed.

I argued in Section I that states have general obligations of justice at the international level that almost certainly exceed their present-day efforts in that direction and that in some cases can be fulfilled only by permitting immigration. Once those obligations have been met, states are not absolutely obliged to accept further immigrants, although respect for the value of autonomy suggests that liberal states should be as accommodating as possible to individuals' wishes about where to live. If, however, a state does decide to accept a greater number of immigrants than it is obligated in justice to take in, it should in general adopt impartial policies that do not discriminate among different cultural groups. A fortiori it should not discriminate on racial grounds, as present-day Germany in effect does.[67] It should be noted that the principle of impartiality among cultural groups may have to be qualified in a number of ways, one of which is that a liberal state is presumably not bound to take in a large number of persons from groups espousing illiberal or undemocratic principles who might, if admitted on a sufficiently large scale, pose a real risk to the existence or character of a liberal democracy.[68] But it would presumably take a manyfold increase in the levels of immigration to, say, the United States or Canada before such a risk could be regarded as anything more than a theoretical possibility.

The second point is that the character and extent of the restrictions that might be necessary to maintain cultural and social stability will vary from state to state, and will be a function of a variety of factors, including prosperity, current cultural makeup, population density, and prevailing social and political attitudes. In so-called immigrant countries like the United States and Canada, the national public culture tends to be more overtly political, and specifically liberal, than in many European countries. It is reasonable to think that the resulting public acceptance of pluralism, together with the greater existing degree of cultural heterogeneity, makes it possible for such societies to tolerate more, and culturally more diverse, immigration than might be the case elsewhere. A less open, culturally more homogeneous society might not be able to absorb the same levels of immigration without the occurrence of social unrest. The present-day example of Germany comes to mind.[69] This does not mean that political authorities in states with intolerant societies (or societies with influential strains of intolerance) should simply accept the social status quo and set immigration policy accordingly. At least in states with liberal political systems, like Germany, it is surely incumbent on authorities to encourage, in noncoercive ways, the development of more tolerant public attitudes.

C. The argument from autonomy

The argument from autonomy, it will be recalled, claims that the possession of a stable cultural context is an important element of individual well-being, and in particular that it is a precondition for achieving autonomy. As in the case of the argument from stability, there is undoubtedly a core of good sense to this claim. Once again, however, it is plausible to think that the requisite degree of cultural stability involves neither homogeneity nor the preservation of substantive aspects of the dominant culture or cultures, but only some measure of cultural continuity. As far as immigration policy is concerned, this means that liberal states should not forbid entry to persons on cultural grounds and a fortiori should not do so on racial grounds.[70] Nor are they entitled to favor one person or group over another on the grounds of greater likelihood of assimiliation into the dominant culture or cultures. They may, however, limit overall immigration, and perhaps impose ceilings on immigration from any one country, with a view to ensuring cultural continuity within the state.

The thesis that governments of liberal states are entitled to take cultural continuity into account in determining immigration policy does not mean that governments may try to shape the nature of cultural change (although this may be permitted by particular theories of liberalism, such as Raz's perfectionist theory).[71] It simply means that they are entitled to ensure that change is sufficiently gradual, whatever direction it ultimately takes, that individuals' "context of choice" (to use Kymlicka's term) is not disrupted. The claim that a cultural context is necessary for both general well-being and the ability to lead an autonomous life seems well-founded. But this does not mean that well-being and autonomy require a *particular* cultural context; there are indefinitely many cultural frameworks that will do. Moreover, cultural change occurs all the time, quite apart from the influences or effects of immigration. Individuals within liberal societies are not entitled to a static and unchanging cultural framework, but only to a sufficient degree of cultural continuity so as to ensure that their "context of choice" is not unreasonably disrupted.

Will Kymlicka has drawn a distinction between the *character* and the *structure* of a cultural community.[72] "Character" refers to the norms, values, and institutions of a cultural community as they exist at any one time. In the case of cultural "structure," however, "the cultural community continues to exist even when its members are free to modify the character of the culture, should they find its traditional ways of life no longer worthwhile."[73] Kymlicka argues that there can be no justification within liberal theory for protecting the character of a culture; doing so would limit rather than protect individuals' ability to choose particular goals, projects, and life plans. Cultural structure, not cultural character, provides the necessary context of choice, and it should accordingly be treated as a primary good in Rawls's sense. Kymlicka then argues that the concern for cultural structure within liberal theory can give rise to differential rights claims on behalf of minority cultures; an example would be the rights associated with the special status of aboriginal peoples in North America, such as the exclusive right to live in certain designated areas (reserves or reservations). If this argument for minority rights is sound, it might well justify certain cultural restrictions or preferences in immigration policy that are intended to protect the structure (but not the character) of minority cultural communities. Such restrictions and preferences in fact exist in Canadian immigration law with respect to the francophone culture of Quebec.[74] One might also argue that the restrictions concerning who can live on aboriginal reserves constitute a kind of internal immigration law that is justified by differential minority rights.

It is not possible to discuss the issue of minority rights at length here. But I would like to suggest that cultural "structure" in Kymlicka's sense can in the end mean no more than cultural continuity of the kind discussed earlier. There is no basis for thinking that it includes certain key or core substantive elements, such as the use of a particular language, since sufficiently gradual cultural change can lead, over time, to a shift from one language to another without undue disruption of the context of choice. In Kymlicka's terms, the use of a particular language is a matter of cultural character, not structure. In fact there is no reason to think that a concern for the context of individual choice will necessarily entail the preservation of a distinct culture, since the context of choice can survive even the assimilation of a culture, as long as the process is sufficiently gradual.

Thus Kymlicka's argument, even if it does justify differential rights claims on behalf of minorities, may not justify minority rights that are particularly robust. Kymlicka makes the sensible points that a person's cultural upbringing is "a constitutive part of who that person is" and that cultural heritage "may affect our very sense of agency."[75] But these claims provide support only for the position that cultural change should not occur too quickly. Thus the minority rights that could be justified by Kymlicka's argument might prohibit coerced assimilation or change,[76] and they might permit measures that retarded the rate of change or assimilation with respect to a particular minority group. But they could not justify measures intended to ensure the long-term survival of a particular culture or of particular elements of a culture, such as the use of its language. Minority rights of the kind permitted by Kymlicka's argument might well justify certain cultural preferences or restrictions in immigration policy, but these would be limited; current immigration practice in Quebec might not be supportable on these grounds, for instance, since the long-term well-being of the francophone culture itself seems to be a key object of present Quebec policy.[77]

This is not the end of the story on minority rights, of course, since there are arguments for such rights other than Kymlicka's, some of which regard the goal of promoting the survival of a particular way of life as morally legitimate.[78] But any such argument is likely to fall within the bounds of a communitarian rather than a liberal political theory, and hence will be closer to the first of the three arguments for the permissibility of cultural preferences in immigration policy that were described earlier than it will be to the argument from stability or the argument from autonomy. As I noted in my brief consideration of the first argument, the validity of general communitarian or perfectionist theories is beyond the scope of this essay, the operating framework for which is liberal political theory.

D. Walzer on membership

Michael Walzer, in one of the seminal discussions of the relationship between the value of cultural community and immigration, has argued that states, on behalf of the communities they help to protect and define, are entitled to regulate immigration in accordance with their own self-understanding.[79] It is important to emphasize that Walzer regards the authority to determine membership as hedged in by moral obligations, deriving from a principle of mutual aid, that coincide with some of the obligations of universal justice that were discussed in Section I. But it is nonetheless clear that there is, for

Walzer, an important area of discretion within which states are entitled to determine their own membership in accordance with their particular cultural values. Such a discretion would apparently permit states to give a preference to would-be immigrants with whom there is a preexisting cultural affinity and to exclude those with whom there is little or no affinity.

Walzer puts forward a number of arguments, not always very clearly differentiated, in support of this general thesis about membership. One is that diversity has value of its own.[80] Walzer does not develop this argument at all, but it would appear that it could take one of three forms. The first is that a diversity of social forms is necessary to ensure that people have a sufficiently wide range of options in life; otherwise, individual autonomy will be unattainable.[81] But the diversity required to underwrite autonomy can be, and indeed must be, located within the bounds of a single cultural community; this argument does not speak at all to the value of having a number of different communities. The second version of the claim that diversity has value would be a Millian instrumental argument to the effect that knowledge of many different cultures contributes, by increasing our understanding of possible ways of life, to social vitality and overall human progress.[82] This argument has a definite appeal, but its empirical presuppositions are questionable. It seems just as plausible to suppose that the Millian goals will be better achieved by a cultural free market, in which interchange and cross-fertilization among cultures are encouraged by permitting relatively open immigration on a worldwide scale. Such a policy would obviously lead to cultural change, but there is no reason to think that it would bring about global cultural homogenization. Even if it did, the resulting culture would not be static; the Millian goals might still be better served by the free flow of people across borders than by the "museum" approach to culture that the argument under consideration envisages. The third version of the diversity argument is the idea that cultural diversity is *intrinsically* valuable, possibly for reasons deriving from a communitarian approach to poltical theory. Walzer provides no argument for such a claim, however, and it is not clear what form such an argument might take.

Another argument that Walzer makes in support of his thesis about membership is this: "If we cannot guarantee the full extent of the territorial or material base on which a group of people build a common life, we can still say that the common life, at least, is their own and that their comrades and associates are theirs to recognize or choose."[83] This argument distinguishes among different goods, access to which is affected by borders. Even if there is no absolute entitlement to the land and natural resources that fall within a state's territory, still, the argument claims, the good of *community* belongs to the community, which accordingly has a collective right to distribute membership as it sees fit. Let me assume that Walzer is right to conclude that

outsiders do not, generally speaking, possess a right to join a cultural community to which they do not already belong; a fairly strong case for this
proposition can, I think, be mustered.[84] But in order to justify the conclusion
that *states* can exclude would-be immigrants on the ground that the good of
community belongs to the community, Walzer needs further premises. The
most promising possibilities are the following two propositions: first, each
cultural community has the right that its distinct character be protected and,
second, the distinctiveness of cultures depends on closure at either the neighborhood or state level (preferably the latter).[85]

Consider the second proposition first. Walzer appears to assume that the
distinctiveness of cultural communities can be preserved only if closure takes
a territorial form, at either the state or neighborhood level. But it is by no
means obvious that this is so. Walzer suggests that the state should be conceived as analogous to a club, which is a social organization that can permissibly determine its own membership, but perhaps the appropriate analogy
is between clubs, which need not have a territorial base, and cultural communities: perhaps the state, or at least the liberal state, should be conceived
of not as a club but as a loose association of nonterritorial clubs. Entry to
the association's territory would not carry with it a right to join one of the
clubs, which control their own membership, so that a fairly liberal right of
entry could be recognized without jeopardizing or questioning the legitimacy
of this control. Walzer dismisses this possibility on the ground that "nations
look for countries because in some deep sense they already have countries:
the link between people and land is a crucial feature of national identity."[86]
But this response equates "community" with "nation," and that simply begs
the question; within North America, for example, cultural communities tend
not to be nations with a territorial base (although such nations do exist there,
of course). Another response is available to Walzer, however: he could claim
that closure at the state level would still be required to preserve the distinctiveness of nonterritorial clubs. At this point our attention shifts to the first
of the two propositions that were suggested for completing Walzer's argument, namely, the claim that cultural communities have a right to the protection of their own distinctiveness.

A right of cultural communities to have their distinctive characters protected could take a number of forms. If the idea is that a cultural community
is entitled to the political protection of its distinctiveness because the culture
is inherently valuable, at least for the members of the community in question,
then we are back to a perfectionist or communitarian claim of the kind that
is beyond the scope of this essay. It should be noted, however, that Walzer
does not himself provide the argument that would justify such a claim.

The notion that communities have a right to have their distinctiveness
protected can also be given interpretations that are compatible with liberalism,

but these make Walzer's argument much more modest than he presumably intends. If we take "distinctiveness" to mean cultural continuity of a kind necessary to preserve either social stability or individuals' context of choice, his argument collapses into either the argument from stability or the argument from autonomy; as we have seen, both arguments turn out to be fairly modest in scope. If we take "protection of distinctiveness" to mean that cultural communities cannot be *coerced* into change, the argument is again compatible with liberalism, but it is not obvious that it justifies any state control of immigration whatsoever. There does not appear to be a *liberal* argument to the effect that cultural communities have the right to be free not just from coercion but from any external cultural influences that might, say, lead members to abandon the cultural community or call upon it to change. Finally, we might interpret the right in question as holding no more than that cultural communities themselves, as opposed to the political communities that contain them, are entitled to take steps to preserve their distinctive characters. But while such a right may well exist, its scope is limited. Its recognition would not take us beyond the entitlement of cultural communities to control their own membership to the further conclusion Walzer requires, which is that the *state* is justified in taking action to protect cultural distinctiveness.

At this point Walzer might wish to say that the preceding considerations apply to pluralist liberal states, which contain a number of cultural communities, but not to states with a single dominant culture. In fact, he asserts that the United States, having at an earlier stage of its history opted for a pluralist society, cannot now ignore the "moral realities" of that society by, say, restricting immigration to white Protestants.[87] He then notes that "the earlier decision might have been different, and the United States might have taken shape as a homogeneous community, an Anglo-American nation-state."[88] The implication appears to be that, under those circumstances, the United States might indeed be entitled to limit immigration to white Protestants. I want to suggest, however, that the crucial earlier "decision" was not the one to become a pluralist state, but rather the one to become a liberal state.[89] The considerations adduced in the preceding three paragraphs apply to all liberal states, whether pluralist or not. It does not matter, in other words, whether the association of clubs I discussed earlier contains several clubs or only one. One might put the point by saying that liberalism rejects Walzer's implicit equation of the nation and the state. Thus a liberal state always contains the seeds of a pluralist society. If this happens as a result of internal change, it cannot legitimately be prevented. If it happens as a result of immigration that is required by the universal obligations of justice, it again cannot be legitimately prevented. Liberal states do have a discretion with respect to immigration, but if they decide to take in immigrants they cannot do so in a way that is intended to preserve a dominant culture. This is, in effect, the moral issue that present-day Germany is facing.

One final argument Walzer makes in support of his thesis concerning membership is this:

Admission and exclusion are at the core of communal independence. They suggest the deepest meaning of self-determination. Without them there could not be *communities of character*, historically stable, ongoing associations of men and women with some special commitment to one another and some special sense of their common life.[90]

The core of this argument, to the extent that it is not concerned simply with continuity (stability), seems to be the value of political association rather than the value of cultural community. The notion of an ongoing association of persons who have a special commitment to one another suggests the form of collective self-determination, discussed in Section I, that gives rise to the possibility of localized rights and obligations within particular states. Cultural communities undoubtedly have a right of self-determination as well, and we have already remarked that they are not under any obligation to accept outsiders as members. But cultural self-determination cannot ordinarily be forwarded, in a liberal state, by means of political power and its attendant use of coercion. Walzer is right to take seriously the aspiration to collective self-determination within an association of persons with a special commitment to one another. The political expression of this aspiration does, moreover, give rise to a limited discretion to exclude. But in a liberal state this discretion cannot be exercised by excluding on the basis of culture. Walzer's argument can suggest otherwise only by ignoring the distinction between cultural and political community.

E. *Cultural communities and inclusion*

I have so far argued that liberal states are not generally justified in shaping immigration policy by preferring certain cultural groups or discriminating against others. This is to look at the issue from the point of view of receiving states. But perhaps we should look at the bearing that culture might have on immigration from the point of view of the would-be immigrant. Can an outsider assert a right to enter a liberal state as a permanent resident because he shares the culture of a community that is flourishing within the state? Or if he does not have a right, can he at least maintain that he has a relatively stronger claim to be permitted to enter (see Coleman and Harding, Chapter 2, this volume)?

It is important to distinguish between a right or claim to belong to a particular cultural community and a right or claim to permanent residence within a state in order to have access to a cultural community. Walzer argues that communities are entitled to exercise complete control over their own membership, and if we understand this claim to apply to *cultural* communities, it may well be defensible. Particular communities are not obliged to recognize or adhere to the liberal values of autonomy and tolerance, and may be perfectly justified, within their own traditions, in shunning or expelling members.[91] Moreover, there are strong arguments to the effect that there cannot be a general right, held by individual members against their cultural communities or against the other members, to the continued existence of the community. Joseph Raz argues that there can be no such right because "the maintenance of a collective good affects the life and imposes constraints on the activities of the bulk of the population, in matters which deeply affect them."[92] It is, according to Raz, difficult to imagine that a set of onerous and widespread duties of this kind could be justified by the interests of a single individual.[93] Denise Réaume offers a different argument. She points out that in the case of goods like cultural membership, an individual needs other persons not just to bring the good into being, but also to enjoy it.[94] Réaume calls these *participatory* goods. She maintains that there cannot be an individual right to such a good because it cannot be enjoyed by an individual independently of its enjoyment by other individuals; the individual has no interest *as* an individual that could be the subject of such a right.

Whether or not there is a right to continue to belong to a cultural community is clearly relevant to the justifiability of the claim that one should be permitted to enter a state on grounds of cultural affinity, but it is not really the heart of the matter. The claim made against the *state* is that one is entitled to get past the gatekeeper at the border and thereby be given a chance to join a flourishing center of one's culture within, and that one has this entitlement even if one can assert no right against the local cultural community itself that it should not rebuff one's attempt to join or, if one does join, that it should continue to exist indefinitely in its present form. The claim, in other words, is to an opportunity of a certain limited kind. Such a claim, however, could plausibly be asserted only by an individual who had been uprooted from another locus of her cultural community, and not by someone who was residing in a center of the culture flourishing elsewhere. In a case of the latter type it becomes implausible to say that the ultimate justification for the claim is the would-be immigrant's own well-being, since by hypothesis she is doing all right where she is (at least as far as cultural matters are concerned). In such a case the best interpretation of the postulated right would be that it is instrumental in character;[95] its ultimate justification is best understood as the welfare of the cultural community itself. But a justification of this kind appears to be profoundly illiberal, since it entails building a preference for one or more cultures into the politics of the state or states with the corresponding duty. This takes us back to the arguments canvassed in our earlier discussion of the relationship between culture and immigration as seen from the point of view of the state, as opposed to the point of view of the would-be immigrant.

Let us consider, then, the case of an individual who has been forcibly uprooted from one locus of his cultural community and now claims a right to be admitted to another. It is important to notice that someone in this situation would ordinarily be a stateless refugee who had experienced setbacks to well-being extending far beyond the loss of cultural ties. I argued in Section I that refugees do indeed have the right to be accepted into some other state as a permanent resident, although the corresponding obligation is imperfect against any given state. It is plausible to think, however, that cultural membership might serve as one relevant factor in sorting out who should go where. Consider the persons of East Indian descent who were expelled from Uganda in the 1970s. It made some sense that they should go to Britain and Canada, where there are flourishing East Indian communities, rather than to countries where there are not. All other things being equal, it is preferable that the refugees a country takes in have affinities with cultural groups who have a presence there. In the case of the expelled East Indians, a concern for their individual well-being clearly made it preferable that they go to countries with flourishing East Indian communities. Even if one cannot speak here of a right to be admitted to such a country, surely it makes sense to say that there is a strengthened claim to be admitted. Furthermore, assuming there are no other refugees with more pressing general needs, it also seems appropriate that countries should offer haven, as an expression of solidarity, to refugees with whom some or all of their citizens have a cultural affinity.[96]

Is an expression of solidarity of this kind illiberal because it favors one cultural group over another? It seems to me that it is not. Such a gesture neither presupposes nor entails the entrenchment of general cultural preferences in the politics of the state. The circumstances in which it would be appropriate are by definition exceptional, and they involve persons who are in desperate need of assistance quite apart from their cultural background. These are individuals with crystallized rights to be granted permanent resident status in some well-ordered state, and the factor of cultural well-being is simply being taken into account, along with other factors, to determine against which states their claim is strongest. This is very different from systematically favoring certain cultural groups in the category of discretionary immigration. It also seems to me to be different from making systematic distinctions on cultural grounds among persons who have a nonspecific claim to assistance, which could take the form of either a transfer of wealth or permission to immigrate, whose claims have not crystallized into rights to be admitted to another state. (Determining the relevance or nonrelevance of culture to the resolution of such nonspecific claims is, however, admittedly less straightforward than in the other situations considered.)

The claim that cultural affinity is an appropriate factor to take into account in determining where refugees should be settled is thus not equivalent to the claim that individuals – even forcibly uprooted individuals – have a right, based only on those aspects of their well-being that flow from cultural membership, to immigrate to states in which their cultural communities have a presence. Suppose that a member of the expelled East Indian community in Uganda is granted asylum in a safe, prosperous country that contains no East Indian community of its own. Does this person have a stronger claim than others to immigrate to a country that does have such a community? Since by hypothesis she is no longer a refugee, it seems to me that her interest in enhanced well-being, rooted in the desire to reestablish ties with her culture, is simply not strong enough by itself to support such a claim. The primary basis for taking in refugees is to alleviate the suffering and to counter the vulnerability to which stateless persons are typically subject. The main problem facing refugees is lack of a viable state, not lack of a viable cultural community. The person with asylum in a safe country does not suffer from lack of a state. To grant a preference to her, on cultural grounds alone, over others who might want to enter a given state begins to take on an illiberal air. On the other hand, such a person has as strong a claim as anyone else to be considered as a candidate for discretionary immigration. Her claim is not for cultural reasons stronger than the claims of others, but neither is it, for those reasons, weaker.

III. Conclusion

I have argued in this essay that liberal states have extensive but not unlimited obligations to admit outsiders as permanent residents. Their obligations are strongest with respect to refugees, understood to be persons who do not have the protection of a state: there is, as we have seen, a strong case for expanding the current definition of ''refugee'' beyond those who are persecuted and who are outside the borders of their home countries. I have also suggested that Western liberal states are almost certainly not doing enough to satisfy their general international obligations, which in many cases they could meet either by permitting immigration or by making direct transfers of wealth to other countries. There comes a point, however, at least in theory, beyond which liberal states are not obligated to take in more immigrants. There are limits to universal justice, and this means, among other things, that liberal states are not obliged to throw open their borders completely. But while states have a discretion as to whether to admit more immigrants, they cannot exercise this discretion by favoring some cultural groups or races or by discriminating against others. There may be some room for recognizing stronger claims by refugees who have ties to cultural communities that are present within a state, but beyond this the cultural heritage of would-be immigrants is not an appropriate ground for either admission or exclusion. States may, however, control the overall flow of immigration, and perhaps also the number of immigrants from any one country, with a view to ensuring that cultural continuity within the state is not disrupted.

Two limitations on the arguments advanced here should be noted. First, I have neither formulated nor defended the comprehensive theory of justice that would be needed to justify fully many of the claims I have made. Instead, I have appealed to intuitively plausible premises and to general constraints that it seems reasonable to require any theory of justice to meet. This is sufficient for a first pass at the problem of immigration, but ultimately the only satisfactory response to the issue must be presented within the framework of a full-blown theory of justice. This would demand, among other things, a more probing explication of the thesis that universal and robust localized obligations of justice can coexist and a more thorough justification of the differential rights to certain goods that could be claimed by insiders over outsiders. The second limitation is related to the first. I have not purported to lay out the details of a legitimate immigration law for any state, but only to provide rather vague guidelines for formulating and assessing policy. Anything more specific would require not only a comprehensive theory of justice, which would yield principles more specific in content than those I have described, but also a great deal more in the way of empirical information. For these reasons, then, this must be regarded as a preliminary study only.

Notes

1 See Michael Walzer, *Spheres of Justice* (New York: Basic Books, 1983), 52–61; Joseph H. Carens, ''Membership and Morality: Admission to Citizenship in Liberal Democratic States,'' in William Rogers Brubaker (ed.), *Immigration and the Politics of Citizenship in Europe and North America* (New York: University Press of America, 1989), 31.
2 Allen Buchanan, ''Justice as Reciprocity and Subject-Centered Justice,'' *Philosophical and Public Affairs* 19 (1990): 227, 228 (emphasis in original).
3 David Gauthier, *Morals by Agreement* (Oxford: Clarendon Press, 1986).
4 Buchanan, ''Justice as Reciprocity,'' 231. As Buchanan notes, somewhat conflicting strands in Rawls's work make it difficult to classify his theory (ibid., 230 n. 6). There are a number of indications that it is a version of justice as fair reciprocity, including his characterization of society as ''a cooperative venture for mutual advantage'' (John Rawls, *A Theory of Justice* [Cambridge, Mass.: Harvard University

Press, 1971], 4, 126). But Rawls's ultimate emphasis on a normative ideal of free and equal personhood makes it more plausible, as Buchanan says, to regard the theory as a Kantian version of subject-centered justice. I shall suggest below that Rawls's characterization of society is nonetheless a significant element in his theory. It is one of a number of elements that together create the possibility of localized rights and obligations that hold, not universally, but within specific societies only. Localized rights and obligations thus turn out not to be unique to justice as reciprocity; subject-centered justice can find a place for them as well.

5 Cf. Allan Gibbard, "Constructing Justice," *Philosophical and Public Affairs* 20 (1991): 264, 271–3.

6 Buchanan, "Justice as Reciprocity," 231–2.

7 Robert Goodin, "What Is So Special about Our Fellow Countrymen?" *Ethics* 98 (1988): 663. See also Brian Barry, "Humanity and Justice in Global Perspective, in J. Roland Pennock and John W. Chapman (eds.), *NOMOS XXIV: Ethics, Economics, and the Law* (New York: NYU Press, 1982), 219 (distinction between justice as reciprocity and justice as equal rights); David A. J. Richards, "International Distributive Justice," in ibid., 275 (distinction between actual reciprocity and moral reciprocity).

8 Goodin, "What Is So Special?" 666–71.

9 Ibid., 678. Like Buchanan, Goodin notes that the logic of a mutual-benefit society should deny social benefits to, e.g., the congenitally handicapped, remarking further that most of us intuitively feel that, morally speaking, it is a good thing that this does not happen.

10 In his discussion of a framework for utopia, Robert Nozick envisages a market of community membership, in which communities compete for members and individuals compete for entry to communities. Communities look to how each individual can benefit them, and vice versa. Robert Nozick, *Anarchy, State and Utopia* (New York: Basic Books, 1974), 302. (Nozick assumes that these communities are all located under the umbrella of the minimal state, but since the communities in question clearly have the unqualified right to admit and reject members, and are for all intents and purposes self-governing, there is no reason not to regard them as political communities in their own right.) Nozick begins with an idealized model of imagined possible worlds in which everyone would find an optimal community for him- or herself. But when the model is applied to our actual world, where the number of communities is necessarily finite, several points of divergence from the idealization appear (ibid., 307–8). One difference that Nozick does not expressly acknowledge is that in the actual world the market for individuals might not clear; i.e., there might be individuals left over whom no community would accept.

11 Goodin, "What Is So Special?" 682.

12 Other institutions, like international bodies of various kinds, may also provide appropriate vehicles for mediating duties. On this general topic see the very helpful discussion by Henry Shue, "Mediating Duties," *Ethics* 98 (1988): 687.

13 Of course, other justifications for the sovereign state have been proposed, some of which do not flow directly from considerations of justice. See, e.g., Frederick

G. Whelan, "Citizenship and Freedom of Movement: An Open Admission Policy?" in Mark Gibney (ed.), *Open Borders? Closed Societies? The Ethical and Political Issues* (New York: Greenwood Press, 1988), 3, 25–6, where arguments based on, first, the fear of universal despotism and, second, the Millian view that general human progress is best advanced by decentralized decision making are discussed.

14 Goodin, "What Is So Special?" 683–6.

15 Jules Coleman and Sarah Harding (Chapter 2, this volume) draw a distinction between two models of distributive justice that closely resemble Goodin's assigned-responsibility and mutual-benefit society models. They view their analogue of the assigned-responsibility model as an unsatisfactory basis for evaluating immigration policies, for two reasons. First, the world's resources are very unfairly distributed, and the notion that current immigration policies can be regarded as helping to rectify that situation is implausible. But these claims about the existing distribution of resources and current immigration policies, while no doubt true, do not call into question the abstract principles of subject-centered justice that must be taken to underlie the second model. They simply suggest that we live in an unjust world and that a radical revision of current policies, including immigration policies, may be in order. Coleman and Harding's second reason for dissatisfaction with their analogue of the assigned responsibility model begins with its allegedly goal-driven character: entitlements to immigrate are said to depend solely on incentive and allocation effects, not on rights; to the extent that individuals do have rights to resources, these can be satisfied by some form of direct wealth transfer; there can thus be, in this model, no fundamental right to immigrate. But even if distributive justice has a maximizing component, as the claim that the second model is fundamentally goal-driven seems to presuppose, this is compatible with the existence of certain nonmaximizing distributive rights, such as a right to a need-based minimum level of resources. Moreover, as we shall see, claims to goods will arise within any plausible subject-centered conception of justice that can best be satisfied by, and in some cases only by recognizing a right to immigrate.

16 For present purposes it does not matter whether the obligations arising on a localized conception of justice are owed directly to one's compatriots or to some mediating institution or set of institutions, such as the state. It should also be noted that, for ease of exposition in comparing different views, I treat the terms "duty" and "obligation" more or less synonymously. For Rawls's distinction between the two concepts see Rawls, *Theory of Justice*, 108–17.

17 The key here is Buchanan's point that justice as reciprocity is not wrong to maintain that rights can be grounded in mutually beneficial cooperative schemes, but only to maintain that they can be grounded *only* in such schemes. To justify localized rights and obligations on the basis of justice as reciprocity would obviously require that this restriction be lifted.

18 Rawls, *Theory of Justice,* 115; see also 335–7.

19 Jeremy Waldron, "Special Ties and Natural Duties," *Philosophy and Public Affairs* 22 (1993): 3, 12–15. Ronald Dworkin argues in *Law's Empire* (Cambridge,

Mass.: Harvard University Press, 1986), 193, that the natural duty of justice does not tie political obligation sufficiently tightly to a particular political community. Waldron's article is a response to that argument.

20 See, e.g., Charles R. Beitz, "Cosmopolitan Ideals and National Sentiment," *Journal of Philosophy* 80 (1983): 591, 593–7; Joseph H. Carens, "Immigration and the Welfare State," in Amy Gutmann (ed.), *Democracy and the Welfare State* (Princeton, N.J.: Princeton University Press, 1988), 207, 214–16.

21 Walzer, *Spheres of Justice,* 33, 45–51. Walzer makes clear in his discussion that the demands flowing from the principle of mutual aid could in fact be quite extensive.

22 Nozick, who accepts (with little argument) a Lockean principle of initial acquisition applicable to individuals, rightly draws attention to the parallel between the individual and the group cases: "We should note that it is not only persons favoring *private* property who need a theory of how property rights legitimately originate. Those believing in collective property, for example those believing that a group of persons living in an area jointly own the territory, or its mineral resources, also must provide a theory of how such property rights arise; they must show why the persons living there have rights to determine what is done with the land and resources there that persons living elsewhere don't have (with regard to the same land and resources)." Nozick, *Anarchy, State and Utopia,* 178.

23 Jeremy Waldron, *The Right to Private Property* (Oxford: Clarendon Press, 1988), 115–16.

24 Waldron's *The Right to Private Property* develops a convincing case for a general-right-based view of property and mounts a powerful attack on special-right-based arguments, i.e, arguments that take an individual interest to be of sufficient importance to justify duties of respect for property on account of the occurrence of some contingent event or transaction (such as an act of initial acquisition), rather than on account of the nature of the interest itself.

25 I have in mind here Nozick's critique of patterned distributive justice in *Anarchy, State and Utopia,* 149–231.

26 Not everyone accepts that this is a principle of justice as opposed to a principle of general morality. See, e.g., Barry, "Humanity and Justice," 243–6. It is implicit in Walzer's assumptions about the nature of justice that he does not regard the principle of mutual aid as a matter of justice. See Walzer, *Spheres of Justice,* 31–3. Rawls seems to me to be ambiguous on this issue. See Rawls, *Theory of Justice,* 108, 115, 347. The point is not an important one for present purposes.

27 I am assuming universal justice to include, in the first instance, negative rights prohibiting, e.g., the use of deliberate force and positive rights of distributive justice relating to material resources and certain other goods. But I am also assuming that justice gives rise to rights to be protected from rights violations by third parties. That is the basis of the fourth constraint discussed in the text. Nozick, among others, has disputed the existence of such rights, but that issue cannot be taken up here. See Nozick, *Anarchy, State and Utopia,* chaps. 2–6.

28 Cf. Shue, "Mediating Duties."

29 Cf. Whelan, "Citizenship and Freedom," 11–13.

30 Henry Sidgwick, *The Elements of Politics*, 4th ed. (London: Macmillan, 1929), 255.
31 Walzer, *Spheres of Justice*, 45–8.
32 This is not to say, of course, that there will not be competing considerations, such as the desirability of preserving wilderness areas as part of the general heritage of humanity. It is also necessary to take account of Joseph Carens's point that a "society's capacity to support its population depends not primarily on its landmass but on its overall capacity to create jobs" ("Nationalism and the Exclusion of Immigrants: Lessons from Australian Immigration Policy," in Gibney [ed.], *Open Borders?* 41, at 58). Thus the moral situation may be quite different between two sparsely populated countries, one of which is industrialized and whose territory is largely nonarable, the other of which is not industrialized and most of whose territory can support agricultural activity.
33 See J. Stackhouse, "Foreign Aid's New Targets," *Toronto Globe and Mail,* June 24, 1993.
34 See Joseph Raz and Avishai Margalit, "National Self-Determination," *Journal of Philosophy* 87 (1990): 439. Consider the examples of the Kurds and the Bosnian Muslims. Given the persecution and suffering both groups have endured, their members have, on the basis of the arguments in the text, a right to be taken in elsewhere. But this might not be the best solution to their difficulties, and it might not be one of which they wish to avail themselves. It would almost certainly involve dispersal and a consequent weakening of their shared culture, a matter that, as we shall see in Section II, is of legitimate moral concern even within liberal theory. It is thus arguable that we would do best by both peoples if we were to help them exercise the right to national self-determination that Raz and Margalit's argument suggests they have, rather than assist them to emigrate from their homelands. Of course, I do not mean to assert that emigration could never be the best solution to the difficulties faced by either group. The point is simply that, depending on circumstances, assistance in situ might be the presumptively preferable solution.
35 Article 1A(2) of the United Nations Convention relating to refugees (189 UNTS 137) defines a refugee as a person who, "owing to a well-founded fear of being persecuted for reasons of race, religion, nationality, membership in a particular social group or political opinion, is outside the country of his nationality and is unable or, owing to such a fear, is unwilling to avail himself of the protection of that country."
36 Cf. Andrew E. Shacknove, "Who Is a Refugee?" *Ethics* 95 (1985): 274.
37 Cf. Beitz, "Cosmopolitan Ideals," 598.
38 See, e.g., Joseph Carens, "Aliens and Citizens: The Case for Open Borders," *Review of Politics* 49 (1987): 251; Carens, "Immigration and the Welfare State."
39 Carens, "Immigration and the Welfare State," 220.
40 Carens, ibid., 214–16; Carens, *Aliens and Citizens*, 255–62.
41 Carens, "Immigration and the Welfare State," 226.
42 "[The difference principle and the principles of equal liberties and fair equality of opportunity] would apply globally, and individuals would design institutions

to implement them – still from the perspective of the original position. Whether such institutions would include sovereign states is debatable, to say the least, but if states existed, they would be states constrained by the principles of justice'' (ibid., 214). In my view David Richards and Charles Beitz, who also advocate globalizing the original position, are likewise best understood as interpreting Rawls's theory as giving rise to universal rights and obligations only (Richards, ''International Distributive Justice,'' 287–93; Beitz, ''Cosmopolitan Ideals,'' 594–7; see also note 47 below). Each mentions the possibility of local rights and obligations, but seems to understand them in something like the weak sense of Goodin's assigned-responsibility model discussed earlier. Brian Barry, by contrast, appears to understand Rawls's theory in terms of justice as reciprocity rather than subject-centered justice (''Humanity and Justice,'' 232–3).

43 See note 4 above.
44 Rawls, *Theory of Justice,* 338–9. On the universal character of natural duties, Rawls says: ''A further feature of natural duties is that they hold between persons irrespective of their institutional relationships; they obtain between all as equal moral persons. In this sense the natural duties are owed not only to definite individuals, say those cooperating together in a particular social arrangement, but to persons generally'' (115).
45 Ibid., 4.
46 As noted in Section I, B, localized rights and obligations can be generated by universally applicable principles.
47 Charles Beitz at one time accepted that the application of the original position required a certain degree of reciprocal interaction among the parties, but argued that there is sufficient cooperation and interaction at the international level to meet this requirement. Charles Beitz, *Political Theory and International Relations* (Princeton, N.J.: Princeton University Press, 1979), 129–36, 143–53. More recently, Beitz has accepted that the requisite degree of international reciprocity may be lacking. But he continues to maintain that the original position can be applied globally, on the ground that Rawls's theory does not presuppose a minimum degree of reciprocal interaction. This assumes, in effect, that Rawls's theory gives rise only to universal rights and obligations (some of which may be localized in the weak sense characterized by Goodin), and not to robust localized rights and obligations of the kind described earlier. See Beitz, ''Cosmopolitan Ideals,'' 595–7; see also note 42 above.
48 John Rawls, ''The Basic Liberties and Their Priority,'' in Rawls, *Political Liberalism* (New York: Columbia University Press, 1993), 289, 299.
49 Ibid., 302.
50 Ibid., 321–3, 332.
51 See note 22 above.
52 Rawls, *Political Liberalism,* 332, 334–5.
53 Ibid., 335.
54 Carens, ''Immigration and the Welfare State,'' 225–6.
55 See H. L. A. Hart, ''Rawls on Liberty and Its Priority,'' in *Essays in Jurisprudence*

and Philosophy (Oxford: Clarendon, 1983), 223. Rawls responds to Hart in "The Basic Liberties."

56 Peter Schuck, "The Transformation of Immigration Law," *Columbia Law Review* 84 (1984): 1, 7, 49–50, 86–90. In this article, Schuck offers a very interesting analysis of the way the two strands of liberal thought that he identifies have shaped and reshaped U.S. immigration law over the past two centuries. See also Peter Schuck and Rogers M. Smith, *Citizenship Without Consent* (New Haven, Conn.: Yale University Press, 1985), 30, 41, 134, and passim.

57 The emphasis within the liberal tradition on consent need not be understood as attributing fundamental significance to the community's power to consent to the membership of particular individuals. Consent, actual or hypothetical, can be understood simply as an indication of an individual's autonomous acceptance of a general political arrangement, so that the obligations it involves can be regarded as self-imposed. See Rawls, *Theory of Justice,* 13. Cf. Jeremy Waldron, "Theoretical Foundations of Liberalism," *Philosophical Quarterly* 37 (1987): 127, 136–7, on the connection between consent and legitimation in the liberal tradition. As remarked in note 4 above, Rawls is probably best interpreted, despite some ambivalent features of his theory, as defending a Kantian version of subject-centered justice. I suggest later that a strong interpretation of the idea that the state has a right to consent to membership – i.e., an interpretation that gives the state an unlimited discretion to determine its own membership – is more compatible with justice as reciprocity than subject-centered justice.

58 Schuck, "The Transformation of Immigration Law," 2, 7, 85–6. Perhaps it could be argued that the population density in the territory of the United States during that period was sufficiently low that constraint 1 on universal justice left no choice but to open the borders.

59 Raz and Margalit, "National Self-Determination," 443–7.

60 Will Kymlicka, *Liberalism, Community and Culture* (Oxford: Clarendon Press, 1989), 164–5. See also Joseph Raz, *The Morality of Freedom* (Oxford: Clarendon Press, 1986), 198–216, 369–99, for a discussion of the relationship between social forms and autonomy.

61 Raz, *Morality of Freedom,* 416–19. Raz's liberal perfectionism is criticized in Jeremy Waldron, "Autonomy and Perfectionism in Raz's *Morality of Freedom,*" *Southern California Law Review* 62 (1989): 1097, 1127–52.

62 Raz does suggest, however, that nonviable cultural communities that reject autonomy can permissibly be assimilated, possibly by force of law. Self-sustaining autonomy-rejecting cultures should be left alone. Raz, *Morality of Freedom,* 423–4.

63 Cf. Bruce A. Ackerman, "The *only* reason for restricting immigration is to protect the ongoing process of liberal conversation itself" (*Social Justice in the Liberal State* [New Haven, Conn.: Yale University Press, 1980], 95; emphasis in original). See also Whelan, "Citizenship and Freedom," 16–23. Whelan discusses instances of the argument referred to in the text that have been put forward by a number of writers, including Thomas Jefferson. Joseph Carens, on the other hand, is of the view that a threat to the welfare state is not a legitimate ground for restricting

immigration from poor countries to rich ones. Carens, "Immigration and the Welfare State," 227.

64 Will Kymlicka argues that Rawls and Dworkin effectively avoid this issue by implicitly presupposing that any given liberal state is culturally homogeneous (Kymlicka, *Liberalism*, 177–8). Joseph Raz has drawn a useful distinction between neutrality concerning the *effect* of state action and neutrality in the *reasons* for it (Raz, *Morality of Freedom*, chaps. 5 and 6). Raz rejects both forms of neutrality. Other liberals are inclined to reject the first but accept the second. See Waldron, "Autonomy and Perfectionism," 1133–8; Will Kymlicka, "Liberal Individualism and Liberal Neutrality," *Ethics* 99 (1989): 883. It is not entirely clear, however, that Kymlicka's endorsement of neutrality of reasons is consistent with his argument for minority rights, which is discussed briefly later.

65 T. H. Green, *Lectures on the Principles of Political Obligation* (1882), quoted in Will Kymlicka, "Liberalism and the Politicization of Ethnicity," *Canadian Journal of Law and Jurisprudence* 4 (1991): 239, 244.

66 See note 64 above. Raz does not accept a neutrality principle, and he argues that governments can noncoercively promote valuable life options (Raz, *Morality of Freedom*, 416–19). But this is very different from saying that they can favor entire cultures. As we shall see in the following section, Kymlicka endorses limited differential rights for some minority groups.

67 Jules Coleman and Sarah Harding observe in their comparative study of immigration policies in Europe and North America (Chapter 2, this volume) that the combined effect of immigration, citizenship, and naturalization laws in several of the European states they discuss is, if we leave aside the generally more liberal treatment of refugees, the preservation of the relatively closed cultural communities that predominate in the states in question. This is particularly true of Germany, where, as Coleman and Harding explain, not only has it become increasingly difficult for immigrants other than refugees to enter the country, but all ethnic Germans have a right of citizenship regardless of where they live and residents of non-German descent face serious obstacles to naturalization. Recently, entry has been made more difficult for those claiming refugee status as well. See "Germany Revokes Right to Asylum," *Toronto Globe and Mail,* May 27, 1993. The German policy of granting a right of citizenship (and hence a right of entry) to all ethnic Germans is obviously contrary to the principle stated in the text. It is interesting that this policy seems to have contributed not to cultural homogeneity within Germany, but rather to greater cultural strife. Insofar as returning ethnic Germans have maintained a German culture at all, they have tended to preserve the culture of their ancestors at the time of emigration. This more traditional culture does not always sit very easily with the cultural patterns that have evolved in modern-day Germany. See W. Bleek, "Germany's Clash of the Cultures More Than Just a Nazi Revival," *Toronto Globe and Mail,* April 13, 1992. This development is not really surprising, since the preferential treatment in question is determined not by cultural ties as such, but by bloodlines. This manner of defining a community is particularly repugnant to liberal principles. See Chapter 4 by Jean Hampton, this volume.

68 See note 63 above. This qualification must itself be carefully qualified. It would not mean that persons could be excluded because their present culture is illiberal in the sense that, say, it does not value autonomy, and this is so even if they intended to continue to adhere to that culture. What would matter is not an individual's or group's preferred way of life, but rather a willingness to accept more general principles of tolerance and democratic rule. More specifically, what would matter is a willingness to live by such principles and treat them as an appropriate charter for public life, whether or not one believes that from the perspective of political theory they really are the best principles. There is an obvious difference between someone who subscribes to, say, Marxism as an intellectual creed but is willing to live by liberal democratic principles, and someone who advocates overthrowing the established government by terrorism or force. One of the underlying issues here is whether, in Rawls's terms, the intolerant should be tolerated, with the further complication that the intolerant are not as yet members of the political community. See Rawls, *Theory of Justice*, 216–21. This is a difficult question, and not one that can be settled here.

69 This is not the place for a sociological analysis of current events in Germany, but it is worth making the point that one of the sources of unrest there may be the failure to integrate foreign residents into German life. Guest workers and refugees tend to be isolated from the rest of the population, and German naturalization policies make it very difficult for foreign residents of non-German descent to become German citizens (see note 67 above). My primary concern in this essay is with the right to become a permanent resident and not with citizenship, but as I noted earlier, there are powerful arguments to the effect that anyone who is admitted as a permanent resident has a moral right, subject only to fairly minimal qualifying conditions, to become a citizen. See note 1 above.

70 The liberal prohibition against racial restrictions on immigration is emphasized by Schuck, "The Transformation of Immigration Law," 88. While generally advocating a generous immigration policy, Schuck also seems to suggest that the preservation of some unspecified degree of homogeneity in the national culture is a legitimate and appropriate goal of immigration law in a liberal state like the United States (ibid., 86–90). In the end this may come down to the maintenance not of cultural homogeneity, but of cultural continuity. Like Schuck, Joseph Carens rejects race as a criterion for determining who can become a resident of a country (Carens, "Nationalism and the Exclusion of Immigrants," 50–6). But in the same paper Carens is surprisingly sympathetic to states wishing to maintain cultural homogeneity (ibid., 56–7).

71 See note 62 above.

72 Kymlicka, *Liberalism*, 166–7.

73 Ibid., 167.

74 Agreements that have been in force between the federal government and Quebec's provincial government since 1978 make clear that immigration to Quebec "must contribute to Quebec's cultural and social heritage, taking into account Quebec's French character" (Gary L. Segal, *Immigrating to Canada*, 9th ed. [Vancouver: Self-Counsel Press, 1990], 89). In accordance with these agreements Quebec has

established its own rules and point system for immigration; the federal government does no more than conduct medical, security, and criminal checks. (Of course, once an immigrant is settled in Quebec there is no legal impediment to her moving elsewhere in the country, just as there is nothing to prevent legal residents, including immigrants, who are currently living in other parts of the country from moving to Quebec.) Quebec's point system allocates, out of a total of 100 points, 15 points to the ability to speak French, 2 to the ability to speak English, and 22 to "adaptability to Quebec" (15 points for personal qualities, 5 for motivation, and 2 for knowledge of Quebec). Most of the other points are for education, job training, occupational demand, and related matters (ibid., 91–2). By contrast, the federal point system for the rest of Canada allocates, again out of 100 points, 15 to proficiency in both French and English (with neither language being favored over the other) and 10 points to "personal suitability" (ibid., 48–9).

Language is often an important attribute of a cultural community, and that is certainly true of Canada's two main cultural groupings, namely, anglophones and francophones. But the assessment of language qualifications for immigrants is complicated by the fact that language serves a functional, coordinating role as well as a cultural one: any association of persons requires a single common language, or at most a very restricted number of common languages, to facilitate communication and cooperation.

75 Kymlicka, *Liberalism*, 175.

76 It might seem that such coercion is independently prohibited by liberal principles, but not all liberals would agree. As noted in note 62 above, Raz thinks the forced assimilation of autonomy-rejecting, nonviable minority cultures is permissible.

77 See note 74 above. The matter is by no means clear-cut, however, since one of the key provisions in Quebec's immigration rules concerns the ability to speak French, and language serves a functional as well as a cultural role.

78 See, e.g., Charles Taylor, "The Politics of Recognition," in Amy Gutmann (ed.), *Multiculturalism and "the Politics of Recognition"* (Princeton, N.J.: Princeton University Press, 1992), 25.

79 Walzer, *Spheres of Justice*, 31–63.

80 Ibid., 39.

81 Cf. Raz, *Morality of Freedom*, 373–7.

82 Cf. Whelan, "Citizenship and Freedom," 33–4.

83 Walzer, *Spheres of Justice*, 48.

84 I argue in the following section that insiders do not have a right to continue to belong to a cultural community. For similar reasons, outsiders do not have a right to join.

85 Walzer explicitly accepts the second proposition and implicitly accepts the first. *Spheres of Justice*, 39.

86 Ibid., 44.

87 Cf. Whelan, "Citizenship and Freedom," 30.

88 Walzer, *Spheres of Freedom*, 40.

89 There was, of course, no decision as such, but rather a series of historical developments.

90 Walzer, *Spheres of Freedom*, 62.
91 There is an ambiguity in the notion of belonging to a cultural community that bears mentioning but need not detain us for long. Raz and Margalit make the point that membership in a cultural community is essentially nonvoluntary: it depends not on achievement but on the sharing of certain slowly acquired characteristics, and it is determined by mutual recognition rather than by formal institutions ("National Self-Determination," 445–7). But someone who belongs in this nonvoluntary sense can still fail to belong in another sense, because other members of the group refuse to permit him to associate with them and to take part in core cultural activities.
92 Raz, *Morality of Freedom*, 203. Raz defines a collective good as an inherent public good, i.e., a public good that cannot be subjected to distributive control only for contingent reasons, such as the availability or existence of an appropriate technology. He gives the example of living in a tolerant society (ibid., 198–9).

   Denise Réaume has pointed out that Raz's argument against rights to collective goods, turning as it does on the relative importance of a single individual's interest as compared with the onerous and multiple character of the corresponding duties, does not depend on anything peculiar to such goods. See Réaume, "Individuals, Groups and Rights to Public Goods," *University of Toronto Law Journal* 38 (1988): 5–6.
93 Jeremy Waldron points out that this argument ignores the fact that the interests in question belong to a large number of individuals in common. To establish a right we must consider individual interests in a nonaggregative, nonutilitarian way, but we must not consider them in complete isolation from one another ("Autonomy and Perfectionism," 1124).
94 Réaume, "Individuals," 8–13. Réaume's own example is not the good of cultural membership but rather the good of a cultured society, i.e., a society that exhibits "a generally higher level of concern for the aesthetic side of life" and that contains appropriate corresponding institutions such as libraries, art galleries, and theaters (ibid., 4–5).
95 On the nature of instrumental rights, see Raz, *Morality of Freedom*, 247–50.
96 Cf. Walzer, *Spheres of Justice,* 41–2, 49–50. Although Walzer suggests at one point that the affinity could be ideological rather than cultural, he seems to assume that the paradigm case is that of a nation-state taking in persecuted nationals who reside elsewhere. But there is also something appropriate and right in a liberal pluralist state expressing solidarity with a particular cultural community within its borders by taking in refugees who share that culture. The shameful episode in which Canada and the United States turned back a boatload of Jewish refugees during the Nazi era is all the more shameful by reason of the fact that there were well-established Jewish communities in both countries.

6

Fear and loathing at the border

LOUIS MICHAEL SEIDMAN

Americans identify with America, and increasingly there are people –
Poles, Italians, Israelis – who identify with two countries. But I do not
know of any other identification that I can make, say, with the condition
of the people of the Sahara. I repeatedly see pictures in the papers of a
starving mother with her child holding out its hand. I think it would be
hypocritical if I didn't say that I would feel a little more compassion if
one of my pet birds had broken a leg in its cage in my own house.[1]

Clare Booth Luce

In their thoughtful and original analysis of the immigration problem, Jules
Coleman and Sarah Harding (Chapter 2, this volume) fail to take sufficient
notice of the very deep emotions on the dark underside of immigration policy.
One would not know from reading their account that the problem is politically
situated in a world increasingly dominated by huge increases in population,
rapidly dwindling resources, and ethnic hatred. The politics of immigration
are driven by fear and selfishness, by prejudice and desperation.

A satisfactory analysis of the immigration problem must be grounded in
this politics. It must incorporate political reality in two separate ways. First,
it must evaluate the moral status of the racial, ethnic, and cultural antipathy
that animates the immigration debate. Second, even if this antipathy is not
morally defensible, the analysis must nonetheless take the fact of its existence
into account in formulating a real-world, second-best solution to the immigration problem.

Coleman and Harding make a start at the first task by defending the right
to membership in a political community. I will argue that the defense is
incomplete, however, because it fails to capture our ambivalence about the
duties we may owe to persons outside our own political community.

Even if I am wrong about this first point and Coleman and Harding's
position is entirely persuasive, their failure to address the second task makes
their guide to immigration policy misleading. One might suppose that the
reality of ethnic, cultural, and racial division would argue for alternative

techniques for redistribution, such as foreign aid, that do not challenge political and cultural boundaries. In this essay, I will defend a different, less intuitively obvious proposition. I will argue that a restrictive immigration policy coupled with very lax enforcement may provide the mix best calculated to achieve real-world justice that transcends ethnic and cultural divisions.

I. The problem of bounded caring

The reason Clare Booth Luce is so infuriating is that she is so right. Anyone in this country who spends money on a pet bird or, for that matter, on dinner at a good restaurant, a movie ticket, or a book about immigration policy must care very little about the welfare of starving children in the Sahara. And that includes just about all of us.

A virtue of the Coleman and Harding essay is that it begins to make some sense of this disquieting reality. Significantly, it attempts to do so without relying on a problematic limitation on the domain of distributive justice. Coleman and Harding reject the argument that the obligation of distributive justice extends only to the borders of a political community. Instead, they claim that membership in a political community is itself a good that should be justly distributed. Claims to membership are important, they argue, because communities provide a context in which individuals can act autonomously and give meaning to their own lives.

Coleman and Harding insist that this right to membership in a political community has consequences for immigration policy. On the positive side, it means that political refugees (members of *no* political community) as well as individuals with family and cultural ties (members of the *same* political community) may have a just claim of access to borders. On the negative side, it means that countries may legitimately exclude other, less worthy candidates for access including, presumably, "mere" economic refugees. This is so even though political borders are in some sense arbitrary. The borders may nonetheless serve as a basis for exclusion because they help to define and protect the communities to which people have a right to belong.

As sophisticated and intriguing as this argument is, it provides only an incomplete justification for the various immigration policies that Coleman and Harding describe. The first and most obvious problem with their position is that it focuses solely on political membership as a good without balancing it against other goods with which it might conflict. Put bluntly, only someone with a full stomach could argue for the primacy of community membership. Granted, such membership fosters autonomy and provides meaning. But in a world overflowing with destitute and hungry people, membership is neither a necessary nor a sufficient condition for autonomy and meaning.

This point is best illustrated by a comparison of the status of an economic refugee, who might appropriately be barred under the Coleman and Harding scheme, with a political refugee entitled to admission. Consider, on the one hand, the starving mother in the Sahara for whom Luce expresses so little compassion. This applicant for admission may well belong to a functioning political and cultural community. But membership in this community is hardly sufficient to yield autonomy and meaning. Plainly, there are some minimal preconditions that must be met before community membership has any meaning at all. At very least, these include a place to live, clothes to wear, and enough to eat.

Compare the plight of the Saharan mother with that of a refusnik in the old Soviet Union. Although adequately clothed, fed, and housed (perhaps barely), the latter has been effectively expelled from her political community. But in this case, membership may not be a necessary condition for autonomy and meaning. I do not mean to denigrate the hardship experienced by persons suffering from political persecution. Yet the very fact of such persecution can provide individuals with a kind of identity and autonomy. Through courage and perseverance, they sometimes succeed in forming an oppositionist community, defined by the persecution they oppose.

Thus one might agree with Coleman and Harding that political membership is a good without also agreeing that it is the only good or that promotion of this good justifies current immigration policy. If we are to take seriously Coleman and Harding's rejection of political boundaries as limitations on the domain of distributive justice, claims to homogeneous political communities might have to give way to more fundamental claims to a just distribution of the world's resources.

One might respond to this line of argument by asserting that the opposition between these two claims is only apparent. There is no intrinsic reason why the requirements of the world's undernourished need be met in a way that undermines political communities. Subsistence for the poor might be achieved by a redistribution of assets rather than people – for example, by foreign aid, free trade, or guest-worker programs – that provides access to resources and labor markets without political membership. In contrast, as long as political communities have a geographic component, the just claims of a political exile can be met only by immigration.

But this response fails to take account of the full force of Luce's position. Her disinclination to aid mothers starving in the Sahara seems unrelated to a desire to maintain the homogeneity of a political community. The lack of compassion to which she confesses would seem to argue as much against foreign aid as against immigration.[2] In short, Luce's position entails what Coleman and Harding reject – a geographic or cultural limitation on the reach of distributive obligations.

Although Luce has chosen to defend this limitation in an especially inflammatory and insensitive fashion, it would be a serious mistake to dismiss her position out of hand. As already noted, virtually all of us behave in the manner that she describes. It is not obvious that when we do so we are behaving badly. Membership in a community – be it a family, a cultural grouping, or a nation – does seem to entail a special concern for the welfare of other members. In the absence of such special concern, all our relationships with others would be abstract, desiccated, and impersonal. We would lack the very sense of belonging and identification that makes community membership a good.

Moreover, this privileging of community members logically implies a comparatively diminished concern for the welfare of outsiders. By their nature, communities must have boundaries, and the boundaries can have meaning only if there is some difference between those situated on either side of them.

It would seem, then, that the community membership that Coleman and Harding defend necessarily implies the bounded distributional obligations that they attack. Furthermore, it is the boundedness of the obligation, rather than the value of membership per se, that lies at the heart of the immigration debate. Of course, the world has too many political refugees seeking asylum. But if this were all there were to the problem, it would be far more manageable than it in fact is. The masses clamoring at our door want to get in not because they don't belong, but because they are hungry. We fail to provide for them not because we belong, but because we don't care.

For these reasons, any analysis of immigration policy that fails to come to grips with Luce's unsettling ethnocentrism is certain to be beside the point. Yet it is also easy to see why one might want to avoid the point. The difficulty is not just that Luce has had the poor judgment to say some things that should not be repeated in polite company. To be sure, one has a sense that she has recklessly and tactlessly opened up a line of argument best suppressed in the name of civic peace. For reasons that Coleman and Harding explore, Luce's argument risks sundering our own fragile and multicultural political community.

I believe, however, that the difficulty with her remarks runs deeper than this. The underlying problem is not that we feel constrained to remain silent about the subject she introduces, but that we hardly know what to say. We are beset by a seemingly unresolvable dualism in our attitude toward those outside our community. If we simply agreed – or disagreed – with Luce's views, they would not rattle us so badly. Her iconoclasm stirs us to anger precisely because we *both* agree *and* disagree with her.

Thus Luce is surely right when she says that our empathy for those outside our community is distinctly limited, but her implicit assertion that these limitations tell the whole story is unfairly reductive. At the very moment that we experience and defend the boundaries of our concern, we are also able to regret and transcend them. Even as we confer special benefits on those closest to us, we also understand that, in some ultimate sense, everyone is entitled to equal concern and respect. Although no one wants to give up the bonds of special caring that hold communities together, we all feel guilt about the exclusionary impact of these bonds. We therefore both recognize ourselves in Luce's description and feel anger at ourselves (and so, at her) precisely because the description is so accurate.

Luce has hit upon an authentic antinomy, and any effort to formulate an ideal immigration policy would require a theory by which the antinomy can be resolved. I offer no such theory in this essay. Indeed, my own view, which I have defended elsewhere,[3] is that such a theory is impossible. It turns out, however, that we may not need a fully worked out theory if we stick to a more modest, yet more import objective – the formulation of a second-best immigration policy in the world that actually exists.

II. Toward a second-best solution

There are two reasons we can get by without a complete theory reconciling our universal obligation to others with our special ties to our own community. First, although we might not be able to agree on a fully worked out theory that properly balanced the two sides of the antinomy in the abstract, we might reach a consensus on where the greater risks lie in the real world. My strong sense is that there is presently little risk that our politics will overstate our altruistic and universalistic impulses. Presumably, not even Clare Booth Luce would argue that we are spending too little money on veterinary care for our pet birds and too much on starving Africans. Even if we grant arguendo that some degree of chauvinism and self-regard is morally defensible, the real-world political risks are that these impulses will be over- rather than under-emphasized.

The second reason we can put to one side questions about the moral defensibility of bounded caring is that, like it or not, these limitations are facts that exist in the world – facts that are unlikely to change more than marginally in the near future. A real-world immigration policy must therefore take account of these facts and work around them.

These observations, in turn, suggest twin dangers for discussion of immigration policy. First, at a minimum, we should avoid further strengthening the hand of those who would defend exclusion and bounded caring. This is so because our natural impulses toward selfishness and ethnocentrism are certain to exaggerate the effect of any argument pushing in this direction. Thus, even if such an argument is theoretically sound, it is likely to yield suboptimal results when filtered through political reality.

Second, although we should not make arguments that strengthen exclusionary impulses, neither should we proceed as if these impulses did not exist. We cannot wholly remake the world, and it is surely a waste of time and effort to bemoan or defend states that are very unlikely to change.

Unfortunately, Coleman and Harding run afoul of both of these cautions. Their defense of political and cultural communities, even if right on its own terms, is likely to provide ammunition for defenders of exclusion and apologists for the status quo. Moreover, the defense proceeds on the dubious assumption that the value of political membership is worth debating rather than an inevitable given around which policy must be organized.

How might we talk about immigration in a fashion that avoids these risks? At first blush, one might suppose that the twin constraints just described would argue for a policy of very limited immigration coupled with generous foreign aid.

This policy is attractive for a variety of reasons. First, even apart from the problems posed by bounded caring, foreign aid redistributes assets with the least dead-weight loss. If I am correct that the desire to move is principally a symptom of an underlying problem in resource allocation, then free immigration is a wildly inefficient solution. Of course, there are some immigrants who wish access to our border because they like our culture, our politics, or our climate. But for the larger number of immigrants who simply want enough to eat, it is far more efficient to feed them where they are.

Second, the inevitable existence of bounded caring makes immigration still more inefficient. This is true for the home country, for the target country, and for the immigrant himself. For the home country, free immigration is likely to result in an inability to internalize the full benefits of social investments. Some of these putative investments will benefit future immigrants and some of these benefits will, in turn, be captured by other inhabitants of the target country. Because of bounded caring within the home country, these investments will be perceived as wasted, producing suboptimal incentives to make them.

Bounded caring also produces suboptimal incentives for the target country. In a regime of free immigration, the target country must share benefits extended to its citizens with outsiders attracted to the country by those benefits. The result is likely to be a "race to the bottom," with no country wishing to raise the living standards of its members for fear that the gains will be dissipated among a horde of outsiders.

Finally, bounded caring imposes considerable cost on the immigrant herself. Apart from the inevitable geographic and cultural dislocation produced by immigration, the immigrant must endure hostility, suspicion, and hatred generated by her outsider status. Romanticized versions of our melting-pot history should not obscure the real and tragic sacrifices made by first-generation immigrants. It would clearly be preferable if these individuals could achieve the benefits of immigration while remaining within their own community.

Thus the argument for redistribution without immigration is a powerful one. Unfortunately, however, the argument once again ignores the admonition to take account of the politics in which the immigration problem is embedded. The case for foreign aid ends up ignoring the very political obstacles to which it is intended to respond. To be sure, if wealthy countries could be persuaded to greatly increase foreign aid, these increases might redistribute resources in the most efficient fashion. But the very bounded caring that makes foreign aid attractive as a solution also blocks its implementation. Precisely because Americans care very little about starving Africans, they are unlikely to authorize much aid to help them.

Thus, despite the inefficiencies associated with it, a regime of liberalized immigration probably constitutes the best solution to resource maldistribution in our actual world of bounded caring. This is true for empirical rather than logical reasons. In our culture, at least, caring seems to be partially associated with physical location within our borders.

I do not mean to deny for a moment the obvious fact of differential caring, even within our borders, based upon cultural and ethnic identity. We have a long and sorry history of persecuting, neglecting, scapegoating, and abusing our immigrant population. Yet it nonetheless seems true that, holding other factors constant, we are systematically less able to ignore the needs of people within our jurisdiction.

The evidence for this is everywhere in our culture. Indeed, many of our practices are incomprehensible unless one understands the empirical link between caring and physical presence. Consider, for example, the Supreme Court's holding that the Constitution grants illegal aliens a right to equal access to public education.[4] The decision is logically anomalous. Illegal aliens have no right to be in the United States and have no right to a U.S. education if they are outside the United States. How can it be that it is constitutional to deport them, thereby depriving them of both a U.S. education and physical presence, but that it violates their constitutional rights to deprive them of a U.S. education without depriving them of physical presence?[5]

The easiest way to make sense of this result is to posit differential caring based upon presence within our physical borders. As long as illegal aliens are here, they are entitled to equal benefits because we care about them equally. But their rights while physically present entail neither a right to physical presence nor a right to equal caring once they are no longer present.

Widespread political opposition to guest-worker programs involving foreigners working without minimum wage and the protection of the Occupational Safety and Health Administration reflects a similar phenomenon. Of course, some of the motivation for this opposition is perfectly straightforward. Domestic workers have an obvious interest in shielding themselves from outside competition that would drive down the price of labor. But although opposition to guest-worker programs is sometimes phrased in terms of protecting domestic workers, opponents more often claim that it is the guest workers themselves who are unfairly "exploited" by the program.

Even if this rhetoric is advanced for the most cynical reasons, it remains puzzling that it seems to resonate with a public that has no special interest in limiting wage competition. Why should anyone believe that a guest worker is "exploited" when he receives higher wages and more protection in the program than he would receive if he remained in his home country?

Once again, the overlap between the geographic boundaries of our country and the psychological boundaries of our empathic capacities helps make sense of this rhetoric. It is true that a worker who remains home may be worse off than a worker who receives subminimum wages in the United States on a guest basis. But as long as the worker remains in his home country, we care very little about his welfare. The worker's presence in this country changes not only his welfare, but also his status as an object of caring. His objectively improved status while in this country is therefore filtered through a lens of differential caring, creating the illusion that the program actually makes him worse off.

It is important to understand that I am not defending the normative attractiveness of this phenomenon. Indeed, precisely because it is normatively unattractive, we need to figure out strategies that will bypass the empirical linkage between physical boundaries and empathy.

The linkage suggests that despite the inefficiencies associated with it, immigration may play an important role in resource redistribution. Paradoxically, however, the linkage also suggests that working for liberalized legal immigration is likely to be futile. There is no obvious way to get the immigration strategy off the ground. To be sure, once immigrants arrive, they will be the beneficiaries of greater caring. But prospective immigrants who might be admitted under liberalized immigration standards remain on the wrong side of our empathic and physical boundaries. The same differential caring that dooms the foreign aid strategy therefore makes the real-world prospects of immigration reform unpromising.

These difficulties might be addressed by emphasizing the role of illegal immigration. The level of illegal immigration is also a function of government policy, but the policy is less open to public scrutiny than are our formal standards for legal immigration. Enforcement levels depend upon budgetary constraints, civil liberties concerns, judgments about resource allocation, and lower-level administrative decisions that to some extent sidestep direct confrontation with our chauvinist impulses. For example, a proposal to amend immigration laws so as to greatly expand the number and categories of legal immigrants would doubtless produce a political firestorm. In contrast, the federal government's failure to enforce the restrictions on the hiring of illegal immigrants went almost totally unnoticed until the recent flap about the hiring practices of presidential appointees.

Underenforcement of immigration laws might produce two desirable consequences. First, the threat of large-scale illegal immigration has the potential to make ethnocentrism work in favor of, rather than against, redistribution. As already noted, a foreign aid strategy for achieving redistribution is blocked by the hold that ethnocentrism has on our politics. But the threat of large-scale illegal immigration might actually provide an ethnocentric incentive for increasing foreign aid. Precisely because we identify less with people outside our borders, we might want to provide them with aid so as to reduce the disparities in wealth that motivate their desire to enter this country. As explained earlier, foreign aid is a far more efficient method of redistribution than is immigration. To the extent that the threat of illegal entry helps overcome the political obstacles to these wealth transfers, it serves a useful purpose.

Second, as the recent amnesty for illegal immigrants suggests, once illegal immigrants succeed in breaching the physical boundary of our country, the bounds on our empathic capacities are much more difficult to sustain. Consequently, even though illegal immigrants have no right to be here, they do have rights as long as they are here. Underenforcement thereby creates possibilities for redistribution that would not otherwise exist.

It would be foolish to suppose that any immigration policy – much less a marginal change in the level of immigration enforcement – would do much to solve the world hunger and population crisis. Moreover, it is worth emphasizing that my argument may support only marginal change. As noted, I do not want to reject altogether the case for bounded caring. I can argue for liberalized immigration only because our current practices are so far removed from anything like the proper mix between universal and particular caring that it is possible to sidestep the dilemma posed by Luce's pet bird. If we moved toward the much more aggressive redistributive efforts that would really make a difference, this dilemma would, of course, reemerge.

These comments should therefore not be taken as anything like a complete response to the immigration problem. What they do suggest is that although community membership plays a crucial role in an analysis of the problem, it is not the role that Coleman and Harding imagine. In a world full of starving people, a right to community membership is too weak a reed to support our disregard for those outside our borders. Membership is important not because it is a moral right that justifies exclusion, but because it is a political reality that blocks inclusion. We should not ignore that reality when we formulate immigration policy. But neither should we reinforce it so as to provide ammunition for those interested in justifying the status quo.

Notes

I extend my thanks to Warren Schwartz and Mark Tushnet for suggestions about an earlier version of this essay.

1 As quoted in William Raspberry, "Mrs. Luce: An Awful Interview," *Washington Post,* September 15, 1982.

2 Luce's empathic limitations are not necessarily inconsistent with a program of free trade. Gains from trade might improve the overall welfare of both the United States and Third World countries without either requiring the admission of foreign nationals into our political community or subsidizing them at our own expense.

There are nonetheless reasons to be skeptical about the possibility that free trade will solve the problems discussed in the text. First, since the welfare gain from free trade is divided between United States and foreign citizens, the internal gains from trade for U.S. consumers may be counterbalanced by the internal losses for U.S. workers and industries that must sacrifice the advantages of protection. To the extent that this is true, people agreeing with Luce would presumably oppose a free-trade regime even if worldwide welfare were increased.

Second, these internal losses are likely to be far more concentrated than the gains. Even if free trade improves the status of the world's poor, it may therefore have undesirable distributional consequences within the United States unless coupled with compensation for the losers. Moreover, the fact that the losses are concentrated is likely to lead to their overstatement by the political system. Thus, even if we put to one side normative objections to the redistribution, as a positive matter, there may be insurmountable political obstacles to free trade.

Finally, although gains from trade might increase the size of the pie, free trade does nothing to provide for a more equitable distribution. A free-trade policy is therefore unlikely to be of much assistance to impoverished countries possessing few resources desired by others.

3 See Louis Michael Seidman, "Public Principle and Private Choice: The Uneasy Case for a Boundary Maintenance Theory of Constitutional Law," *Yale Law Journal* (1987): 1006, 1042, 1053–9.

4 See *Plyler v. Doe,* 457 U.S. 202 (1982).

5 The *Plyler* Court offered a double-barreled response to this argument. First, the Court pointed out that state governments "enjoy no power with respect to the classification of aliens," because this power "is 'committed to the political branches of the Federal Government.' " 457 U.S., at 225 (quoting from *Mathews v. Diaz,* 426 U.S. 67, 81 [1976]). Second, although conceding that the children were illegally within the country, the Court observed that "there is no assurance that a child subject to deportation will ever be deported." 457 U.S., at 226.

Neither argument fully justifies the Court's holding. Although the federal government unquestionably has the power to preempt state laws that contradict federal immigration policy, the state law invalidated in *Plyler* was wholly consistent with the federal decision to exclude the aliens in question. The case is therefore fundamentally different from cases like *Graham v. Richardson,* 403 U.S. 365 (1971), where the Court has invalidated state laws imposing disabilities on *legal* aliens whom Congress has chosen to admit. Nor is the Court able to point to any indication that Congress intended to "occupy the field," thereby preempting even those state laws that complemented federal policy. Cf. *Decanas v. Bica,* 424 U.S. 351 (1976) (state has complementary power to regulate illegal aliens when state regulation mirrors federal objectives).

Of course, the Court is correct when it observes that a particular child who is legally subject to deportation may nonetheless never be deported and that some illegal aliens eventually gain legal status and even become citizens. But it is difficult to see how the child's de facto presence alters her current legal rights, even when that presence is coupled with the possibility of a future change in status. Whatever the future holds, the children in question have no *current* right to be present in the United States. If the children have no current right to physical presence, then it would seem that they also have no current right to benefits that are properly conditioned on physical presence.

7

Immigration policy in liberal political theory

MARK TUSHNET

May a liberal state have a relatively restrictive immigration policy? How could we go about answering that question?

In writing of "immigration policy," I refer to policies that restrict access to certain benefits to people who are geographically "connected" to the liberal state's territory.[1] The benefits I will discuss are (a) the material resources that the state controls, either because those resources are physically located in the state or because the state has taken control over them through its tax policies, and (b) participation in the political processes that constitute the liberal state. Relatively restrictive immigration policies deny access to state-controlled physical resources to many people who are geographically connected to the state.[2] They also, and perhaps independently, may deny access to participation in some liberal political processes.

We could try to determine whether liberal states may, consistent with their liberalism, adopt restrictive immigration policies either by examining the practices of states that all agree are sufficiently liberal or by attempting to figure out what liberal political principles imply about access to material resources and political participation. The first approach might be called the survey, the second the principled, approach. The survey approach identifies actual practices of liberal states and attempts to infer justifications for those practices that make the practices consistent with liberal political theory. So, for example, it appears that few liberal states impose significant restrictions on the rights resident aliens have to free speech, while many do restrict access to the right to vote.[3] This might suggest that voting is connected to membership in a liberal political community in a way that free expression is not.

The difficulty with the survey approach is most apparent in what all observers agree are ethnocentric restrictions on access to resources, like those the United States historically imposed on entry by Chinese immigrants. These clearly demonstrate that racism has been an important element of immigration policy.[4] The survey approach must somehow exempt restrictive policies that are the residues of preliberal or antiliberal commitments, such as racism, from its search for justifications for existing policies; otherwise it runs the risk of providing ostensibly liberal justifications for policies that a liberal state ought not adopt.

The difficulty with the principled approach is the patent arbitrariness of the geographic lines that define the states developing immigration policy. In Chapter 2 of this volume, Coleman and Harding argue that territorial boundaries have moral significance because they define the contours of organized political communities, membership in which is an important human good. Conceding that territorial boundaries may well be arbitrary when established, they argue that after boundaries are created and political communities organized, members – "citizens" – come to attach particular value to their membership in "their" community.[5] Yet to defend any sort of exclusionary immigration policy, Coleman and Harding would have to establish that the value a citizen properly attaches to membership in a particular community would be reduced in a morally relevant way if immigration occurred without restriction.

I believe it impossible to establish that proposition. Even if membership is a liberal value, and even if restrictions on access to membership are consistent with liberalism, there is a further difficulty. Once geographic lines are drawn, the lumpy distribution of the world's material resources means that even if states are useful administrative bodies for maximizing the use of the resources located within them, it is no longer apparent that worldwide distributive justice concerns can be satisfied by immigration policies that restrict access to material resources (unless, as Coleman and Harding note, those policies are supplemented by foreign aid policies designed to achieve whatever worldwide distributive justice requires).

The survey and the principled approaches can lead to irresolvable conflicts. Consider, for example, the widespread immigration policies designed to deny access to a state's territory to those who would be a net drain on the state's resources – those who would become public charges. If those thereby excluded are entitled by principles of worldwide distributive justice to a greater share of the world's material resources, it is unclear how the state's restrictive immigration policy *could* be justified. (Nor would a supplementary foreign aid policy help in this example, because foreign aid, to be sufficient to achieve whatever worldwide distributive justice requires, would have to impose the same net drain on the state's resources that would occur if immigration were freely allowed.)

Determining whether liberal states can have restrictive immigration policies is further complicated by the history of immigration policy. Although people have moved from one place to another in the world from time immemorial, "immigration" became a social issue in the modern world under particular circumstances. Those circumstances were so far removed from the conditions of justice that the solutions to immigration problems have not been on the order of second best, but rather on the order of fifteenth best or worse. Because of this, even the principled approach is far less likely to offer insight into contemporary problems of immigration policy than an intensely practical and detailed focus on the situation in today's sending and receiving countries.

I. A critique of the survey approach

The survey approach requires us to determine *which* states ought to be included in the survey. The first approximation, illustrated by Coleman and Harding, examines nation-states. Why *they* are the relevant units is unclear. The survey's results would be rather different if it took into account subnational units like the states of the United States. Including such units in the survey would make restrictive immigration policies seem anomalous, for under U.S. constitutional doctrine these subnational units may not impose substantial restrictions on the access of new entrants (who are already citizens of the nation) to local material resources or participation in the local political community. For example, Alaska could not distribute income from taxes on local oil production to residents in amounts that varied depending on how long they had been in the state.[6] Nor can states limit the right to vote in local elections to long-term residents; they may impose short durational residency requirements, but only to allow the states time to process the voter registration materials.[7]

The example of including subnational units in the survey again indicates the arbitrariness of the geographic lines that are prerequisites for analyzing immigration policy. By proliferating the units in the survey, we can make unrestricted immigration seem the norm; by restricting the units, we can make restrictions seem common.

Suppose the problem of which units to include in the survey were solved. If we assume that contemporary practices attempt to accomplish morally valuable ends, a survey of those practices might provide us with the basis for refining our understanding of what justice requires, so that we could propose modifications to align practices more closely with justice's demands. For example, Coleman and Harding's survey suggests a widespread effort to offer admission to those whose contributions seem likely to enhance a nation's economic performance and a less widespread effort to confine offers of admission to those who share the values presently widely shared in particular nations. We might infer from those practices that economic considerations properly predominate in determining immigration policy, with community-preserving policies playing a secondary role.

That inference would be proper, however, only if present practices can be ''plausibly construed as implementing'' justice, as Coleman and Harding put it. A more realistic view, informed by the history of immigration policy, would be more skeptical about such policy. Rather than admirable efforts to enhance economic performance and preserve morally valuable communities, present immigration practices seem racist and ethnocentric. They appear to be efforts to restrict the material benefits of advanced liberal societies to people whose parents contributed to the creation of those benefits, by working with the material resources that happened to be located in those societies when the parents were productive. One would need a complex liberal theory of family rights to explain why the children are entitled to those benefits; more common liberal theories suggest that those resources should be available for distribution to those entitled to them under liberal principles of distributive justice.[8]

Perhaps we might attempt to refine present practices to remove the racist and ethnocentric elements, and see what remains. Yet once we introduce this possibility, we have moved a long way in the direction of the principled approach. We might then use the results of the survey not to develop principles liberal states can adhere to, but as examples of the kinds of problems states have faced and the solutions they have devised, examples that must nonetheless survive whatever principled scrutiny liberal theory subjects them to.

II. Political morality and territorial borders

Immigration policy rests on answers to two questions. The first question, and I believe the more important, is, Why do people move from one place to another? The second is, Why do organized political communities have territorial borders that they seek to enforce by means of immigration policy?

A. Immigration and worldwide distributive justice

People move from one place to another for two basic reasons – to avoid famine and to escape tyranny. The first reason for moving arises from the fact that the distribution of the world's resources is lumpy. Unlike Bruce Ackerman's manna, which falls from the heavens without regard to territory,[9] the world's resources have real physical locations. People move from one place in response to the lumpy distribution of those resources. In more general terms, in the absence of immigration policies, people would prefer to place themselves where they were best able to combine their personal talents with the local resources to maximize their satisfaction.

The central image of famine-induced migration can be misleading, however. Suppose we had a theory of justice in the distribution of material goods and a mechanism for accomplishing that distribution.[10] Then immigration policy would be uninteresting insofar as people relocated to maximize the satisfaction they took from material goods.[11] The policy would be free migration coupled with a mechanism of foreign aid[12] to produce the distribution of material goods required by the theory of distributive justice.[13]

If we knew what worldwide distributive justice required, and sought to achieve it, immigration policy would surely seem quite secondary. The reason it seems important, in the absence of worldwide distributive justice, is that there appear to be free-rider problems on both sides of the issue.

Some people, the residents of areas favored by nature in the distribution of resources, receive benefits from the mere chance of finding themselves in those areas. They use their talents to produce more, though there is no good reason to think either that they have produced more than would have been produced had others happened to reside in the favored territory, or that they have produced more than they would have had they found themselves elsewhere (in places whose resources better matched their particular talents). In any event, the fact that these areas have been favored by nature has a multiplier effect. Then potential immigrants seek to benefit from the investments the residents have already made. Not surprisingly, the residents tend to believe that immigrants are not entitled to a share of the wealth that has resulted from the combination of nature's gifts and their own efforts.

I confess to being skeptical that any theory of worldwide distributive justice would give substantial weight to these free-rider problems. Rather, it would specify appropriate shares, taking effort into account and discounting for the luck of finding oneself in favored or disfavored areas. Thus, to the extent that migration occurs because of the maldistribution of the world's resources, the proper response lies not in devising immigration policies that take the views of the beneficiaries of nature's bounty into account, but in revising the distribution of wealth. The incentive effects of exclusionary practices, I believe, are likely to be quite small: present residents are unlikely to work significantly less intensely because new residents have access to previously produced resources, and whatever reduction occurs is likely to be offset by the greater intensity with which the new residents are likely to work.

B. Political justice and territorial boundaries

People move for a second reason. Once political communities are organized territorially, some communities may offer forms of political organization that some people find more attractive than those offered by others. Yet once again it seems peculiar to address this as a matter of interest for immigration policy. The first-best solution surely is to replace the tyranny with a form of political organization that satisfies the requirements of justice in politics. Immigration policy may contribute to that solution indirectly: by confining people to the

land controlled by their tyrannical government, restrictive immigration policies might increase their incentives to rebel or might increase the internal
pressure on the government to accommodate dissenters.

In dealing with immigration policy more generally, I begin by noting that
principles of liberalism ought to find certain kinds of restrictions quite troubling. Assume that the state does admit people for permanent residence. If it
denies them access to membership in the political community no matter how
long they reside, two kinds of problems are likely to arise. Because they lack
membership in the political community, other residents are likely to use political power systematically to exploit them. In addition, precisely because
membership in the political community is valuable, denying membership establishes something worse than "second-class citizenship." In permanently
denying the possibility of becoming a member, the state *creates* a caste system of a sort inconsistent with liberal principles. At some point, then, liberal
states must either admit residents to full membership or terminate their residency.

Suppose we confine our attention to the question of immigration from one
liberal state to another, thereby avoiding the question of how liberal states
ought to respond to the existence of tyranny elsewhere. I assume that a range
of modes of political organization can satisfy the requirements of justice in
politics and that individuals have preferences for particular modes. People
may find themselves located within a territory governed in a permissible way,
yet might prefer to live in one governed in another permissible way. I find
it difficult to see why the place to which they are attracted ought to be
allowed to exclude them, particularly in light of the fact that the very reason
for relocation is that the immigrants share the values that have put their
preferred mode of government in place.

This point may gain support from the fact that immigration policy is a
relatively recent development in the modern world. It is a by-product of
nationalism, itself a relatively recent phenomenon.[14] Of course, territorially
organized political communities have frequently distinguished between members and nonmembers resident in the territory, and these distinctions have
operated as costs imposed on migration. Yet compared with the costs inherent
in uprooting and relocating, the costs that were historically imposed on recent
immigrants seem to me relatively small. Until recently, territorially organized
political communities have rarely attempted to discourage entry by such severe measures as deportation.[15] The first permanent U.S. law regulating entry,
for example, was enacted in 1875.[16]

There is no conceptual connection between having an organized political
society and identifying that society with a specific territory. Similarly, there
is no conceptual connection between being a people and having a territorially
defined nation. These points have two implications. First, even if we assume

that membership in a polis or a people is a fundamental human right, enjoying that right need not implicate residing anywhere in particular. Some peoples, such as the Gypsies, exist only in what might inappropriately be called the diaspora. And some organized political communities have been known to claim universal jurisdiction; the universal church in the Middle Ages might serve as an example, as might the now-vanished tradition of proletarian internationalism.[17] So we need to distinguish the benefits that flow from membership in a people and those that flow from membership in an organized political community.[18]

Once we do so, the role of geographic boundaries becomes even more arbitrary – except, as discussed later, in connection with liberal states themselves. European and African borders divide peoples, and devising modes of political organization that deal appropriately with so-called ethnic minorities has been nearly impossible. Some existing nation-states are so geographically extended that the sense in which people in one region are co-members of the same "people" with those in another is quite problematic, although they may be co-members of the same polis. Perhaps we either inevitably do, or are entitled to, weigh the interests of friends and neighbors – those who are of the same "people" as we – more heavily than we weigh the interests of strangers. Yet there is little reason in some nations, including, I believe, the United States, to believe that every co-*citizen* is more a friend and neighbor in the relevant sense than many people outside the nation's borders.[19] In short, the closeness of the fit between co-residence in a polis defined by arbitrary geographic borders and co-membership in a people is an empirical question. If, as I believe, the fit is relatively loose, immigration policies geared to geographic borders are unlikely to promote the ends promoted by membership in a people.

Just as the question of immigration policy would seem very different – perhaps even disappear – if the world's societies were organized to achieve distributive and political justice, so too it would seem very different if territorially organized political societies had more appropriate boundaries. Even if borders are arbitrary, however, the creation of borders may set in train processes that produce modes of social and political organization that have intrinsic value. Borders, in short, can come to constitute a polis.

Here we arrive at the exception involving liberal states mentioned earlier. Insofar as immigration policy has some bearing on how particular polities are constituted, liberal states ought to impose no limits on immigration. The reason is straightforward: limitations on entry attempt to preserve the existing distribution of values in a society, in a way inconsistent with a liberal state's commitment to the possibility of revising its own values as the values of its members change.

Without such a policy, communities may exclude potential entrants who are not "like us" in the sense that they do not share our values to a sufficient degree. I believe that an alternative understanding of the value of community membership is better and provides a different perspective on the question of immigration policy. According to the alternative understanding, what gives membership in a politically organized community value is the fact that it is so organized. Recall that we are here considering the immigration policy appropriate to a liberal state in a world where all states are sufficiently liberal and where principles of worldwide distributive justice are satisfied.

There are, I believe, two difficulties with the view that communities can properly exclude those who are not enough "like us."[20] First, it overlooks the fact that migrants have chosen to come here rather than go elsewhere at least in part because *they* believe that their values are more compatible with ours than with either those of their country of origin or those of any alternative destination.[21] Consider that immigrants to the United States have demonstrated quite literally the get-up-and-go that is such an important value in the United States.[22]

Second, and perhaps more important, value-based exclusions assume that the values constituting a polity are fixed, yet that assumption seems unfounded and arguably inconsistent with liberalism's basic commitments.[23] Take the United States and Canada as exemplary liberal states. As Coleman and Harding discuss, they differ from other countries at least in part because they are constituted by commitments to liberal toleration. Now consider a broader implication of that observation. Communities in which membership is morally valuable are constituted by a complex blend of values and decisions. Among the decisions that constitute a community are decisions about whom to admit to membership. Yet no matter how hard a community tries, some people it admits to membership will have values different from those held by the people making the admission decision: think here only of changes in community that result from generational change, when children have values different from their parents'. This shows that the values that contribute to the constitution of a morally valuable community must be revisable in response to the values of new members. As a result, there is no good reason to exclude people simply because they do not share the full range of values that contribute to the constitution of the existing community. Liberals are rightly troubled by policies like Germany's, which require an immigrant to "become *a* German," as if there were some predetermined essence of Germanness that all Germans must share.

Current residents often believe that admitting people who are different will "destroy" the existing polity. Of course it will not. Rather, admitting them will *transform* the polity. Thus, while membership in some polity is a fundamental human value, membership in a polity constituted in a particular way is not. There is therefore no principled reason to object to the transformation of the polity that will occur when those with different values enter.[24]

III. Conclusion

Communities are historically contingent entities. Membership in some community is morally valuable. Membership in a community constituted in a particular way is not.[25] Nor is membership in a community defined with reference to existing territorial boundaries. Immigration policy, in contrast, is an issue only because members of existing territorial communities believe otherwise. Liberals should work to eliminate unjust regimes and achieve an appropriate worldwide distribution of wealth. Restrictive immigration policies may be sensible strategies for eliminating tyrannies, since restrictions force opponents of unjust regimes to deal with those regimes, and vice versa. Restrictive immigration policies seem less sensible strategies for dealing with wealth distribution issues, for they appear to respond to a desire by the relatively well off to preserve what they have, and thus are unlikely to be accompanied by foreign aid policies that might rectify injustices in worldwide wealth distribution. Discussions of immigration policies appropriate to liberal states ought to focus on such strategic questions. As a matter of principle, liberals ought to be committed to relatively unrestricted immigration policies.

Notes

1 I write "connected" to avoid peripheral questions about the rights of citizens who happen to be located outside the state's geographic territory. For example, may a liberal state deny the right to vote to members who are outside its boundaries on the day voting occurs? This and similar questions are interesting but answering them would not, I believe, shed much light on more basic questions.

2 Questions of access to the state's resources by those who are not geographically connected to it raise issues that I describe as "foreign aid" issues.

3 It bears noting, however, that on some theories of free speech the beneficiaries of resident aliens' right to free speech are the state's citizens.

4 The recently abandoned national-origin quotas were only marginally more subtle in their racism; the present quota system is, I believe, a classic "disparate impact" form of race discrimination.

5 Note that this is essentially a historical process, and Coleman and Harding need not contend that the process has proceeded to the same degree everywhere in the world.

6 *Zobel v. Williams,* 457 U.S. 55 (1982).

7 See, e.g., *Dunn v. Blumstein,* 405 U.S. 330 (1972).

8 These principles would take incentive concerns into account by denying the state's

power to redistribute resources made available only because parents worked so hard precisely in order to make resources available to their children and not to anyone else.

9 Bruce Ackerman, *Social Justice and the Liberal State* (New Haven, Conn.: Yale University Press, 1980).

10 In Chapter 6, Michael Louis Seidman argues that people (inherently) have differential sympathy for those closer to them. I suspect that this draws an unjustified analogy from the fact of greater sympathy for those genetically close to us to the hypothesis of greater sympathy for those geographically close to us. In any event, if there were a worldwide mechanism – "government" – to achieve distributive justice, I doubt that mere geographic proximity would have much psychological bite.

11 It might have some impact on people with preferences for particular scenery, the Austrian Alps being unavailable anywhere else (and, arguably, having no sufficiently close substitutes that could be combined with a monetary payment to achieve equivalent satisfaction for people with preferences for the Austrian Alps).

12 Under these circumstances the sense in which the aid would be foreign is unclear.

13 Coleman and Harding note that using the world's resources most effectively might require the creation of boundaries as convenient administrative units. They also note the possibility of foreign aid under these circumstances. It is unclear to me, however, why these convenient administrative units would have a legitimate interest in excluding those who sought to immigrate. With a foreign aid mechanism in place, it is not clear that so many people would want to relocate – given that, by hypothesis, they would be receiving the shares to which they were entitled by the theory of distributive justice – that the administrative capacity of these units would be overwhelmed.

14 See Eric Hobsbawm, *Nations and Nationalism since 1780: Programme, Myth, Reality*, 2d ed. (Cambridge University Press, 1992).

15 I put aside the obvious exception that they have tried to discourage mass entry in the form of military invasions.

16 The Alien Act of 1798 was "short-lived." Abba P. Schwartz, *The Open Society* (New York: Morrow 1968), 100. In 1875 began the pattern of identifying classes of excludable aliens: criminals and prostitutes at first, later expanded to include "standards of physical and mental health" and, after 1903, political criteria. Starting in 1882, the United States regulated entry by Chinese immigrants under a series of statutes. These facts suggest, once more, the difficulties attendant on the survey approach.

17 Calling these "political" might be contested.

18 Of course, there are contingent historical connections between territories and community membership. For example, Zionism was a historical creation linking the aspirations of some Jews in the Diaspora with the territory of Israel. It arose in response to developments in Europe in the nineteenth century and gained greater support in the aftermath of the Holocaust. Yet for more than a millennium Jews thought it largely irrelevant to their present membership in the community of Jews that Jews reside in any particular territory. Similarly, the vision of proletarian

internationalism suffered crippling blows during World War I. Again, a detailed historical analysis seems likely to illuminate the contingent connections between territory and community membership.

19 For example, I believe that I have a closer connection – genetic as well as social – to people who live in Ukraine than to those in Montana.

20 I put aside the problem, which I think likely to be quite substantial, that the value-based exclusion might serve as a mask for a race-based exclusion: we might say that some people are "not like us" because of their values when we really believe that they are "not like us" because of their race.

21 Obviously the real-world analysis is complicated by the fact of maldistribution of wealth.

22 For this reason, arguments that recent waves of immigration differ from older ones because the new immigrants are more unskilled than in the past miss the mark. For a popular presentation, see George Borjas, *Friends or Strangers: The Impact of Immigrants on the U.S. Economy* (New York: Basic Books, 1990). Unskilled they may be, but they are also motivated.

23 I have benefited here from Jeremy Waldron, "Minority Cultures and the Cosmopolitan Alternative," *University of Michigan Journal of Law Reform* 25 (1992): 751.

24 The question is even less serious in light of the preceding point, that people choose the nation to which they move at least in part because they share the values of the target nation.

25 This is subject, of course, to the qualification that the community must satisfy minimum norms of political justice – the "no tyranny" requirement.

8

The welfare economics of immigration law

A theoretical survey with an analysis of U.S. policy

ALAN O. SYKES

Much like tariffs and quotas, immigration restrictions are a form of protectionism, insulating domestic workers from competition in the labor market. Yet even the most ardent supporters of open markets usually stop short of advocating the abolition of immigration controls. Efforts to reduce barriers to the migration of labor were conspicuously absent, for example, from the Uruguay Round of GATT negotiations.[1] It seems clear that immigration policy will remain a bastion of national sovereignty in international economic relations,[2] ensuring the persistence of a wide range of uncoordinated and typically restrictive national regimes.

This essay considers whether restrictive national immigration policies have sound economic justification. The heart of the inquiry is normative, embracing the conventional tools and assumptions of modern welfare economics to analyze the efficiency of immigration controls. An ancillary aspect of the inquiry is positive, exploring whether current policy can be understood as an effort by unconstrained sovereigns to pursue the national economic advantage, perhaps at the expense of other nations. The current immigration policy of the United States receives close attention.

The economic issues are difficult to resolve, though more at an empirical than a theoretical level. Ultimately, any economic justification for immigration restrictions must rest on the presence of adverse external effects upon the world as a whole or the country of immigration. Theory identifies a variety of possibilities, though many are at best conjectural and fail to provide compelling support for a restrictive policy. Probably the most plausible argument for restrictions rests on the existence of entitlement programs in wealthier nations that may, depending upon how they are structured, induce inefficient migration from poorer nations. The most direct and efficient solution to such problems lies in changes to entitlement programs rather than in immigration policy, but legal constraints may in some cases make immigration restrictions the only alternative. There is little basis, however, for barring the immigration of those who are not allowed to or are unlikely to participate in entitlement programs or to vote themselves a right of participation.

This proposition has implications for, inter alia, the perceived problem of "illegal aliens" in the United States. The curtailment of programs to admit certain categories of temporary workers to the United States most likely has much to do with the growth of illegal immigration. It is not easy to fashion a convincing economic argument against an open door policy toward temporary workers with employer sponsorship, and thus illegal immigration may be in large part the result of economically unsound U.S. policies. Furthermore, because illegal aliens participate only minimally in entitlement programs, do not vote, and usually pay taxes much like other workers, it is by no means clear that their presence should be viewed as a "problem." Without an appropriate policy regarding the admission of temporary workers, illegal immigration may be a "second-best" response to the resulting economic inefficiencies.

Section I of this essay surveys the theory, raises the key empirical questions, and notes the existing empirical evidence. Section II then examines U.S. policies toward permanent immigration, temporary workers, and undocumented aliens, and offers a tentative assessment of their economic soundness from the global and national perspectives. It also suggests some options for reform. Section III presents the central conclusions.

I. The efficiency of international migration: theoretical and empirical issues

The decision to migrate is no different from any other – people migrate because their expected gains exceed the costs. Barring misinformation that exaggerates the quality of life abroad, therefore, it follows that migrants benefit from the opportunity to migrate and that government restrictions upon migration in the home country or the country of immigration can only lower their welfare. Hence the economic justification for such restrictions, if any is to be found, must rest upon some adverse consequence of migration for nonmigrants.

The simplest economic models of migration, drawn from standard models of international trade, suggest that migration is a net benefit to the world as a whole and to the country of immigration – any adverse consequences for nonmigrants are limited to the country of emigration. This proposition is at odds with the observation that restrictions upon immigration are more common that restrictions upon emigration. The disparity is perhaps less a failing of policy than a failing of the simple models, which omit potentially important external consequences of migration, as well as some other complications. Once these considerations are incorporated, the possiblility of inefficient migration from the world perspective and especially the national perspective emerges.

The inquiry then moves to empirics. Some empirical research has been done, and the results tend to suggest that migration is frequently a source of gains to the world and to the country of immigration, though assuredly not always. Furthermore, one cannot assume that the historical experience with immigration necessarily serves as an accurate predictor of the future, especially if immigration policies change. In particular, complete abolition of immigration restrictions would most likely be inefficient for many countries, including the United States. The optimal immigration policy from the national perspective is more difficult to characterize, however, partly because the set of feasible alternatives is unclear, partly because the empirical issues are difficult and unresolved, and partly because the unabashed pursuit of national self-interest generally collides with substantial moral objections.

A. A preliminary note on the normative significance of efficiency analysis

This essay is concerned with the "efficiency" of immigration policy. The term "efficiency" here refers to Hicks–Kaldor efficiency, defined in the familiar way: policy A is Hicks–Kaldor superior to policy B if those who benefit from switching to policy A from policy B could in principle compensate those who suffer from the switch and still remain better off themselves. The phrase "in principle" is used because compensation is not actually paid, and indeed the transaction costs of providing compensation might well dissipate the aggregate gains. Thus efficiency in the Hicks–Kaldor sense rests upon aggregate cost–benefit analysis, without regard to the impact of policy alternatives upon the distribution of wealth.

The normative relevance of this efficiency concept has been debated extensively in many settings, and I have no desire to rehash that debate at length here. In my view, the strongest argument for attaching normative significance to Hicks–Kaldor efficiency lies in an old-fashioned utilitarian instinct – if aggregate "wealth" measured in monetary units increases, it is frequently plausible that human happiness increases, because most of us prefer greater wealth, other things being equal. The standard caution is that some policy changes may cause redistribution from poor to rich, and thus even if aggregate wealth rises we may suspect that human happiness has diminished because the marginal utility of wealth is greater for poor people.[3] Nothing in this defense of Hicks–Kaldor analysis indulges the fiction that compensation will actually be paid to the losers, however, or that if it is not, the reason lies in a high-minded decision by a benevolent government to withhold compensation on grounds of distributional equity. Rather, all that is required is an increase in aggregate wealth, coupled with the absence of *systematic* redistribution from poor to rich.

Furthermore, it is not necessary to suppose that Hicks–Kaldor efficiency is the sole criterion of normative interest to find its welfare implications normatively useful. One need only assume that aggregate wealth is of some interest in policy making, possibly among quite a number of other things. Put differently, even if one may favor inefficient policies at times, it would be quite peculiar to assert that the aggregate economic costs of such policies are irrelevant to assessing their wisdom.

Some additional comfort may be taken from the fact that arguments from the Hicks–Kaldor perspective are widely used and widely accepted by many, particularly with reference to international economic policy. The economist's argument for free trade, for example, rests on the fact that protectionism is detrimental to the economy as a whole – it can hardly be denied that it benefits certain import-competing groups. Likewise, it can hardly be denied that those who suffer as a result of trade liberalization are not in general compensated or that the failure to compensate them does not reflect a thoughtful decision against compensation by some benign central authority.

With particular reference to immigration policy, there are additional arguments as to why any adverse impact of efficient immigration policies on the wealth of particular individuals or subpopulations may not provide a convincing argument against such policies. First, the most substantial costs and benefits of policy changes often tend to be borne by similarly situated individuals. An inefficient restriction on the immigration of inexpensive labor from abroad may benefit certain low-wage laborers domestically, for example, but much of the burden will be borne by low-wage workers abroad who are most likely even poorer.[4] More generally, as long as one cares about all individuals affected by immigration policy, there is little reason to suppose that efficient policies systematically redistribute wealth from poor to rich. And even if one cares more about citizens of one's own country than about foreigners, other means of preserving an acceptable domestic wealth distribution may well exist that are less costly than inefficient immigration restrictions. Finally, empirical studies of the effect of immigration on wage rates (the probable source of any adverse distributional impact) tend to suggest, with some exceptions, that even at the considerable levels of immigration experienced in the United States in recent decades, downward pressure on wages has been minimal.[5] Thus the effects of changes in immigration policy upon the wealth distribution may well be fairly modest, at least as long as any such changes are not too drastic.

A troubling ethical question on which the analysis to follow takes no position is suggested by my reference to poor foreign workers – is it acceptable, in the formulation of national policy, to give more weight (or even exclusive weight) to the welfare on one's own citizens or residents? If so, does a would-be immigrant count as a "foreigner" until after his arrival, or even longer (say, until naturalization)? On the one hand, it seems perfectly coherent and high-minded to claim that citizenship or residency ought to have no moral significance. On the other hand, it is clear that in the formulation of many public policies, nations do appear to prefer their own people quite strongly over people who are not presently citizens or residents (the U.S. government gives much greater assistance to the domestic poor, for example, than to the more destitute poor in Ethiopia). To avoid the need to consider the ethics of such preferences, the analysis here simply addresses the welfare of three groups – migrants, original residents of the country of immigration, and those individuals left behind in the country of emigration. It discusses the welfare consequences of immigration from both the "global" perspective (aggregating all three groups) and the "national" perspective (focusing only on non-migrants in each country). I leave to the reader the choice between these perspectives, noting only that both have a long and distinguished tradition in the discussion of international economic policy.[6]

I also note that any ambivalence over the choice between the "national" and "global" perspectives is not fatal to our ability to draw some firm conclusions from the welfare economic analysis. In particular, the two perspectives overlap to a considerable degree on one potentially important source of inefficiency in the incentive to migrate – cross-national variations in the public sector.

B. Immigration in traditional trade models

The possible benefits of migration to a migrant fall into two categories: (a) the labor market in the country of immigration provides better opportunities; and (b) the country of immigration is more attractive because of psychic considerations (e.g., migration permits family reunification or allows the migrant to escape one form or another of persecution or social unrest in the home country). Of course, both types of gain may be present in a given instance, and these categories to some degree overlap (e.g., persecution may reduce labor market opportunities at home). Most economic discussions of migration focus on the first source of gains, and the discussion to follow is written with that emphasis as well. It will note in due course, however, why the analysis does not change when the gains to the migrant are psychic rather than monetary.

International trade theory devotes considerable attention to the reasons for cross-country variations in factor returns in general and returns to labor in particular. The formal conditions required for international "factor price equalization" have been studied in models of increasing complexity and are shown in the end to be fairly complex.[7] Intuitively, when goods and services are exchanged freely in international trade with no trade barriers or transport costs, their prices equalize across countries. If countries also have access to the same technologies, then the productivity of the various factors of production, and their associated compensation in real terms, can (though by no means must) converge. By the same reasoning, differences across countries in factor returns can be attributed to differences in technology, to governmental barriers to trade, to transport costs and the related fact that some goods and services are not "tradable" (certain perishables, haircuts), and to the possibility that in some countries but not others particular factors may be in surplus.

These observations suggest one reason for inefficient migration, at least in a "first-best" sense. Suppose, for example, that a tariff in one country artificially raises the returns to some type of labor and depresses the return to that type of labor abroad. Not only may the pattern of human capital investment around the world be distorted as a consequence, but an artificial incentive to migrate may arise under conditions where, but for the tariff, the costs of migration would exceed the benefits. The world could gain if the tariff were removed and the migration did not occur. The problem might arise for other reasons as well, such as an inefficient restriction on technology transfer.

If such distortions are taken to be immutable, however, migration can be a "second-best" adaptation to them. The product price distortion across countries because of a tariff, for example, can diminish as factors move from the country with the low price to the country with the high price. Indeed, the flip side of factor price equalization brought about by trade in end products is end product price equalization brought about by factor flows.[8] Inefficient incentives for human capital investment can diminish as well.

Thus, whenever the incentive to migrate is the product of a distortion, the "efficiency" of migration in response to it turns in one sense on whether elimination of the distortion is feasible. If migrants have rational expectations about the likelihood of the distortion persisting, perhaps the occurrence of migration suggests that it is indeed a second-best adaptation. But even this proposition is open to challenge. Conceivably, for example, if the incentive to migrate arises because of protectionist trade policies, restrictions on migration might increase political pressure for the elimination of protection and thereby promote the first-best outcome. Alternatively, in the case of migration driven by persecution in the home country, it is conceivable that restrictions on the ability of people to flee would heighten the prospects for reform. In the discussion to follow, however, I generally put such possibilities to one side on the plausible assumption that they are not very important, and treat the source of the incentive to migrate as "exogenous" to immigration policy.[9]

On this assumption, it is possible to adapt standard trade models to the study of migration. The simplest of these models suggest that migration is a source of net gains to the world as a whole and generally suggest that migration either benefits or leaves unharmed the original residents of the country of immigration.

We begin with migration in the *absence* of trade. Consider first a "Ricardian" model, in which countries differ in their technologies. There is only one factor of production (call it labor), constant returns to scale (CRS), and competition. Because trade between countries is of no interest at the moment, suppose that there is only one end product (call it a "widget").[10] Let workers enjoy utility from widget consumption and from leisure. Workers everywhere have one unit of labor, and its price in the home currency is 1. An incentive to migrate will arise in this model because one country has superior technology. A unit of labor might produce two widgets in country A and three in country B, for example. The price of widgets in country A would then be .5, while it would be only .33 in country B. Workers in country B would then enjoy a larger consumption possibilities set and a higher level of welfare for any utility function that led them to consume positive amounts of widgets. Thus workers in country A would like to move to country B.

In this simplest of models, the only individual affected by migration is the migrant. Workers who remain behind in country A can still purchase widgets for a price of .5 and attain the level of welfare they attained before. Likewise, the consumption possibilities of workers in country B are unaffected. Migration has simply allowed the migrants to gain access to the superior technology used in country B and thereby to enhance their consumption opportunities. Worldwide welfare thus rises by the amount of the gain to migrants, and the welfare of nonmigrants is unaffected.

Although this model is plainly lacking in generality, it is useful to establish a benchmark case. When technology in a competitive economy exhibits CRS, migration *may* simply shift the locus of production from country to country without having an impact on nonmigrants. More precisely, if all factors are paid their marginal product (which exhausts total output exactly under CRS), and if migration does not affect the marginal products of factors owned by nonmigrants (as it cannot in the earlier one-factor CRS model), then the only individuals affected by migration are the migrants.

This proposition immediately suggests two reasons why migration can affect the welfare of nonmigrants. First, if technology is not CRS over the "relevant range," it is well known that factors cannot be paid their marginal products, because the sum of payments no longer adds up to the value of output. With increasing returns to scale (marginal products above average products), factors must on average receive less than their marginal products. If immigrants are paid in this fashion, they will add more to national output in the country of immigration than they receive in compensation, and thus confer a benefit on the original residents. The reverse condition holds if technology exhibits decreasing returns to scale (average products above marginal products) so that factors on average are paid more than their marginal products. Perhaps one can dismiss these possibilities as unimportant for immigration policy on the premise that the assumption of CRS ''over the relevant range'' is a plausible approximation of reality in most industries, or on the premise that it is impossible to observe departures from marginal product factor pricing attributable to the shape of the production function and thus impossible to fashion an acceptable policy response. Some authors suggest, however, that scale economies are in fact quite important in trade, and such models dominate much of the modern trade literature. In a number of these models, consistent with the result noted here, an inflow of any factor is potentially beneficial to the nation that experiences the inflow because it allows greater scale economies to be realized.[11] The claim has also been advanced that such benefits of immigration are empirically demonstrable, though the evidence is not entirely convincing.[12]

Another departure from the assumptions of this simple model relates to the possibility that migration affects the marginal productivity of factors owned by nonmigrants even under CRS. Consider the simplest of ''Heckscher–Ohlin'' models, for example, in which technology is assumed for simplicity to be the same across countries, as are consumer tastes. Two factors of production exist (call them ''labor'' and ''capital''), which are used to produce two end products under CRS. Factors everywhere are paid their marginal product, but factor endowments differ across countries. The country with the higher capital–labor ratio is ''capital-abundant'' and the other ''labor-abundant.'' The central insight of these Heckscher–Ohlin models is that when trade begins between the two countries, the capital-abundant country can specialize in the capital-intensive good and export it, and the labor-abundant country can specialize in the labor-intensive good and export it. The world production possibility set expands, and the consumption possibilities set expands for residents in each country (hence, gains from trade), raising the welfare of both.[13] In this model, however, trade does influence factor prices, since it causes the real price of labor in the labor-abundant country to rise and the real price of capital in the capital-abundant country to rise, while the price of the scarce factor in each country falls (the Stolper–Samuelson theorem).[14]

A moment's reflection suggests that these results apply directly to the analysis of immigration. Continuing for now with the assumption that the countries of emigration and immigration do not engage in trade, simply define the group of immigrants as "country A," and let the original residents of the country of immigration be "country B." Suppose that the immigrants bring with them their labor, but relatively little capital, so that country A is labor-abundant and country B capital-abundant. Immigration is then equivalent to the opening of trade between countries that differ in their factor endowments. Both nations will enjoy gains from trade, although the real returns to labor fall in country B and rise in country A, with the opposite pattern in the returns to capital.

But what about those left behind in the country of emigration (call them "country C")? Precisely the same reasoning allows us to view immigration as the *cessation* of trade between country A and country C. If those countries differed in relative factor abundance, gains from trade were present, and the cessation of trade causes those gains to disappear. Country C is then unambiguously hurt by emigration. As for the immigrants (country A), they have losses from their cessation of trade with country C and gains from the opening of trade with country B – on balance the gains must exceed the losses or immigration would not occur. Thus immigration benefits the immigrants, benefits the original residents of the country of immigration (in the aggregate), and hurts the residents who stay behind in the country of emigration (in the aggregate). It should also be intuitive that the effect on world welfare is positive by virtue of the immigrants' opportunity to locate where the gains from trade are greatest.[15]

A special case of this model, in which migrants own labor only and all returns to capital are captured by nonmigrants in the countries of emigration and immigration, has been discussed widely. Migration occurs because the marginal product of labor is higher in the country of immigration. A non-infinitesimal amount of migration then causes the marginal product of labor to fall in the country of immigration and to rise in the country of emigration. Returns to capital move oppositely. Original residents in the country of immigration experience a net gain because the marginal product of the last immigrant, equal to the wage paid to all immigrants, is below the average product of the immigrants. All the gains (and then some), of course, are captured by the owners of capital, and any nonmigrant who owns labor only will be hurt as the price of labor falls.

The situation in the country of emigration is exactly the opposite. Owners of labor, who formerly competed with the emigrants, benefit, and owners of capital suffer. The net effect is adverse, because the wage formerly paid to the immigrants (their marginal product) was below their average product. The net effect on the world is favorable, however, because migration allows workers to locate where their marginal product is the highest, and thus world production expands.[16]

Such analysis implies that for a nation interested in maximizing its national advantage, emigration is a source of concern.[17] Immigration, by contrast, is to be welcomed as long as aggregate economic welfare affords the proper metric for evaluating alternative policies.

As noted at the outset, the conclusions do not change when the gains to the migrant are psychic rather than monetary. Psychic gains to the immigrant may simply be regarded as a "fringe benefit" to employment that is part of the total compensation package in the country of immigration, and may likewise be regarded as part of the social marginal product of the immigrant. Thus they are simply social gains that are captured in full by the immigrant, and there is no reason to suppose that their existence will affect the returns to factors owned by nonmigrants.

The analysis does change materially, however, when migration occurs in the presence of international trade. Intuitively, migration alters world demand patterns, in part because of the attendant population shifts and in part because migrants do not in general have the same tastes in consumption as the indigenous population. It also alters the factor endowments of affected countries. All of these changes can alter the pattern of trade and the terms of trade – the relative prices of imports and exports. The result that factor mobility is beneficial to the world as a whole is not changed, but the net impact upon the welfare of nonmigrants can change because of terms-of-trade effects. In general, however, an inflow of (or exogenous internal growth in the supply of) a factor that is used intensively in the import-competing sectors rather than the export sectors will tend to benefit the country that experiences the factor growth. The reason is that an increase in such a factor makes import-competing goods cheaper to produce at home, and thus lowers demand for imports and their price, improving the terms of trade.[18] The country of emigration then experiences a worsening in terms of trade. It is possible to posit settings in which other forms of immigration occur, however, that might worsen the terms of trade for the country of immigration. For example, the migration of skilled labor to a country that exports high-technology goods might well cause a fall in the relative price of its exports. No general conclusion is possible, therefore, although the models with trade included arguably tend to reinforce the conclusions of the models without it, and certainly do not provide any reason to suppose that the residents of the country of immigration would *systematically* lose as a consequence.[19]

Still further complications can arise if the returns to nonmigrating factors of production are owned by foreigners. In the simple Heckscher–Ohlin illustration, for example, where labor migrates but capital does not, suppose that a significant percentage of the capital in the country of immigration is owned by foreigners. Then the result that the country of immigration benefits can easily be reversed – the gains are realized by the owners of capital, and if a significant number of those individuals are foreign, the original residents can plainly lose. The problem would be compounded if residents of the country of immigration held capital investments in the country of emigration, because emigration lowers the returns to capital abroad.

A parallel concern arises because of the mobility of domestic capital. Suppose that the most efficient location for a new factory is domestic, with many workers at the factory coming from abroad. But if immigration restrictions prevent foreign workers from migrating to work at the factory, investors may choose to build it in a foreign country. A loss of global welfare occurs because investment does not occur at its most efficient location. A loss of national welfare may also occur because domestic investors are not able to maximize their returns. That problem may compound once the public sector is introduced, as noted later.

In summary, therefore, the theoretical picture is fairly complex, although the analysis does permit a few generalizations to be made. First, any adverse effect of immigration on aggregate *global* welfare must rest on the existence of consequences omitted from the simple models of conventional trade theory – most likely the existence of nonpecuniary externalities.[20] The basic theorem of welfare economics that competitive equilibria are efficient survives in the presence of international boundaries as long as its assumptions continue to hold, a claim that is hardly startling.

The welfare effects of migration upon individual countries need not be strictly favorable even in the competitive model without nonpecuniary externalities, however, because the pecuniary externalities do not affect them uniformly. The simplest theoretical models suggest that the country of immigration benefits and the country of emigration loses, but these propositions are not always robust to complicating assumptions. Terms-of-trade effects and foreign ownership of nonmigrating factors, perhaps among other things, have the potential to change the conclusions.

Conceivably, all of these effects are empirically unimportant. It is often argued that the gains and losses that the models without trade identify are likely to be very small,[21] and the probable significance of terms-of-trade effects and foreign ownership of capital is quite unclear. In any case, the models discussed to this point, coupled with the current state of empirical knowledge, do not make a convincing case for immigration restrictions even on the part of a nation that is concerned solely with the welfare of current residents or citizens. At best, they identify some possible adverse consequences, but are equally adept at identifying possible favorable consequences.

C. Externalities and the public sector

Nonpecuniary externalities from migration can arise for a variety of reasons. An inflow of population can exacerbate common-pool problems when property rights are incomplete, for example, or result in greater pollution of the local environment when transaction costs impede the formation of markets to correct the problem. Opportunities to commit crimes may attract immigrants from nations where those opportunities are less attractive, either because victims are poorer or law enforcement is better. If direct corrections for such externalities are infeasible or ineffective for some reason, one cannot exclude a priori the possibility that immigration restrictions are a second-best response from the perspective of the country of immigration or that emigration may generate significant positive externalities for those left behind. These familiar types of negative externalities tend not to be emphasized in most discussions of migration, however, perhaps because they are thought to be relatively insignificant empirically (or impossible to measure), perhaps because other policy instruments are assumed adequate to address them, or perhaps because they are more related to broader concerns such as population growth and law enforcement policy.

Negative externalities may also arise if the labor market, or some portion of it, does not clear. When involuntary unemployment exists as a disequilibrium phenomenon, an influx of new workers can reduce the probability that existing workers will find a job.[22] The externality arises because some of the expected returns to migration here are a transfer from existing workers to the new workers. An obvious source of this problem is the minimum wage, which may create a pool of unemployed workers that may simply grow with the immigration of less skilled workers. Of course, an influx of new immigrants also raises aggregate demand, which ameliorates unemployment problems, other things being equal. Thus, even in an economy where disequilibrium involuntary unemployment is significant, immigration is by no means clearly undesirable. But the immigration of workers who are close substitutes for groups of workers that already suffer high unemployment may well be detrimental from both the national and global perspectives.

It is also possible to imagine positive externalities from migration. Perhaps the most obvious are associated with family reunification. These externalities are social gains from the world perspective and gains from the perspective of the country of immigration if all existing residents "count" in the national welfare function. Some authors have argued that other positive externalities arise because migrants enrich the lives of original residents by exposing them to different cultures and that migrants may bring specialized knowledge to the labor market that would not transfer as quickly without migration.[23] These externalities are clearly extraordinarily difficult to quantify, and it is difficult to say more about them than simply to note their existence.

One class of externalities that seems especially significant, however, and with respect to which some empirical evidence may be assembled, arises from the activities of the public sector. There can be little doubt that tax policies and entitlement policies can affect the incentive to migrate, perhaps inefficiently. Indeed, these externalities lie at the center of many popular and academic discussions of immigration policy. In this section, I consider the theoretical issues raised by different aspects of public sector activity and note as appropriate the existing empirical knowledge.

As before, the discussion in this section treats public sector policies that affect the incentive to migrate as exogenous and migration decisions as endogenous. This assumption is perhaps realistic when the level of immigration is modest, but becomes increasingly suspect as the immigration flow increases and the balance of political power between new immigrants and original residents changes. Accordingly, it will be relaxed below in Section I, D for the area of policy that is perhaps most likely to be affected by immigration – redistribution policy.

1. Taxation. Putting aside the fictional device of "lump-sum" taxation, all methods of taxation create distortions of one sort or another. The possibility of migration simply adds some further possible distortions to an already lengthy list.

Return for a moment to the simple Ricardian model of Section I, A, in which migration is beneficial because it allows the migrant to expand her consumption possibilities set after moving to the country with superior technology (country B). Suppose, however, that this country now imposes a tax on the production of widgets, and suppose further for a moment that tax collections are wasted by the sovereign with no benefit to the citizenry. The effect is to create the conventional labor–leisure choice distortion for all workers, because the private marginal product of labor falls below the social marginal product, and also to reduce the returns to migration, other things being equal. Plainly, if the tax becomes high enough, migration will not occur.

Of course, country A may also impose a tax on widget production, and if the tax rate is the same in the two countries, labor will always do better in the country with the superior technology and some incentive to migrate will survive for any tax rate. But because migration in reality is costly, taxation clearly has the potential to destroy the incentive to migrate even when the increment in social marginal product exceeds the costs of migration. The problem is compounded if the country with the higher social marginal product of labor imposes a higher tax rate. Indeed, one can easily construct scenarios in which differences in tax policy cause migration to flow in the wrong direction.

The assumption that government provides no benefits to its citizens is obviously too strong, however, and it remains to consider what the migrant will receive back from the government in reality. Although the manner in which the benefits of public sector activity are distributed in practice is not likely to solve the problem of the labor–leisure choice distortion, it may assuredly diminish any distortion in the incentive to migrate attributable to taxes, and even reverse it. Consideration of government expenditures will also suggest other ways that migration may impose positive or negative externalities upon nonmigrants.

2. *Government expenditures, assets, and obligations.* If there are no other distortions in the incentive to migrate, the existence of the public sector will create such a distortion if what a migrant must pay in taxes[24] (at the privately optimal level of work effort) does not equal what the migrant will receive back from the government in the form of benefits from government programs, in either the home country or the destination country.[25] When taxes paid exceed benefits received (and perhaps even when they do not; see the discussion of public goods below), the presence of the migrant confers an external benefit upon nonmigrants. In the reverse case, an external cost may be present. Thus consider the most important likely sources of divergence between taxes and government benefits.

(i) Variation in the earning capacity of migrants. Regardless of how the benefits from government programs are distributed to residents, the balance of taxes and government benefits will most likely vary among them because taxes are invariably related to ability to pay. If one imagines that government expenditures and revenues over the long run will be approximately equal, for example, it is plausible to suppose on the basis of tax rate progressivity alone that low-income individuals will receive more in benefits than they pay in taxes, and high-income individuals will receive less. Indeed, even proportional taxation can produce such a result.

This possibility is reinforced by the fact that many government programs afford benefits only to low-income individuals by design. Income support, medical assistance, and other public safety net programs exist in the United States and elsewhere, funded by the relatively more affluent for the benefit of the relatively less affluent. It is certainly plausible that unrestricted migration into developed countries such as the United States, coupled with full entitlement for all immigrants to the public safety net programs, would create a sizable incentive for migration quite apart from any labor market opportunities, particularly for residents of countries with low standards of living and few safety net programs. Such migration could assuredly be inefficient from the world perspective (the gains to the migrant being a transfer rather than a social gain) and inefficient from the perspective of the country of immigration.[26]

(ii) International variation in other entitlement programs. Safety net programs are not the only possible source of inefficient incentives to migrate
due to entitlement programs. Even relatively affluent individuals might be
induced to migrate by the opportunity to receive benefits under a national
health care system, for example, if they are ill and their home country provides no comparable program. Programs for the elderly, for both income
maintenance and health care, can produce similar inefficient incentives depending upon their design. An older person might be induced to migrate to
the United States inefficiently, for example, if the entitlement to Social Security benefits vested after a few years in the work force and the return on
contributions paid into the system were actuarially unfair in favor of the
retiree.[27]

(iii) Education. Many countries provide "public education" to children
up to a point. They also subsidize higher education to some degree. If such
educational subsidies were financed in full by taxes on parents while the
student was in school, subsequent emigration of a public school graduate
would impose no cost on any other residents except the members of the
immediate family of the migrant. But if one imagines instead that the educational subsidy is repaid by the public school graduate through taxation after
graduation, emigration appears potentially disadvantageous to all those left
behind. To be sure, it may remain efficient from the world perspective to the
degree that the migrant maximizes the returns to human capital and the incentives for governments to invest in human capital accumulation (assuming
such investment to be desirable) are not too greatly diminished.

For the most part, this observation suggests why countries might seek to
restrict emigration to promote the national advantage, but does nothing to
justify restrictions on immigration. Thus, in particular, the much-celebrated
U.S. Supreme Court decision in *Plyler v. Doe*,[28] which held that states cannot
discriminate against undocumented aliens in the provision of public primary
and secondary education, need not be contrary to the pursuit of the national
advantage. Only to the extent that children of undocumented aliens may be
expected to leave the country subsequently would the provision of an educational subsidy become worrisome. And although some such children may
by choice leave the country, perhaps the greatest danger is that they will be
deported at some point along with their parents, a form of emigration that
need not occur at all. These observations also bear directly on aspects of the
recent "Save Our State" initiative in California.

The possibility that an immigrant may stay only long enough to take advantage of an educational subsidy is perhaps greater with respect to temporary
residents in subsidized portions of the higher educational system. Even here,
however, the cultural and educational benefits to permanent residents from

the opportunity to interact with foreign nationals affords an offsetting consideration.

(iv) Public goods. With true public goods (perhaps national defense is an example), consumption is nonexclusive and the presence of additional residents does not diminish the value of the public good to others. Thus, to the degree that a migrant contributes to the funding of public goods through taxation, migration is a loss to the country of emigration and a gain to the country of immigration.

(v) Congestion of public facilities. Related and opposite, access to many publicly owned facilities is underpriced (national parks, beaches, highways), resulting in the presence of congestion externalities. Additional residents exacerbate the problem. Of course, congestion externalities may arise in the use of privately owned property as well if access is underpriced but such underpricing is perhaps rare enough that the problem is not very significant.

(vi) Returns to net public assets. More generally, one must ask who earns the returns to publicly owned assets, sometimes termed "public capital" in the literature. As a first approximation, one might suppose that those returns accrue pro rata to the citizenry, so that an immigrant imposes a negative externality on those already present by capturing a pro rata share immediately. Upon reflection, however, the issue is much more complicated.

A pro rata share of the returns to public goods, as noted, creates no negative externality, because consumption is nonexclusive. For facilities subject to a congestion problem, by contrast, the negative externality is clearly present. Many public facilities do not fall neatly into either category, however, and the proper allocation of "returns" to such facilities, and even the conceptual measurement of those "returns," is problematic.

Consider, for example, the postal system. Who earns the returns to the investment in post offices, airplanes, trucks, and so on? Perhaps those returns are captured by the postal workers union or by politicians who influence the location of post offices and hiring. At the other extreme, the returns might be realized by postal consumers, who pay a lower price for service because the cost of capital is not reflected in the price (equivalently, perhaps the price is lower than it would be if the service were supplied privately).

Similar conceptual issues arise with respect to police stations, fire stations, the Department of Commerce building in Washington, and on and on. Consider a representative federal building. Who paid for it? Was it financed by earlier taxpayers, so that the returns to its operation (think of them as savings on rent that the government would have to pay currently if it were renting a privately owned building) are passed on to current taxpayers in the form of

lower rates? Or should we think of it as financed by a bond issue that is
repaid over the life of the building out of current tax revenue, so that there
is no intertemporal transfer reflected in the tax burden? Depending on the
answers, a new immigrant, paying taxes currently but not in the past, might
or might not be viewed as contributing to the cost of its construction. And
there remains the problem of determining who presently receives the returns
from its existence – government employees? politicians? all current taxpayers
on a pro rata basis? some current taxpayers? beneficiaries of the programs
that the agency sponsors? Depending upon how these questions are answered,
and they are no doubt unanswerable in practice, the immigrant's presence
could have a favorable or unfavorable effect on the rest of the populace with
respect to a given facility.

The reference to intertemporal transfers suggests a more general point. Just
as the value of publicly owned assets can be considerable, so can the value
of public debt. And the migrant who captures a share of returns to public
assets may likewise be viewed as capturing a share of the obligation to repay
public debt. For example, if the value of public assets were equal to the
national debt, and if the rate of return on public assets were equal to the rate
of interest on the debt, a pro rata share of the returns to *net* public assets
would be worth nothing.

With these remarks as background, a paper by Usher argues that immigration may be quite harmful to the country of immigration (and by implication quite beneficial to the country of emigration) because of the ability of
immigrants to capture a share of the returns to public capital and "mixed"
capital, the latter being all capital the returns to which are subject to tax.[29]
His "back of the envelope" calculations for the United Kingdom are quite
peculiar, however, because he assumes that all workers capture the marginal
product of their labor (no tax on labor) and that each member of the population receives a pro rata share of the returns to public capital (estimated as
its net value times a market rate of return) and revenue from taxes on privately owned capital. As a result, migrants who arrive with labor and no
"capital" almost inevitably reduce the welfare of prior residents because they
pay no taxes yet capture a pro rata share of the returns to all government
activity.[30]

Simon takes a different approach to the problem, abandoning any effort to
allocate directly the returns to public assets.[31] Using data for the United
States, he estimates the tax payments made by immigrants and compares them
with their readily measurable consumption of public services (payments to
them under entitlement programs, but excluding their use of public education,[32] national parks, etc.). He then concludes that immigrants on average
pay more in taxes than they receive in public services, so that their net effect
on the rest of the population through the activities of the public sector is

positive rather than negative. The exception is the immigrant who is *employed* by the government, since government employees are assumed to capture the returns to the capital with which they work (the postal workers union example mentioned earlier). But because the number of immigrants so employed is small, Simon argues, this appropriation of returns to public capital from prior residents is quite small, and vastly smaller than the effect calculated by Usher.

Neither approach is entirely satisfactory in light of earlier remarks, although Simon's approach seems far closer to the mark. A proper accounting of the effect of immigrants on natives through the activities of the public sector would account for all taxes paid by immigrants over their life span and would value all services received by them through the public sector over their life span at their proper economic cost (including imputations for congestion externalities, ordinary economic returns foregone by the government when it sells goods or services at a subsidized price, the value of public education, etc.). Simon's analysis, putting aside any objections to his data, plainly understates the typical immigrants' draw upon public services and facilities for failure to include the imputations just noted but arguably overstates the effect of immigrants who are public employees on the rest of the population.

(vii) Other considerations. The introduction of government taxation and expenditures affects the analysis not only of the efficiency of migration by workers, but also of the efficiency of migration by other factors. Some of these effects have direct bearing upon immigration policy.

Let us return to the earlier example of a factory that, from a global welfare perspective, is best located domestically but is best staffed with foreign workers. We assume that immigration restrictions prevent foreign workers from migrating to work at the factory and that as a consequence the factory is built abroad. Suppose further that if the factory were built domestically, the taxes that would be paid on the returns to investors in the factory would exceed the incremental costs of government services necessitated by its presence. Then immigration restrictions would impose a net loss on the domestic economy, other things being equal, because they would induce capital investment abroad with a resultant loss of net government revenues.

3. Summary and a further note on the empirical literature. The theoretical discussion suggests difficult empirical issues, only a few of which have been examined closely and some of which are probably impossible to examine in practice. If one assumes away the general problem of allocating returns to public assets, however, and focuses only on direct payments to migrants in relation to the taxes that they pay, the available evidence for the United States suggests that migrants *on average* pay their way, and then some.[33] This conclusion is reinforced by the fact that immigrants are often young adults (although they may bring their children) who have received their education at the expense of someone abroad and who will not participate in entitlement programs for the elderly for many years.

Of course, the available empirical information reflects the national experience with migration under past immigration policies. One cannot infer that the same conclusions would necessarily hold had immigration been less restrictive or based upon different criteria. Quite clearly, for example, an open door policy, coupled with immediate right to full participation in public entitlement programs, might well become a source of considerable financial drain on the national treasury. Likewise, the fact that immigrants on average pay their way does not establish that all of them do, and one must ask whether policies intended to minimize immigration driven by a desire to participate in transfer programs are adequate.

It is important to remember, however, that immigration law is not the only policy instrument available for addressing externality problems. If externalities arise because of entitlement programs, for example, changes in those programs may dominate any change in immigration policy. Yet that perspective on the problem may be naive, for it presupposes that the appropriate modifications to entitlement programs are legally feasible and that the political system will be equally adept at effecting the needed changes irrespective of the level of migration. Indeed, the assumption that public sector decisions in general are exogenous to migration policy is generally somewhat suspect. These issues warrant further attention.

D. Entitlement programs revisited: public choice and altruism

Even when immigrants cannot participate in the political process, a substantial influx of immigrants can affect the allocation of resources in the public sector – witness current U.S. policies toward illegal migration. The potential impact of immigration upon public policy is far greater, of course, if immigrants have the power to influence policy directly. In the democracies, that power comes largely through the voting franchise.[34]

It has been argued that full political membership for immigrants with sociopolitical backgrounds that differ from those of existing residents may threaten the possibly fragile and poorly understood institutional structure that makes the country of immigration more successful than the country of emigration.[35] This possibility perhaps cannot be ruled out but it seems equally plausible that the participation of immigrants in the political system will strengthen the commitment of the polity to preserve the vital institutions of the country of immigration. Individuals who have abandoned one country for another may well have both a greater appreciation for the differences between the two that make their new country a source of greater economic opportunity and a greater commitment to preserving the sources of that opportunity.

Likewise, with respect to the political resolution of many specific policy issues, there seems little reason to suppose that the franchise for immigrants will have an adverse impact on the rest of the population. The preferences of the "median voter" may shift a bit, to be sure, and decisive new coalitions may emerge on some issues. But in the end, it seems quite unlikely that important national defense programs will be undermined or that valuable highway construction, police and fire services will grind to a halt. Rather, as long as immigrants pay their way – returning to the issues discussed in the preceding section – their right to vote on many matters of mutual concern need not concern the rest of the citizenry.

I do not mean to claim, however, that completely unrestricted immigration into any nation would have no impact on democratic decisions. An obvious concern, though probably not the only one, again relates to transfer and entitlement programs. A wave of new, poor immigrants may well gain the capacity to vote themselves a substantial transfer from original residents. The problem here, of course, is nothing but a slight variant of the one discussed earlier. Because the generosity of entitlement programs is in reality endogenous to immigration policy, any distortion that they create can grow with immigration if the composition of the immigrant flow is such that immigrants benefit from entitlement programs more on average than original residents.

The issue becomes more complex if one views entitlement programs not simply as coerced transfers to organized interest groups, but as the product at least to a degree of altruism on the part of more affluent residents. One possibility of relevance here, modeled in the public finance literature that addresses redistribution within a federal system,[36] is that citizens "care" more about local poor than distant poor. Precisely why this should be so is not clear – perhaps the affluent gain more utility from helping those with whom they have more frequent encounters, or perhaps ethnic racial biases are present. In any event, this structure of preferences coupled with legal constraints on the exclusion of new residents from redistribution programs may justify immigration restrictions as a second-best means to facilitate "efficient redistribution."

The situation can be illustrated using a simple model adapted from the work of Pauly. Suppose that a country is initially composed of a single affluent altruist and a number of identical poor residents.[37] The altruist contemplates a program of redistribution. Assume further that redistribution will induce immigration unless it is prohibited, that legal constraints require equal transfers to all poor people, and that they preclude the exclusion of immigrants from the transfer system. Let the altruist have total income I and utility function $u(y, w, p)$, where y is the altruist's own consumption, w is the transfer payment to each poor resident, and p is the number of poor residents who receive transfers. The altruist's budget constraint is thus $y + pw = I$.

To keep the analysis as simple as possible while developing the essential points, assume that the initial population of local poor is p^* and inquire whether the altruist would prefer to restrict p to p^* by prohibiting *any* immigration of additional poor people.[38] This question can be answered by solving the problem in which the altruist chooses y, w, and p to maximize utility subject to the budget constraint and to the constraint $p \geqslant p^*$. Let γ be the Lagrange multiplier associated with the latter constraint. The altruist will prefer to prohibit immigration if γ is positive at the optimum.

The pertinent first-order conditions, which I assume to be sufficient, can be written

$$u_w = u_y p \tag{1}$$

$$u_p = u_y w - \gamma \tag{2}$$

Assuming that a positive amount of redistribution is to occur, equation (2) confirms the obvious point that γ will be positive if u_p is sufficiently small. That is, if the marginal utility of adding another person to the transfer rolls is small enough at the population level p^*, the altruist will prefer to exclude any new recipients. The possibility that the altruist may not care much about the nonresident poor is conceptually similar to the situation in which u_p is small or zero (though it must be conceded that the discontinuity implicit in that description of preferences would require a more elaborate set of first-order conditions).

Further, on the assumption that the marginal utilities of y, p, and w are diminishing, equations (1) and (2) imply that allowing the altruist to limit p to p^* when that outcome is preferred by the altruist leads to a larger transfer payment w than if immigration could not be restricted and redistribution had to be undertaken over a larger population. Thus the use of immigration restrictions will benefit the existing poor residents, who will receive greater transfers. It follows that immigration restrictions can enhance national economic welfare (that of the altruist and the original poor residents) – indeed, such restrictions can yield a Pareto improvement for them.

Even if altruists care equally about local and distant poor, an argument for limiting redistribution to the current domestic poor might be based upon transaction costs. It is certainly plausible that the transaction costs of redistribution rise as the number of transferees rises, other things being equal, and that the transaction costs of redistribution domestically are lower than the costs of redistribution abroad.[39] Quite plausibly, altruists would then prefer both to limit transfers to domestic residents and to limit the number of eligible transferees domestically to reduce the proportion of the redistributive budget consumed by administrative costs. Once again, if transfers induce immigration and legal constraints preclude the exclusion of new immigrants from transfer programs, a case for immigration restrictions might again emerge.

Of course, it remains to inquire whether immigration restrictions are in fact the only viable way to limit participation in transfer programs. As noted earlier, the more direct solution would be to allow immigration but to deny transfer payments to those who immigrate, at least for some considerable period of time. This solution would have the advantage of eliminating the source of the distortion in the incentive to migrate without concurrently generating the labor market inefficiencies that attend immigration controls.

As a practical matter, however, appropriate corrections to entitlement programs may be infeasible or of limited effectiveness. In the United States, for example, the courts have been quite hostile on constitutional grounds to substantial residency requirements as a condition for participation in entitlement programs.[40] The exclusion of resident aliens from state welfare programs has also been struck down, with alienage now treated as a suspect classification.[41] The fact that resident aliens can quite easily become citizens further constrains efforts to exclude them in any way.[42] Not only is it impermissible to exclude citizens from entitlement programs, but new, disadvantaged aliens who become citizens might well develop the political power to force an increase in payments under such programs. Hence there is considerable reason to believe that immigration restrictions may be useful for preventing inefficient migration by those who would avail themselves of transfers, at least in the United States.

To summarize, the assumption that important aspects of the entitlement programs are "endogenous" to immigration policy because of the voting power of immigrants, the preferences of those who wish to engage in redistribution, or the transaction costs of assisting an increasing population of beneficiaries simply strengthens the conclusions developed earlier about the dangers of an open door policy in nations that are relatively generous to the disadvantaged. To the extent that political or legal constraints preclude the exclusion of immigrants from these programs, respectable arguments can be formulated from both the national and global welfare perspectives for immigration policies designed to ensure that immigrants can pay their way.

E. Further notes on pursuit of the national advantage and efficient rationing of the right to immigrate

Whatever the net impact of immigrants upon the country of immigration under current immigration policies, it is interesting to explore further the question of how a nation can employ immigration controls to maximize its national advantage. For example, various devices might be employed to tax away some of the rents earned by immigrants, a policy that is feasible for nations with a degree of "monopsony power." Alternatively, even if the permissible level of immigration is set without reference to any monopsony power of the country of immigration, the manner in which a limited number of entry permits is rationed among those who wish to immigrate can have important efficiency implications from both the national and global perspectives.

1. Monopsony power. In mentioning devices for the extraction of rents from immigrants, I do not mean to advocate them, and in fact some appear quite unseemly. But a discussion of them is nevertheless useful for an understanding of how a nation can maximize its gains from immigration, and as it turns out, these devices are not altogether dissimilar to policies that are in effect today in some countries. Even the United States uses a crude rent extraction device as the basis for allocating a few of its visas for permanent immigrants.[43]

A question that surfaces here once again is whether the welfare of immigrants "counts" in the computation of national welfare immediately upon their arrival, or whether a rent extracted from a prospective immigrant is instead a gain for the nation because the immigrant is excluded from national welfare until some time after any tax or charge is paid. Without advocating any particular position in response, I shall simply proceed on the assumption that a plausible view of the national advantage excludes prospective immigrants until such time as they have actually arrived and "paid the price of admission," if any.

On this assumption, one device for enhancing the national advantage is analogous to the "optimal tariff" in international trade.[44] Because the supply of immigrant labor to a large country like the United States is unlikely to be perfectly elastic, large countries have a degree of monopsony power in the international labor market, which they may choose to exploit. This monopsony power is enhanced if immigration is restricted by other countries, so that potential immigrants cannot readily go elsewhere because of legal impediments. For the simplest case, suppose that immigrant labor is homogeneous, that immigrants supply nothing but labor, and that discrimination across immigrants is infeasible. The private demand for immigrant labor, reflecting the value of its marginal product under competition, is downward-sloping. In the presence of any externalities from immigration, this private demand relation can in principle be adjusted to reflect them, thereby to create a "social demand" curve indicating at each point the wage payment at which the welfare of original residents is unaffected by another immigrant (the social marginal product of immigrant labor). With an upward-sloping supply curve, a marginal cost of labor function lies above the labor supply function, and a monopsony optimum exists where the marginal cost of labor function intersects the social demand function. To reach it, a tax equal to the difference between the supply price of immigrant labor and the marginal cost of immigrant labor at the monopsony optimum might be imposed.[45] Of course, if immigration yields sufficiently large positive externalities, the optimal tax might be negative (a subsidy).

The assumption that immigrant labor is homogeneous is surely incorrect, however, and thus a model involving a single uniform tax on all immigrant workers is too simplistic. Rather, the preceding exercise would at a minimum have to be repeated for different types of immigrant labor, just as the optimal tariff varies across imported goods.

In addition, even greater gains for original residents can be obtained through price discrimination. In the limit, if it were possible to observe the gains to immigration for each immigrant, the optimal tax on each (from the perspective of the original residents) would extract those gains but stop short of discouraging immigration altogether.

These taxes could be imposed in various ways. A tax on wages paid to immigrant workers would suffice, although such a tax regime would have the quality of a discriminatory wage tax based on alienage or national origin, and thus appear particularly unseemly.[46] A charge for "admission" to the country could serve much the same function, and such charges are not unknown in practice.[47] Even a discriminatory charge might be structured in such a way as to avoid offending sensibilities. For example, the immigrant doctor might be charged more than the immigrant farm worker.

Another device is the auction, which has been advocated by some economists in the past (though not necessarily for the purpose of extracting monopsony rents).[48] By computing the number of immigrants that maximizes national welfare and then auctioning that number of entry permits, an auction could roughly replicate the effects of an entry tax. Depending upon how the auction was conducted (whether there were separate entry permits for different categories of immigrants, whether some bidders would pay more than others within a category), it might also allow price discrimination.

Of course, just as with the use of optimal tariffs in trade, the strategic reaction of foreign countries must be considered. Here, however, the likelihood of retaliation seems modest. Earlier analysis suggests that those left behind by emigrants may well lose from emigration, and to that extent they would be unlikely to object to policies that discouraged it. The rents extracted here come mainly at the expense of actual immigrants, and at the expense of a limited group of foreign nationals who would choose to immigrate in the absence of rent extraction policies.

Nevertheless, all these strategies for extracting monopsony rents (save perfect price discrimination), if successful, are potentially detrimental to global welfare notwithstanding their benefits to the country of immigration.[49] Explicit or implicit agreements to eschew such behavior might well be in the global interest. Short of such agreements, however, these policies may indeed promote the national advantage defined as before, and as noted some nations already employ them in one variation or another.

2. *Efficient allocation of a fixed supply of entry permits.* There may well be good reasons not to engage in calculated policies to extract rents from immigrants, both moral and economic. But there may be equally good reasons, associated with negative externalities, for eschewing an open door policy. And in any case, most countries in practice limit immigration. It may not be a bad first approximation at times, therefore, to suppose that the amount of immigration is fixed by exogenous political considerations and to explore the problem of how to ration the fixed number of entry permits as efficiently as possible from the national and global perspectives.

The auction has possible virtue here as well. Even if the number of entry permits to be auctioned is set by noneconomic criteria, the auction mechanism nevertheless distributes them to potential immigrants who are willing to pay the most. In turn, these individuals have the most to gain from immigration and, other things being equal, allowing them to immigrate will tend to maximize global welfare in a "second-best" sense, taking the possibly inefficient restrictions on the total volume of immigration as given. As noted, an auction also allows existing residents to extract rents from immigrants, which may well make them more willing to accept immigration and lead to a relaxation of restrictions that might otherwise hold the volume of immigration to an inefficiently low level.

As before, a fixed charge in lieu of an auction can in principle achieve much the same result. Such a charge need not be calculated to achieve the monopsony optimum, but can instead be set to clear the market at any desired level of immigration. And as with an auction, such a system tends to admit those willing to pay the most and to provide a payment to original residents that may make them more tolerant of immigration. Whether such transfers are viewed as an independent benefit from the national perspective again depends on whether new immigrants "count" in the computation of national welfare before payment of the entry fee.[50]

To be sure, some imperfections would persist under either an auction system or a fixed-charge system. If some of the gains to the migrant are a transfer rather than a social gain, for example, willingness to pay for entry can be distorted upward just as the incentive to migrate is excessive. At least with payment for entry, however, some of the anticipated transfer is recaptured and the problem is ameliorated. Alternatively, if immigration yields a positive externality to original residents that varies across potential immigrants, the possibility arises that a payment system may discourage the immigration of those who would benefit the country of immigration the most. In addition, any payment system may exhibit the usual tension between Hicks–Kaldor efficiency and utilitarianism – those who might appear to have the most to gain from immigration to a utilitarian (perhaps a close family member of an existing resident or a poor refugee) may not exhibit the greatest willingness to pay. These problems might be addressed within an auction or price system by distinguishing categories of immigrants and maintaining a separate auction or price system for each. Categories of immigrants whose immigration is deemed especially desirable for humanitarian reasons might be excluded from the pricing mechanism altogether.

Notwithstanding the possible virtues of a pricing mechanism, however, such devices are fairly uncommon. Most nations nevertheless retain limits upon immigration, and thus some other means for rationing entry must be devised. It is instructive to conclude this section by asking what criteria, other than willingness to pay for entry, will most efficiently ration entry.

Possible considerations in the design of such criteria plainly include the likely earnings capacity of the immigrants. For nations with a progressive tax structure and public safety net programs, immigrants with a greater earnings capacity are more likely to be a net benefit to other residents, other things being equal. Greater earnings capacity may be inferred from information about the immigrant's occupation and from other variables such as education and accumulated wealth.

Another pertinent consideration is age. The young adult who has been educated abroad, and who is many years away from participation in any entitlement programs for the elderly, is more likely to afford a net benefit to other residents as well, other things being equal.

Family reunification and refugee cases suggest two other important factors. Family reunification affords substantial psychic benefits to existing residents, and entry for refugees allows existing residents the satisfaction of an altruistic policy. Although these benefits are difficult to weigh against conventional pecuniary considerations, it is clear that the immigration of family members and refugees confers more benefit upon other residents than the immigration of individuals in neither category, other things being equal.

II. An analysis of U.S. immigration policy

Immigration policy includes not only the law affecting the immigration of permanent residents, but also laws granting temporary entry to workers, students, and others. Policies concerning "illegal" immigration are also at issue. Finally, laws that govern the taxation of immigrants and their rights to par-

ticipate in public safety net and other entitlement programs must be understood as part of the overall immigration policy.

A. Permanent immigration

Although the numerical limits changed significantly with the Immigration Act
of 1990, the basic structure of U.S. immigration law has remained largely
the same for some time. Under U.S. law, an "immigrant" is a person who
comes to the United States with permanent resident status. Such persons may
elect to become citizens thereafter ("naturalization"), but no commitment to
naturalization is required. Although the rights of citizens and permanent resident aliens differ, they are treated similarly by the public sector on most
matters of interest here (taxation, public education, participation in entitlement programs). The major qualification in this regard is that family-
sponsored immigrants are for a time treated as part of the sponsoring family
for purposes of qualifying for some means-tested assistance programs.[51]

After the 1990 act, the nominal ceiling on annual immigration was 700,000
per year through 1994. Of this total, 520,000 visas were for family reunification according to a kinship priority system, 140,000 for employment-based
immigration, 40,000 for a "transitional diversity" program, and some others
for a miscellany of other "transition" programs. The allowable immigration
level was scheduled to fall to 675,000 in 1995, with 480,000 family reunification visas, 140,000 employment-related visas, and 55,000 "diversity"
visas for residents of countries that have been underrepresented in the flow
of U.S. immigrants previously.[52] The actual level of immigration will exceed
these ceilings, however, because refugees are not counted against the ceiling,
and spouses, minor children, and parents of U.S. citizens are allowed to enter
the country in unlimited numbers that count against the family reunification
ceiling only up to a point.[53]

The "diversity" system is new, and in any event modest in size. Consequently, the 1990 act will not significantly change the fundamental system
of immigration that has prevailed for many years: the great majority of immigrants will be relatives of current citizens and permanent residents. And
while the employment-based category was expanded significantly and often
said to have been the primary impetus for the act,[54] employment-based immigration will nevertheless represent only about 20% of total immigration.
Indeed, total employment-based immigration will exceed only modestly the
average number of refugee and asylee immigrants during the 1980s.[55]

1. Family reunification and refugee immigration. The emphasis on family
reunification and the absence of formal restrictions on refugee admissions
under U.S law may be questioned, but arguments against them are hardly
conclusive. Plainly, a system that allows immigration with little regard to any

of the factors that reflect the earning capacity of the immigrants ignores important indicators of possibly inefficient immigration. Recent work by Borjas indicates that under an immigration policy dominated by family reunification for several decades, the average educational skills of U.S. immigrants have declined, and immigrants rely increasingly upon public safety net programs.[56] He further argues that other nations do more to pursue immigrants with greater earning capacity, and thus do better at promoting the national advantage than the United States.

Unquestionably, a policy that allocated the fixed number of visas with greater attention to educational background and similar factors could enhance the skill composition and earning capacity of immigrants, increase their tax payments, and reduce their welfare participation rate. Focusing exclusively on dollar returns from immigration to original residents, therefore, there can be little doubt that an alternative system of priorities would yield higher returns.

Borjas's work indicates, however, that welfare participation rates are not dramatically higher for immigrants than for natives (about 1 percent higher for immigrants as a whole). Total welfare payments to all immigrants in 1988 were only about $2.3 billion.[57] Nothing in his work is inconsistent with the empirical proposition advanced by Simon and others that immigrants as a whole are a source of net gains to the rest of the nation even if those gains might be increased through alternative policies.

Further, and surely most important, any failure to pursue the national advantage measured narrowly in dollars may well be offset by the psychic gains to existing residents from the admission of refugees and family members. This possibility is certainly not subject to disproof.

Over the longer term, to be sure, the possibility arises that the family preference system may allow immigrant groups with high participation rates in transfer programs to grow rapidly through family reunification once they establish a "toehold." The evidence that this problem is now significant is scant, however, and it probably warrants no more than continued monitoring. Further, statutory modifications are a possible response to it should it develop. U.S. law already includes the statutory authority to exclude aliens likely to become a public charge.[58] Because of this provision, families already on welfare will have great difficulty bringing in their relatives. If such measures prove inadequate and some reform appears desirable, perhaps family reunification visas might be conditioned on an extended prior period of satisfactory employment status for current family residents or, alternatively, satisfactory employer sponsorship (as discussed later) for prospective new immigrants of working age.

2. Employment-based immigration. The 1990 act increased the number of employment-based visas to 140,000 per annum from its previous level of

54,000. The total includes dependents. Out of the 140,000 limit, 40,000 visas are allocated to "priority workers." These include persons of "extraordinary ability" who can demonstrate through substantial documentation that they have enjoyed "sustained international acclaim." The legislative history generously allows that sufficient recognition can result from a onetime achievement, such as "receipt of the Nobel prize."[59] "Priority workers" also include "outstanding professors and researchers" who are recognized internationally, and executives and managers who have been employed overseas by an affiliate of a U.S. company. Admission of an individual in the latter two groups requires a petition from the prospective employer. Nobel Prize winners and others of "extraordinary ability" are allowed to look for a job after they arrive (and even to be self-employed, an option denied to most other employment-based immigrants).[60]

Another 40,000 visas are available for "immigrants with advanced degrees" (beyond the bachelor's level) and others of "exceptional ability in the sciences, arts or business." These visas too include a requirement that a job offer be extended before immigration, subject to a waiver in exceptional cases. Because of the fairly stringent requirements under these first two categories, the anticipation is that the visa ceilings here will not be a binding constraint.

The third category of workers, with an allocation of 40,000 visas plus the number of unused visas in the first two categories, is "skilled and unskilled workers." A "skilled worker" must have a bachelor's degree or the ability to perform a job that requires at least two years of training. Only 10,000 visas may be used for "unskilled" workers. All workers in this category require an employer sponsor and a "labor certification." The labor certification is a determination by the Department of Labor that there "are not sufficient workers who are able, willing, qualified, . . . and available" at the place where the alien seeks to work to perform the work in question, and that employment of the alien will not adversely affect the wages and working conditions of other workers.[61]

A fourth category, with 10,000 visas, is reserved for special workers, such as ministers, employees of the embassy in Hong Kong, and several other groups. The fifth category, also with 10,000 visas, is for "foreign investors," who must invest at least $1 million in starting a new enterprise and must thereby create at least ten jobs. Permanent residence in this instance is conditional on maintenance of the investment for at least two years after arrival.[62]

Aside from the few special preferences in the fourth category and a maximum of 10,000 visas in the third, the structure of the preference system is plainly aimed at workers who are relatively skilled or, as in the last category, relatively wealthy. Because such workers are likely to pay higher taxes and are probably less likely to participate in public safety net programs, such an allocation system seems a reasonable method of allocating a fixed number of employment-based visas. The employer sponsorship requirement further reduces the chances that the immigrant will become a drain on other citizens.

The labor certification process, by contrast, has little to commend it. Unless the local labor market is characterized by significant involuntary unemployment, there seems to be little reason to second-guess the judgment of an employer that an alien is best qualified for a position. Compounding the problem is the fact that the Labor Department grants certification not with reference to whether an alien is the most qualified applicant for a position, but with reference to whether workers are available locally who meet the *minimum* requirements for the job. Further, it seems unlikely that labor certification serves any valuable function because of the failure of the labor market at times to clear. In the presence of substantial unemployment, the likelihood that an employer would be inclined to hire someone from abroad seems minimal since the employer can draw on a local pool of labor populated with individuals who can be interviewed personally and whose language skills and work history, for example, are readily verifiable. Nevertheless, the law requires direct notice to affected unions and provides that nonunion employers must post conspicuous notice of the intent to hire an alien so that interested third parties may supply information to the Department of Labor.[63] Thus the likely effect of labor certification is simply to allow domestic workers to exclude competition.

In addition, it is certainly questionable whether *any* ceiling on the number of visas for skilled immigrants with employer sponsorship is in the national interest. As noted, the most obvious concerns about immigrants' ability to pay their way are allayed for this group, and the case for immigration restrictions then becomes highly conjectural. To a lesser degree, one may question whether limitations on the permanent immigration of unskilled workers with employer sponsorship are desirable. One caveat is the possibility that employer sponsorship may be a sham, and indeed that employer sponsors have been in some way bribed to offer it. Ex post checks and penalties seem preferable to up-front exclusions as a solution to this problem, however, and at least when an employer is paid to offer sponsorship there is some capture of rents domestically to offset any possible loss that arises otherwise.

The investor category, added to U.S. law for the first time by the 1990 act, is quite intriguing. Because the ability to invest $1 million perhaps signals scant likelihood that the immigrant will end up on welfare, this criterion for admission has some resonance with the concerns about educational attainment and employer sponsorship that dominate employment-based immigration. The requirement that the immigrant invest considerable sums domestically in a new enterprise, however, is the key feature of this category. From a global welfare perspective, conditioning immigration upon a particular investment pattern seems inefficient – greater gains arise from allowing all factors to migrate to their best use. From the national welfare perspective, however, a requirement of domestic investment as a condition of immigration, given that the returns to capital are taxed (doubly in some instances under the corporate form), may be an implicit device for taxing away some of the rents from immigration and will no doubt yield added benefits to original residents for reasons discussed earlier.

The further requirement that a ''new enterprise'' be formed with at least ten new jobs, however, is more difficult to justify even from the national welfare perspective. Indeed, it would seem that the domestic tax on the immigrant's returns to capital would be maximized by allowing the immigrant to invest domestically wherever the returns are highest. Still greater gains might be realized by simply charging the immigrant a fee for admission, and allowing him to select the best investment opportunity, whether foreign or domestic. Thus, although this category arguably reflects some movement toward an effort to tax away some of the returns to migration, the particular method it employs is suspect and seems impossible to justify short of political constraints that make the superior options infeasible.

B. Temporary workers

U.S. immigration policy is not as restrictive of the ability of employers to purchase labor services from abroad as a focus solely on permanent immigration would suggest. In fact, before the 1990 act, the number of various kinds of temporary or ''nonimmigrant'' workers admitted annually regularly exceeded the number of permanent residents admitted under employment-based criteria.[64]

The visa options for nonimmigrant workers are too complex to be fully described here. The most important categories, however, are three. The E category encompasses treaty traders and investors, the former defined as employees of entities present to conduct ''substantial trade'' with the United States and the latter encompassing individuals needed to direct the operations of an enterprise in which the qualifying entity has invested substantial capital.[65] These individuals must be from a country with a friendship, commerce, and navigation treaty with the United States, or its equivalent, and by definition are sponsored by an existing enterprise. The law imposes no ceiling on the number of such admissions, and in recent years they have considerably exceeded 100,000 per year (including dependents).[66]

The second category of importance is the L category for intracompany transferees, working as managers or executives or having specialized knowledge. These visas allow employees of companies with U.S. operations to bring employees from their foreign operations to the United States for up to six years. Again, the law imposes no ceiling, and on the order of 100,000 new category L visas are issued annually (including dependents).[67]

The third and largest category of nonimmigrant workers is the H category, for "temporary workers." Admissions in this category exceed 100,000 workers (not including dependents) annually.[68] The law divides the category into four components: H-1A – nurses, covered by a separate set of statutory provisions; H-1B – workers in specialty occupations, having a bachelor's degree or higher; H-2A – seasonal agricultural workers; and H-2B – temporary non-agricultural workers in positions that no unemployed residents are capable of performing. The law imposes ceilings for H-1B visas and H-2B visas. It also creates a new requirement for Labor Department certification in the H-1B category, pursuant to which the employer must certify that it will pay aliens the same wage as that paid to other workers of like skill and authority, and that no labor strike or lockout is in progress.[69] A requirement for labor shortage certification was already present for the agricultural subcategory. Obviously, all of these categories require employer sponsorship. The H-1B visa is limited to six years, and the H-2 visas are limited to the duration of the temporary or seasonal work. Admissions under the H-2 categories have been modest in recent years, on the order of 35,000 for the two combined.

Taken as a whole, the temporary worker visas are heavily weighted toward highly skilled or educated workers, and in practice leave few opportunities for the admission of unskilled workers. Admissions in the latter category are for short-term employment, and because of the transaction costs of obtaining a visa coupled with the limited certifications for labor shortages in the agricultural sector, employers often find that these visas are not worth the effort to procure.[70] This was not always so, and in the heyday of the temporary-worker programs many hundreds of thousands of such workers entered the United States annually. A rather dramatic correlation exists between the decline in the admission of temporary agricultural workers (from more than 430,000 in the late 1950s to less than 10 percent of that figure by the mid-1980s) and the rise in the estimated number of undocumented aliens.[71]

Because all of these worker categories require employer sponsorship, it is again difficult to fashion compelling justification for explicit or implicit ceilings (in the form of labor certification and high approval costs) on the number of admissions. Temporary workers are even less likely than permanent immigrants to be a net drain on the public sector, given that these workers pay taxes just like anyone else, federal funds cannot be used to provide them with public safety net benefits,[72] and their right to remain in the country generally depends on continuing employment. Further, for reasons noted earlier in the discussion of permanent immigration, the likelihood that temporary workers would enter in substantial numbers in competition with unemployed domestic workers seems minimal – other things being equal, employers are likely to prefer an unemployed domestic worker whose skills are more readily verifiable and for whom the transaction costs of obtaining a visa are avoidable.[73] An additional argument, as discussed later, is that temporary-worker status is most likely preferable to undocumented status from the national perspective. If current restrictions on temporary visas are indeed producing a larger number of undocumented workers, an even stronger argument can be made for eliminating those restrictions.

A possible objection is that the children of temporary workers born in the United States have citizenship status and become potential burdens on the public treasury. Likewise, the citizen children can petition for family reunification (currently when they reach age 21), and their parents may receive discretionary permission to remain in the country for humanitarian reasons after their visas lapse. These concerns are not without some force, especially as to low-skilled workers in the agricultural sector who may lack the capacity to support themselves and their children once seasonal work terminates. One solution is simply to exclude the spouses of temporary workers in certain categories, or to establish some system whereby expectant families can be expelled during a pregnancy. Both options are harsh on humanitarian grounds, yet they may be better for all concerned than policies that exclude workers with employer sponsorship simply because of the possibility of childbirth while they are present.

C. Undocumented aliens

Estimates of the number of undocumented aliens in the United States vary, but all are in the range of several million. The debate is whether the range is 3–4 million or 5–10 million.[74] A hefty number of undocumented aliens are not Mexican, but are individuals from other nations who entered legally but overstayed their visas. The majority are from Mexico, however, and despite the efforts of the Immigration Reform and Control Act of 1986 to sanction employers who hire undocumented workers, the market for their services remains strong. Apprehensions of individuals attempting to enter illegally remain on the order of 1 million per year.[75]

Undocumented workers tend to be considerably less skilled than workers who enter legally and are no doubt considerably less skilled than those who enter under existing permanent or temporary employment-based visas.[76] Moreover, they are plainly not screened in accordance with the statutory exclusion relating to aliens likely to become a public charge. Not surprisingly, the concern most often expressed about undocumented aliens is that they will in one way or another overwhelm the social services system.

The effects of illegal immigration on the welfare of those legally residing in the United States, however, are by no means clearly unfavorable. Indeed, it is impossible to rule out the possibility that undocumented workers often contribute more to the rest of the population than legal immigrants. Studies reviewed by the Select Commission on Immigration in 1981 concluded that roughly three-fourths of undocumented workers pay Social Security taxes and have federal taxes withheld,[77] and of course as consumers they pay sales taxes. Other studies report even higher percentages of tax withholding and Social Security tax payments by undocumented workers, on the order of 80 to 90%.[78] This is not surprising, since the tax laws make no exception to the obligation of employers to pay payroll taxes or withhold income tax when their workers are undocumented.

In addition, the participation of undocumented workers in old-age entitlement programs is negligible, and indeed any such participation would have to be based on Social Security numbers fraudulently obtained. Public expenditures on educating their children may yield positive net returns to society in the long run, as noted earlier. Likewise, undocumented workers are ineligible for public safety net programs that are supported by federal funds, save for emergency medical care under Medicaid.[79] States are free to provide such assistance on their own, of course, and no doubt some instances of fraud arise. Also, physicians at publicly supported facilities may well provide health care to undocumented workers regardless of the prospect of reimbursement, and in fact medical ethics may require it.[80] But in the end, there is no clear evidence that undocumented aliens as a group are a net drain on the public treasury once their contributions to tax revenues are taken into account.[81]

Even if undocumented workers are a source of net benefit to other residents, however, it does not follow that illegal entry into the United States is not in some ways costly. At a minimum, considerable resources are devoted to the apprehension and deportation of illegals along the Mexican border and to the detection of undocumented workers in the workplace. These expenditures could be reduced if workers desiring employment in the United States could enter readily as temporary workers. An expansion of the temporary-worker program would most likely facilitate better matching of employer needs with employee skills. One can readily imagine the emergence of employment agencies around the globe to perform this function. By contrast, when employers hire illegals, they must search in a potentially thin and possibly clandestine local market in which worker's backgrounds, experience, and work histories are generally unverifiable.

As noted, the fact that temporary workers are ineligible for participation in public safety net programs is by itself perhaps sufficient to eliminate any inefficient incentive to migrate that these programs might otherwise create. If not, a system of employer sponsorship without the need for labor shortage certifications as under current temporary-worker programs would provide a high level of comfort that the worker will be gainfully employed. An expanded temporary-worker program would also make it easier to ensure that migrant workers paid taxes on the same terms as permanent residents. Presently, in cases where employers are willing to hire undocumented workers despite the threat of sanctions, they may also be willing to risk the consequences of omitting them from the payroll for purposes of the payroll tax and tax withholding. The studies already noted suggest that this behavior occurs to some extent, and the consequence is a tax subsidy for hiring the undocumented worker to the extent that the anticipated sanction falls short of the tax savings (as it must or the employer would prefer to comply with the tax laws). A distortion in the hiring decision will then arise.[82]

It must be conceded that, as in the past, temporary workers might be tempted to overstay their visas, then becoming illegal immigrants. It is surely naive to suppose that an expanded temporary-worker program would eliminate illegal immigration. Nevertheless, by allowing employers access to a pool of foreign workers who could be employed legally to perform the tasks now performed by illegals, presumably at comparable wage rates, the demand for illegals' services would decline considerably, and their incentive to come to or remain in the United States would diminish accordingly. Indeed, there is real doubt that existing policies to control the *supply* of illegal workers have any significant impact – particularly with respect to illegal Mexican immigrants, those deported incur little cost by returning at their earliest opportunity. Thus, if illegal immigration is to be reduced, policies to reduce the demand for illegals hold far greater promise.

In sum, although many argue persuasively that permanent immigration should be expanded, an even stronger case can be made for the enhanced availability of nonimmigrant visas for individuals who seek work in the United States. Such expansion might begin by continuing the employer sponsorship feature of current policy while abolishing "labor shortage" and other labor certification requirements. Even employer sponsorship might prove dispensable in the end given the inability of temporary workers to participate in most of the public safety net programs.

If changes along these lines are politically infeasible, then perhaps a reallocation of enforcement resources is in order. Rather than devoting so much energy to the apprehension of workers at the border and to punishing employers who hire them, enforcement efforts might be better directed at preventing welfare fraud and fraud by employers in relation to their tax obligations. As long as undocumented workers are paying taxes and excluded from entitlement programs, as noted, there is no reason to suppose that they are less desirable than other immigrants. Likewise, the analysis here provides no support for increased expenditures on apprehension and deportation.

III. Conclusion

By far the most convincing argument against free immigration from the global efficiency perspective relates to cross-national variation in entitlement programs. There can be no doubt that if wealthy nations extend these programs to new immigrants from poor nations, inefficient migration can result. That inefficiency is compounded at the national level in the country of immigration, where what appears to be a transfer from the global perspective is an efficiency loss from the perspective of the original residents.

Other concerns arise if one embraces the national perspective. The simplest models of immigration suggest that the country of immigration benefits from a finite inflow of immigrants who can then be hired for their marginal product, because their average product will be greater. But terms-of-trade effects and cross-national ownership of other factors make this conclusion uncertain, and the complications increase greatly once the public sector is taken into account. Little can be said with certainty in the end, although in my view a convincing case that immigration is injurious to national economic welfare arises only in the case where immigration also raises concerns from the global perspective – again, when it is driven by cross-national differences in entitlement programs.

It does not follow, however, that an open door to all except prospective welfare recipients is the *best* a nation can do for itself. Just as trade theory suggests ways that individual nations may intervene to promote their selfish interests at the expense of others through devices like the optimal tariff, so does it suggest opportunities for them to do so in factor markets. Immigrants earn rents that can be taken from them without destroying the incentive to migrate.

Yet, although devices for the extraction of rents from immigrants are observed occasionally, the right to immigrate is more often rationed in such a way that allows immigrants to keep most of the rents. That approach is certainly dominant under U.S. law. Hence it does not appear that one can explain most immigration restrictions, such as those in place in the United States, as a purely selfish pursuit of the national advantage. The explanation instead no doubt lies with interest-group politics and a set of positive considerations omitted altogether from the discussion here.

Furthermore, if U.S. immigration policy is to remain a system that allows immigrants to retain the gains from immigration, a strong suspicion arises that higher levels of immigration, particularly of workers with substantial educational attainment or employer sponsorship, would enhance the economic welfare of existing U.S. residents in the aggregate. The present immigration system instead attaches great weight to family reunification, a policy that may have some efficiency justification if one weighs psychic gains heavily, but even then the system proves difficult to justify in its particulars.

Finally, putting aside changes in policy toward permanent immigration, the expanded use of temporary workers could yield substantial benefits to the U.S. economy. As it stands, the tight limits on permanent immigration and the admission of temporary workers have apparently contributed significantly to the growth in the population of undocumented aliens. Although there is no convincing evidence that undocumented workers are a net drain on the rest of the nation, a policy to allow more legal, temporary workers would have considerable merit. Not only would such a policy ameliorate labor market inefficiencies caused by existing restrictions on legal immigration, but it would reduce the demand for the services of illegals and perhaps facilitate a significant reduction in the enforcement resources devoted to the perceived problem of illegal immigration.

Notes

In addition to many valuable comments from the participants in the Justice in Immigration Conference, I have received thoughtful comments from Lucian Bebchuk, Alan Deardorff, David Friedman, Louis Kaplow, Gerald Neuman, A. Mitchell Polinsky, Eric Rasmusen, and Warren Schwartz and from workshop participants at Harvard University and New York University. I am grateful to the Olin Foundation for financial support.
1 An agreement on trade in services may have ancillary implications for the temporary immigration of professionals in covered sectors, but is not likely to affect the ability of foreign workers to obtain employment from domestic employers or their ability to obtain permanent residence or citizenship. See GATT Secretariat, "Final Act Embodying the Results of the Uruguay Round of Multilateral Trade Negotiations, Annex IB (Trade in Services)" (1994) ("annex on movement of natural persons providing services under the agreement").
2 Recent developments within the European Community afford an exception. See N. Green, T. Hartley, and J. Usher, *The Legal Foundations of the Single European Market* (New York: Oxford University Press, 1991), 91–196.
3 An extended discussion of the ethical significance of "efficiency," including a development of the utilitarian argument and its caveats, can be found in D. Friedman, *Price Theory* (Cincinnati, Ohio: South Western, 1990), 440–5. Another interesting treatment is that of M. Polinsky, "Probabilistic Compensation Criteria," *Quarterly Journal of Economics* 86 (1971): 407.
4 A recent study of world hunger, for example, argues that restrictions on the ability of workers to emigrate from developing countries contributes greatly to the perpetuation of hunger in those countries. See Kirit Parikh, "Chronic Hunger in the World: Impact of International Policies," in Jean Dreze and Amartya Sen (eds.), *The Political Economy of Hunger* (New York: Oxford University Press, 1990), 1: 114, 140–2.

5 See G. Borjas, *Friends or Strangers: The Impact of Immigrants on the U.S. Economy* (New York: Basic Books, 1990), 79–96; J. Abowd and R. Freeman (eds.), *Immigration, Trade and the Labor Market* (Chicago: NBER, 1991), 167–320.

6 The argument for free trade is again illustrative: Hicks–Kaldor efficiency from the global perspective generally supports free trade, while Hicks–Kaldor efficiency from the national perspective may support such measures as the "optimal tariff," a device for the exploitation of national monopsony power by large trading nations at the expense of trading partners.

7 For a factor price equalization result in the simplest of Heckscher–Ohlin models, see P. Kenen, *The International Economy* (Englewood Cliffs, N.J.: Prentice-Hall, 1985), 73–7. More complex models with many factors and commodities are discussed in A. Dixit and V. Norman, *Theory of International Trade* (Cambridge University Press, 1980), 110–25; W. Ethier, "Higher Dimensional Issues in Trade Theory," in J. R. Jones and P. Kenen (eds.), *Handbook of International Economics* (Amsterdam: North Holland, 1984), 1: 131.

8 Models in which the distorting effects of a tariff are undone by factor flows are well known in the literature. See, e.g., J. Bhagwati and T. N. Srinivasan, *Lectures on International Trade* (Cambridge, Mass.: MIT Press, 1983), 291–2.

9 The exception is Section I,D below, in which I discuss the possibility that certain public sector policies, some of which are distorting, may be endogenous to migration policy.

10 Of course, in Ricardian trade models, two or more end products exist and trade occurs to allow each nation to exploit its technological comparative advantage. The single-end-product assumption would make no sense in a trade model, but does no violence here where trade is not at issue.

11 See E. Helpman and P. Krugman, *Market Structure and Foreign Trade* (Cambridge, Mass.: MIT Press, 1985), 204–5; P. Krugman, *Rethinking International Trade* (Cambridge, Mass.: MIT Press, 1990), 20–1. In Krugman's model, however, the "wrong" country may grow to the detriment of world welfare.

12 See J. Simon, *The Economic Consequences of Immigration* (Oxford: Basil Blackwell, 1990), 167–82. Simon argues that population increase allows economies of scale to be realized through greater specialization of the work force, but his empirical evidence is, in my view, weak. He first argues that more populous developing countries have higher labor productivity rates, but this fact is consistent with causation running in the other direction, or with the explanation relating to a number of omitted variables (e.g., large countries may have more liberal trading regimes because they have participated to a greater extent in reciprocal trade negotiations, and they may also have attracted considerably greater foreign investment per capita). He also shows that productivity in the developed world has grown over time along with population, but again the causal relation is hardly clear – technical progress may have raised living standards and encouraged population growth, or may have occurred at much the same rate irrespective of population growth. Finally, he refers to the well-documented learning-by-doing phenomenon in certain industries, but the cases he mentions (airplanes, color tel-

evisions, air conditioners) are all exportables, so that demand will be much the same regardless of the number of domestic consumers. Likewise, there is no reason to suppose that any desirable expansion of the labor force in these industries could not occur through a contraction of other domestic industries where scale economies are absent.

13 See Kenen, *International Economy*, 65–77, for an elementary exposition.

14 See ibid., 75–7.

15 Though the exposition here differs, the result is a standard one from the economic literature on immigration. See, e.g., A. Berry and R. Soligo, "Some Welfare Aspects of International Migration," *Journal of Political Economy* 77 (1969): 778; D. Usher, "Public Property and the Effects of Migration upon Other Residents of the Migrants' Countries of Origin and Destination," *Journal of Political Economy* 85 (1977): 1001.

16 A simple diagrammatic exposition of this argument can be found in Bhagwati and Srinivasan, *Lectures on International Trade,* 304–7.

17 The extensive literature on the "brain drain," inquiring whether the emigration of skilled professionals from the developing world may injure those nations, began as an outgrowth of this simple model. A number of essays on the brain drain can be found in J. Bhagwati, *Essays in International Economic Theory*, Vol. 2: *International Factor Mobility*, ed. R. Feenstra (Cambridge, Mass.: MIT Press, 1983), and in J. Bhagwati (ed.), *The Brain Drain and Taxation* (New York: North Holland, 1976).

18 The original insights on these matters stem from the literature on "immiserizing growth." See Bhagwati and Srinivasan, *Lectures on International Trade*, 249–60; Dixit and Norman, *Theory of International Trade*, 133–7.

19 A survey of much of the pertinent literature can be found in J. Bhagwati and J. Rodriguez, "Welfare Theoretical Analyses of the Brain Drain," *Journal of Developmental Economics* 2 (1975): 195; reprinted in Bhagwati, *Essays in International Economic Theory*. A model of migration with terms-of-trade effects is also developed in Dixit and Norman, *Theory of International Trade*, 146–9.

20 Nonconvexities in production are another possibility. See Krugman, *Rethinking International Trade*. Likewise, one can no doubt imagine various scenarios involving the exercise of monopoly power by a nation in which either immigration or emigration might affect its ability to earn monopoly rents.

21 See, e.g., Usher, "Public Property."

22 On the possible explanations for "involuntary" unemployment, see G. Akerlof and J. Yellen, *Efficiency Wage Models of the Labor Market* (Cambridge University Press, 1986); L. Summers, *Understanding Unemployment* (Cambridge, Mass.: MIT Press, 1990).

23 See Simon, *Economic Consequences*, 182–3.

24 These taxes include those nominally paid by employers of a migrant, such as payroll taxes.

25 Even when taxes and government benefits balance, of course, the incentive to migrate will not be "first best" because of the labor–leisure choice distortion and any other distortions attributable to the method of raising government revenue. I

put such complications to one side on the assumption that any appropriate policy responses lie elsewhere.

26 Whether medical care that is provided charitably might be a source of a negative externality is an interesting question. Although the burden of the poor on charitable hospitals may be considerable, the fact that care is provided at no charge perhaps suggests that the care providers (medical personnel who work for free or who are supported by charitable donors) gain more psychically from the provision of care than it costs them to provide it. Thus any extra burden of immigrants upon charitable providers of medical care and other benefits seems to be a source of positive rather than negative externalities. The only counterargument, rather unseemly at that, is that the providers of charitable services do not care about anyone except those whom they encounter personally or who are local residents, so that suffering abroad has no psychic cost to them.

27 There is good reason to believe that this circumstance has arisen at times in the past for the Social Security system as a whole, and especially for lower-income participants. See generally T. Marmor and J. Mashaw (eds.), *Social Security: Beyond the Rhetoric of Crisis* (Princeton, N.J.: Princeton University Press, 1988); C. Weaver (ed.), *Social Security's Looming Surpluses* (Washington, D.C.: AEI, 1990).

28 457 U.S. 202 (1982).

29 See Usher, "Public Property."

30 The only offsetting benefit to the original residents in Usher's framework is that mentioned in Section I,A – the marginal product of labor falls due to immigration, and the rest of the population gains something because immigrants are paid their marginal product, which is less than their average product. But this gain is dwarfed by the migrants' ability to appropriate a share of returns to capital.

31 See Simon, *Economic Consequences,* 143–64.

32 The exclusion of public education might seem a glaring omission, except that if immigrant children are expected to remain in the country and to pay back their educational subsidy in future years through taxes, the education subsidy will later be recovered.

33 A useful review of the empirical evidence, with further references to the literature, can be found in Simon, *Economic Consequences,* 105–42. A brief discussion of the effect of immigrants upon net public revenues can also be found in P. Lindert, *International Economics,* 9th ed. (Homewood, Ill.: Irwin, 1991), 541–2.

34 The right to vote in the United States, for example, is typically restricted to citizens. Permanent residents are allowed to become citizens, however, and thus under current U.S. policy, virtually all permanent immigrants can obtain the franchise if they so choose in reasonably short order. See L. Tribe, *Constitutional Law,* 2d ed. (Minneapolis: West, 1988), 1545.

35 See Chapter 3, by Buchanan, this volume.

36 See M. Pauly, "Income Redistribution as a Local Public Good," *Journal of Public Economics* 2 (1978): 35.

37 Ibid.

38 A more general formulation of the problem might specify that $p = p(w)$ without

immigration restrictions, and model immigration controls as the altruist's choice
of p subject to the constraints $p^* \leq p \leq p(w)$.

39 I have also encountered a number of arguments for domestic redistribution to a
limited population that seem fallacious. For example, it is possible that the affluent
would prefer that a certain minimum standard of living be achieved by the beneficiaries of transfer programs. A plausible basis for this preference would be a
belief that the marginal utility of wealth to the poor is locally increasing – perhaps
it does more good to give 10 poor families $100 than to give 10,000 families a
penny. If so, a case could be made for restricting the size of the transferee population. But an argument for immigration restrictions does not follow, because on
this information alone it would do just as well to give the $100 to 10 foreign
families as to 10 domestic families.

40 See Tribe, *Constitutional Law*, 1380–4.

41 Ibid., 1544–5.

42 Most legally resident aliens may become citizens after five years by taking an
oath of allegiance, renouncing other allegiances where allowed by foreign law and
demonstrating English language proficiency. See generally 8 U.S.C. § 1421 et.
seq.

43 See Section II,A.

44 On the use of optimal tariffs see, e.g., Dixit and Norman, *Theory of International
Trade*, 168–75.

45 The diagram is so familiar that I omit it. A discussion of a labor market mon-
opsonist can be found in J. Henderson and R. Quandt, *Microeconomic Theory*, 3d
ed. (New York: McGraw-Hill, 1980), 190–2.

46 Indeed, under U.S. law, such a tax would most likely be unconstitutional unless
imposed at the federal level. See generally Tribe, *Constitutional Law*, 1544 et.
seq. and cases cited therein (especially *Mathews v. Diaz*). The legal difficulties
would be compounded insurmountably for any tax imposed on immigrants after
they became naturalized, but an up-front charge for admission would not be subject to this problem.

47 See Borjas, *Friends or Strangers,* 226. The nation of Belize, for example, at one
time allowed the purchase of citizenship through the posting of a $25,000 bond,
half nonrefundable. See Simon, *Economic Consequences,* 146. And a number of
countries (including the United States) allow immigration based on the prospect
of the immigrant making a substantial investment in the domestic economy. This
device for rationing entry bears a close relation to charging for admission, as
discussed further later.

48 See, e.g., Simon, *Economic Consequences,* 329–35. An early auction proposal
was made in unpublished work by Gary Becker, and has recently been reiterated
by Becker in ''An Open Door for Immigrants: The Auction,'' *Wall Street Journal*,
October 14, 1992.

49 I say ''potentially,'' because it is by no means self-evident that such schemes
would be worse than existing policies.

50 If the concept of payments for entry seems peculiar, note that the argument in
their favor is analogous to the argument for the use of tariffs or auctioned quotas

in international trade instead of conventional quotas. When a market is protected from foreign competition, price rises and a "rent" exists relative to the competitive price. A quota system, administered so that foreign suppliers hold the right to import a limited quantity, allows them to capture this rent. A tariff or auctioned quota, by contrast, allows the domestic treasury to capture the rent, and thus the adverse effect of protection upon national welfare diminishes.

Similarly, immigration restrictions exist in part as protection for factors of production that are close substitutes for those supplied by immigrants, and a policy of rationing entry allows those who immigrate to collect the resulting rent. An auction or other system that charges for entry can capture part or all of that rent for the national treasury.

51 See Borjas, *Friends or Strangers*, 155.
52 See generally S. Yale Loehr (ed.), *Understanding the Immigration Act of 1990* (Washington, D.C.: Federal Publications, 1991), 1-1–1-4.
53 Ibid.
54 See H. Sklar and S. Flinsky, *The Immigration Act of 1990 Handbook* (1991), 3-1.
55 From 1985 to 1992 the average number of refugees and asylees granted permanent resident status per annum was approximately 101,000. See *Statistical Yearbook of the Immigration and Naturalization Service* (Washington, D.C.: U.S. Government Printing Office, 1988), 63 (hereafter *INS Yearbook*).
56 See Borjas, *Friends or Strangers*, 156–62.
57 Ibid., 160.
58 See 8 U.S.C. § 1182(a) & § 1255a.
59 See H.R. Rep. 101-723, Part I, 101st Cong. 2d Sess., at 59 (1990).
60 See 8 U.S.C. § 1153.
61 See 8 U.S.C. § 1182(a)(5).
62 See 8 U.S.C. § 1153(b)(5).
63 See Loehr (ed.) *Understanding the Immigration Act of 1990,* 3-9
64 See *INS Yearbook,* table 40. As indicated in the text, my use of the term "temporary worker" does not correspond precisely to a single immigration category, but rather is meant to refer to workers under several types of visas that are permitted to remain as long as they remain appropriately employed or until a visa of fixed duration expires.
65 8 U.S.C. § 1101(a)(15)(E).
66 See *INS Yearbook,* table 44.
67 Ibid.
68 Ibid.
69 8 U.S.C. § 1184.
70 See generally Hearing on Proposal to Amend the Immigration and Nationality Act, House Committee on Education and Labor, Subcommittee on Labor Standards, 98th Cong., 1st Sess., April 13, 1983.
71 See ibid., 27–28; *INS Yearbook,* table 40. I am hardly the first to notice this correlation. See e.g., B. Chiswick, "Illegal Immigration and Immigration Control," *Journal of Economic Perspectives* 2 (1988): 101.

72 See note 79 below. The exception is unemployment insurance.
73 This argument rests on an assumption that the legal requirements affecting em-
    ployers of domestic workers – such as the minimum wage – would apply equally
    to employers of temporary immigrants.

    The argument here is not undermined by the possibility that temporary immi-
    grant workers may have a lower reservation wage than domestic workers who
    might fill the same positions. If so, it is in general efficient from both the national
    and global perspectives for the domestic workers to seek employment elsewhere.
    The caveat is that inefficiency may arise where the higher reservation wage for
    domestic workers is attributable to some distortion of the labor–leisure choice
    decision, such as subsidized unemployment insurance.
74 A review of the empirical estimates and estimating techniques can be found in
    Borjas, *Friends or Strangers,* 61–6.
75 See *INS Yearbook,* table 59.
76 See Simon, *Economic Consequences,* 287; Borjas, *Friends or Strangers,* 69.
77 See *Staff Report, Select Commission on Immigration and Refugee Policy* (1981).
    The evidence is also reviewed in Simon, *Economic Consequences,* 289.
78 See Hearing on Immigration Reform and Control Act of 1983, House Committee
    on Energy and Commerce, Subcommittee on Health and the Environment, 98th
    Cong., 1st Sess., at 116 et. seq. (1983) (henceforth cited as Hearing).
79 See 42 U.S.C. § 1396b(v) (Medicaid benefits limited to emergency care); 42
    U.S.C. § 602(a)(33) (Aid to Families with Dependent Children); 42 U.S.C. §
    1436a (public housing assistance); 26 U.S.C. § 3304(14)(A) (unemployment in-
    surance limited to legal aliens, permanent or temporary); 7 U.S.C. § 2015(t) (food
    stamps).
80 Expenditures on health care for undocumented workers are probably the greatest
    component of social expenditures on their behalf and are sometimes said to be
    quite large. See, e.g., statement of Dr. Martin Finn, in Hearing, 110–11. Finn
    asserts that in fiscal year 1982–3 the Los Angeles County Department of Health
    Services incurred unreimbursed costs of $99.5 million for health care to undoc-
    umented aliens. The basis for this assertion is not made clear. On whether the
    consumption of charitable services by aliens should be viewed as a negative ex-
    ternality, see note 26 above.
81 The literature is reviewed at some length by Simon in *Economic Consequences,*
    288–96.
82 Of course, if undocumented workers presently pay considerably more in taxes
    than they receive in benefits, the argument can be made that some reduction in
    their tax burden is desirable and that without it too few of them will be hired.
    But the current system, under which many of them pay taxes at the usual rates
    while others pay none, is hardly an appropriate correction. Furthermore, from the
    national perspective, a requirement that they pay taxes in excess of public benefits
    received may be a beneficial device for rent extraction.

9

Just borders

Normative economics and immigration law

GILLIAN K. HADFIELD

First off, a disclosure: I am an immigrant. And I am a Canadian. This brings me to the topic of the economics of immigration law with two, at times competing perspectives. First, my inclination is to view immigration law from the perspective of one who has in fact migrated, at least temporarily, and not out of a desire to improve my lot in life or change my nationality. This perspective tends to make the boundary between "native" and "immigrant" seem unimportant, annoying, arrogant, the product of selfish impulses to hoard and protect resources. Second, however, I admit to nationalistic moments not unusual among Canadians and generally aroused by discussions not of immigration but of trade policy. This perspective tends to make borders seem vital, constitutive, culture-defining, the product of a desire to protect a vision of social life and justice from the fray of competition. I mention all of this at the outset because the framework for a welfare economic analysis of immigration law that I will suggest in this essay, although defensible in more objective terms, is nonetheless informed by these perspectives.

I. Positive and normative welfare economics

To approach the "welfare economics of immigration law," it is necessary first to enter upon a historical debate among welfare economists: Is welfare economics a positive or a normative enterprise? The minority view sees welfare economics as an exercise in working through the positive implications of a change in the status quo for a given criterion, specifically an efficiency criterion.[1] According to this view, welfare economists merely inquire into whether a policy proposal will in fact increase the range of choices available to some without decreasing the range available to others. While economists may call an increase in the range of choice an increase in "welfare," proponents of this view argue, this choice of language should not be understood to reflect deeper normative claims. Having nothing to contribute to the normative justification of the efficiency criterion, welfare economists *qua* economists do not take the further step of *recommending* the adoption of a policy proposal based on the outcome of the positive analysis. All they can do is offer the results of their work to those who do make normative recommendations.

The majority of welfare economists, however, have rejected the claim that welfare economics involves only positive analysis. Welfare economics makes distinctive normative claims about human well-being. Most fundamentally, economists contribute to normative debate on the basis of the essential claim that the welfare of "society" is to be determined by aggregating individual subjective welfare. To do welfare economics is to take the stand that social welfare resides not in abstract entities like "a country" but in individuals and that the individual provides the metric for his or her own well-being.

The normative nature of welfare economics is reflected in the exclusive focus on two individualistic normative criteria against which welfare economists assess proposed changes in the status quo. The first is the completely familiar Pareto criterion. Understood in its narrowest sense (which is not the sense in which it is always applied), the Pareto criterion recommends a change in the status quo in a circumstance in which at least one person, by his or her own lights, is made better off by the change and no one worse off. The Pareto criterion is not a complete normative system. Rejecting the possibility of interpersonal comparisons of utility, it has nothing to say about changes that do make some individuals worse off. When each is sovereign over the evaluation of his or her own welfare, there is no metric by which to calculate whether one's losses are outweighed by another's gains. This metric can be provided only by a social welfare function, and economists *qua* economists do not adopt or defend a particular social welfare function except to argue that it should satisfy the Pareto criterion.[2]

The Pareto criterion, it has long been recognized, is of limited practical use in normative debates. Since the great majority of proposed changes to the status quo *do* involve losses to some, and since ordinarily there is no exogenously given social welfare function to apply, the welfare economist is left either mute or searching for an alternative normative criterion with which to practice his or her art. Economists have largely opted for the latter, adopting a modification of the Pareto criterion. This modification, the Kaldor–Hicks efficiency criterion, recommends a change in the status quo if the change could *potentially* make at least one person better off and no one worse off, even if in fact some are made worse off. The Kaldor–Hicks criterion recognizes that, conceivably at least, even though we cannot compare absolute levels of well-being, we can measure – in some numeraire, usually dollars – an individual's subjective gain or loss. The Pareto criterion would recommend any Kaldor–Hicks-approved change to which was appended the requirement that gainers give to losers an amount that losers perceive will compensate them for their losses. The Kaldor–Hicks criterion merely recommends that as long as gainers would be willing to do this if they had to, the change should be made in any event. If a society judges that the Pareto requirement of compensation is the only defensible normative position, then it can simply accomplish the necessary compensation through its tax and subsidy policies. Alternatively, society can select some other stance with respect to redistribution as determined by its social welfare function.[3]

I have belabored these familiar points about welfare economics in order to make obvious the normative content of welfare economics. Economists contribute to normative debate by their defense of the Pareto or Kaldor–Hicks criterion as a standard against which to judge the ethical implications of policies. Proponents of the Pareto criterion defend it as a largely noncontroversial ethical stance, especially when it is used only to recommend changes that give rise to Pareto improvement – and not to recommend against changes that involve a loss in welfare to some – and only to assess proposed changes that do not have a significant impact on values not captured in the "goods" allocated to each individual.[4] The Kaldor–Hicks criterion retains the noncontroversial status of Pareto to the extent that it can be paired with simultaneous redistribution to achieve the Pareto outcome. It becomes a highly contestable normative stance, however, if it is interpreted to mean that redistribution is unnecessary: all that matters is aggregate welfare and not its distribution.

In most cases of applied welfare economics, these normative claims are implicit and in such a setting the distinction between positive and normative welfare economics is minor indeed: yes, yes, I think Kaldor–Hicks efficiency is the appropriate ethical basis for making policy recommendations; now let's get on to the positive analysis of whether minimum wages/patent licensing/ excuse doctrines in contract law will be Kaldor–Hicks improvements. The claim I want to develop in this essay, however, is that when we turn to the normative economic analysis of immigration law, we have to reconsider explicitly the normative justification for the criteria on which we rely for conducting our positive analysis. It is when an analysis fails to give a normative defense of the criteria against which it assesses the "welfare" implications of immigration law that I would characterize the analysis as "positive." As I will explore, however, if we do engage directly the normative questions conventionally left implicit in applied welfare economics, we are led to see some difficulties in the standard defense of the Pareto and Kaldor–Hicks criteria in the immigration context. We are also led to a fundamentally different perspective on how an adequate social welfare function might be constructed for purposes of answering normative questions about immigration law.

II. Who counts? The logical priority of immigration law

At first the normative question raised with respect to immigration law appears to be, Who should we let in? But if we press on this characterization of the issue, I think we will see that it begs a deeper question: Who are "we"? From the perspective of distributive justice, letting someone "in" is fundamentally about giving him or her access to resources: those distributed through markets (including not only consumer goods but also the resources that increase the productivity of labor or ideas), those distributed through governments, and those, like clean air and military defense, available to all within their reach as a consequence of their nonexcludability. "We" are the ones who have access to these resources and thus "we" are the product of some immigration policy.

In the context of doing normative welfare economics, we can make this point sharper. The essential idea is this: immigration policy, the existence of borders that mark some as insiders and others as outsiders, is *logically prior* to the normative defense of conventional welfare analysis.[5] Both the Pareto and the Kaldor–Hicks criteria require the welfare economist to assess the impact of a proposed change in the status quo on the well-being of a set of individuals. This presupposes the definition of the set, that is, an answer to the very normative question we are asking: Who is in and who is out? Whose losses, whose gains count? From the perspective of positive welfare analysis, there is, of course, nothing wrong with presupposing this answer. But if our objective is to contribute as economists to the debate on the underlying normative question, it is simply incoherent to proceed on the basis of a social welfare function that reflects an a priori judgment about who is entitled to a share in society's resources.

This is the problem I have in calling an analysis of optimal immigration policy that adopts the perspective of "original" residents in a country "welfare economics."[6] The Pareto criterion with respect to original residents recommends a change in immigration policy even if it imposes losses on potential immigrants. The Kaldor–Hicks criterion with respect to original residents does not ask whether the losses for potential immigrants are potentially compensable. A social welfare function defined over original residents presumes rather than demonstrates that original residents are the people among whom resources should be distributed.[7] While coherent as a form of positive analysis, this is obviously inadequate as a contribution to the normative debate about ethically defensible policy with respect to immigration. The lines we draw to define our social welfare functions are not just borders.

The normative significance of the definition of the social welfare function we use as the basis for assessing immigration policy is highlighted if we imagine the adoption in other policy settings of social welfare functions analogous to the "original residents" function adopted in some analyses of immigration. Consider the following. The bulk of empirical research on immigration in the United States, adopting a form of the "original residents" welfare function, focuses on the impact of immigration on the wages and employment of "native" Americans as a result of an increase in the labor force.[8] Now, immigration, of course, is not the only potential source of increased labor supply; in recent decades, an increasing number of women and baby boomers have joined the labor force. And in fact these latter sources of increased labor supply swamp immigration by at least a factor of 10: "New immigrants of all ages contributed only 2.5 million extra persons to the labor force [in the 1970s], compared with the concomitant increase of 20 million workers aged 32 or less that was caused by the baby boom and increased labor force participation by young women."[9] How are we to assess the desirability of women's entry into the labor force or the growth in domestic population? It is immediately apparent that to approach either of these questions with a social welfare function that reflects the well-being of men alone or current workers alone is to assume away the ethical issues raised. This is precisely why a social welfare function that focuses exclusively on the impact of immigration on current residents cannot be the basis for the economist's participation in a normative debate on immigration.

III. "Global" social welfare

If economists are to participate in the normative debate over immigration, it seems to me that there can be no starting point other than a global social welfare function. Only a welfare function in which everyone at least potentially counts avoids the question begging raised by a national social welfare function. For observe that adopting the global social welfare function is not, for the economist, equivalent to taking the ethical stance that every citizen is entitled to a share in global resources. Just as the national social welfare function may attach zero weight to the welfare of some of the nation's citizens, so may the global welfare function discount the welfare of those who do not matter in some ethical frame. All that the normative welfare economist requires is that the relatively noncontroversial status of the Pareto or Kaldor–Hicks criterion remain intact and that there be no a priori restriction on distribution policy.

It is, however, a controversial form of the Kaldor–Hicks criterion that comes into play in an analysis that assesses the global welfare implications of immigration policy on the basis of international trade models.[10] First, as a matter of practice, international trade models address the question of whether free trade in products expands the production possibilities set. They do not address distribution. More important, as a theoretical matter, distri-

bution takes on a wholly different aspect when trade is of factors rather than
of products.

The welfare analysis of international trade, explicitly done in a "global"
context, asks the question: Will a reduction in trade barriers result in gains
to trade between two countries? The defense of free trade rests on the demonstration that both *countries*, independently, gain from the reduction of
barriers. A move to freer trade satisfies a national Kaldor–Hicks criterion:
gainers *in each country* could satisfy the losers among their compatriots. The
broad normative appeal of this analysis rests on the feasibility of internal
redistribution, if it is thought to be ethically required, to compensate for the
losses some might suffer as a result of increased trade.

In the immigration context, however, the focus on the aggregate welfare
impact on each country lacks this normative justification. Welfare resides not
in "countries" but in the individuals who are counted in countries. Factor
migration can have net negative consequences for those left behind in the
country of emigration; and clearly immigration restrictions have negative
consequences for those who, but for the restrictions, would migrate. Unless
one wishes to adopt the strong form of Kaldor–Hicks – distribution doesn't
matter – it is necessary to give some account of how the redistribution called
for by Pareto or some other distributive criterion will be accomplished. Often
the decision to ignore the distributional consequences of immigration is justified by the standard appeal to tax policy as the appropriate locus of distribution. This overlooks, however, the point that international, and not merely
domestic, distributional consequences arise. But unlike domestic redistribution, global redistribution, as a matter of fact, is plainly not a significant part
of our world order. A failure to give an account of global redistribution, then,
leaves one, normatively speaking, stranded on a rather lonely island where
the ultimate distribution of wealth is morally irrelevant.[11]

If we consider the matter more closely, it becomes apparent that this is not
simply an observation about current policy with respect to global redistribution through, for example, foreign aid or debt repayment subsidies. Rather,
it goes to the heart of our understanding of what a conventional social welfare
function represents. As Kenneth Arrow's work has emphasized, at its most
basic level welfare economics is about the political aggregation of individual
preferences. The social welfare function is the result of some decision process, such as majority voting, which accomplishes this aggregation. And although it is easy to overlook this fact in the standard domestic context, we
assume that this decision process takes place within a political jurisdiction
with the power to fashion binding rules. In Arrow's terms, "The fundamental
problem of public value formation is the construction of constitutions" where
"a constitution is a rule which associates to each possible set of individual
orderings a social choice function, that is, a rule for selecting a preferred

action out of every possible environment.''[12] The commitment inherent in the concept of a rule is essential here. For if the function is not binding (at least as long as it takes to carry out some particular policy change), then the social decision process collapses into one that violates Arrow's own claim that a proper social welfare function cannot be characterized by dictatorship: without commitment, the social welfare function simply selects the preferred action of some subset of individuals such as the executives of public policy. Clearly, to derive judgments about optimal social policy on the basis of a dictatorial welfare function is to roam far from the safety of the relatively noncontroversial claims welfare economists ordinarily make.

The difficulty in the Kaldor–Hicks approach to global welfare, then, stems from the absence of global political jurisdiction and thus the difficulty of presuming that global redistribution can be separated without significant normative consequence from the maximization of aggregate global welfare. The global structures are simply not in place to enforce the redistribution that a Pareto or other criterion of distributive justice might require.

IV. Toward a positive political economy approach to immigration law

I have argued that unless economists wish to abandon their reliance on relatively noncontroversial claims in their contribution to the normative debate on immigration, they must begin with a social welfare function that, at least potentially, counts the individual welfare of every citizen of the globe. Moreover, in the absence of a binding global political process that we could treat as presumptively legitimate, economists must confront directly the normative legitimacy of a particular social welfare function.

I want to suggest in this final section a framework for developing an economic contribution to the normative analysis of immigration law. Starting from the global perspective on social welfare but presuming the infeasibility of binding international agreements, the question we can ask is, What restrictions on immigration would the citizens of a hypothetical global society choose to achieve their productive and redistributive goals with respect to global resources? The question, of course, raises a bevy of further questions concerning the form and legitimacy of the process out of which this choice might emerge. I wish, however, to leave those normative questions to the political philosophers and to focus on what an economist might be able to contribute, particularly one who drew as much as possible on conventional welfare economics and the emerging fields of organizational theory and positive political economy. In what follows I do not profess to provide any kind of definitive contribution myself to the solution of this hypothetical problem, which in any event seems too large a project for one person. But I do wish to offer a few conjectures.

The first question seemingly raised by the hypothetical is, Why borders at all? Why are we not all truly citizens of the earth? One answer is immediate: borders economize on the costs of administering a political system.[13] If the political process is intended to be a method of aggregating individual preferences to determine and then to execute policy, there conceivably are limits to doing so. We can take this idea further. Developing policy requires not only the collection of information about preferences, but also the collection of information about possibilities. The actual costs of collecting such information may be lower for those close to the territorial site of policy. (For example, the development of optimal waste disposal policy may depend on the relative availability of land versus the cost of incineration in a particular locality, and this information may be more cheaply obtained by individuals living in the region than those at a distance.) Moreover, there are the bureaucratic costs of executing policy, many of which increase with the size of the territory over which authority is exercised. For as the scale of territorial authority increases, so do the layers in a bureaucracy that bring with them the loss of information as it is transmitted both to and from the central authority.

But it is possible to imagine borders created for such administrative purposes that impose no immigration restrictions whatsoever. What would such a world look like? Obviously, there would be no constraints on physical migration. More important, however, there would be no legal constraint on participation in territorial political processes.[14] Indeed, assuming that the ultimate distribution of resources falling within physical borders will be governed by a territorial social welfare function,[15] the limits on political participation that determine whose interests will be counted in the function are the most important features of immigration law from an economic perspective. The interesting observation here is that it does not follow from the fact that a social welfare function is territorial (in the sense that it determines the distribution of resources falling within physical boundaries) that political participation is territorial also. We must be careful not to overlook the theoretical possibilities that may escape us because we in fact live in a world where borders are overwhelmingly territorial. Borders controlling access to resources are relational but the relations they establish need not, in theory, be territorially based. They may as feasibly exist in the abstract as on the ground.

Once we begin to recognize that our hypothetical global citizens have more to decide than simply where to draw lines on a map – they must determine the importance of those lines for resource use and distribution – we open a new basis for inquiry into immigration restrictions. By restricting access to the political process to a subset of individuals, we allow diversity in social welfare functions. Policies may be tailored to address the needs of majorities and minorities, which majorities and minorities come into definition through the drawing of a boundary. Various groups may make different trade-offs between production and redistribution. The immigration question becomes, How permeable are the boundaries of these groups? Who may join? Who may participate in the production and distribution scheme created?

One of the more interesting issues raised here concerns the strategic incentives of political groups to adopt various production/redistribution policies. It is not clear a priori which way these incentives will cut in the face of differing immigration policies. On the one hand, particularly in light of the empirical evidence which suggests that high-skill individuals migrate from more to less egalitarian systems of income distribution, whereas low-skill individuals migrate from less to more egalitarian systems,[16] it would seem that immigration restrictions may be necessary to protect the incentives to promote productive efficiency and distributional equity. On the other hand, it also seems possible that immigration restrictions, because they hamper *emigration*, would dull the incentives of some countries to achieve productive efficiency and distributional equity: those exploited by a highly unequal distribution and therefore suffering the consequences of low productivity have nowhere to go and thus the loss of an important "resource" is not threatened. The existence of emigration restrictions in the former Communist states (with low productivity and apparently very high income inequality between the vast majority of the population and a tiny governing elite) may be testament to this. And it is interesting to ask what the domestic political, ultimately economic, consequences for some poorer countries might be if mass emigration were facilitated by reduced immigration restrictions in the developed countries.

There are other reasons to wonder whether conventional, territorially based immigration restrictions would emerge in the interests of global welfare. As the current focus on global environmental issues emphasizes, the consequences of many national policies do not respect borders. Again it seems that these concerns create strategic incentives that cut in two directions for the choice of worldwide immigration policy. On the one hand, the extraterritorial effects of pollution suggest that those beyond the "borders" should be entitled to participate in the political process of an otherwise territorially bounded political entity in order to avoid the externality their political silence creates. On the other hand, there are environmental consequences of migration – pollution, congestion, soil depletion and erosion, and so on – that cut both in favor of and against immigration. From a strategic perspective, the environmental policies of different countries will obviously be sensitive to the immigration regime.

Without providing anything more than a series of questions and conjectures, these brief observations are intended to suggest where we might go with the welfare economics of immigration law. Recognizing the need to base the economist's contribution to the normative debate on immigration law on a global social welfare function has suggested a rich research agenda. For we can see that ultimately our normative analysis will depend on a set of positive political economy questions that are obscured by an analysis that begins with national social welfare functions. This suggests to me at least that even while deferring the meatier ethical issues to the political philosophers, economists may yet have something substantial to contribute to the normative analysis of immigration law.

Notes

I am enormously grateful to Eric Rakowski for reading a rough draft of this essay. The analysis and exposition have been greatly improved by his comments. I am also very grateful to Peter Menell for helpful discussions as I was developing the ideas and to David Caron for comments.

1 G. C. Archibald, "Welfare Economics, Ethics and Essentialism," *Economica* 26 (1959): 316–27; P. Hennipman, "Pareto Optimality: Value Judgement or Analytical Tool?" in J. F. Cramer, A. Heertjie, and P. Venekamp (eds.), *Relevance and Precision: From Quantitative Analysis to Economic Policy* (Amsterdam: North Holland, 1976), 36–69. See generally Mark Blaug, *The Methodology of Economics or How Economists Explain* (Cambridge University Press, 1980), 129–56.

2 This is Arrow's original "Condition 2," the requirement that there be a positive association between individual and social values. Kenneth J. Arrow, *Social Choice and Individual Values*, 2d ed. (New Haven, Conn.: Yale University Press, 1776), 25–6.

3 The welfare literature has long recognized a formal difficulty with the Kaldor–Hicks criterion, which is that the criterion may simultaneously recommend both a change from the status quo and a return to the status quo. See generally E. J. Mishan, *Introduction to Normative Economics* (New York: Oxford University Press, 1981). This results if the change is sufficient to alter distribution and relative preferences such that original gainers can compensate original losers in the change from the status quo *and* original losers can compensate original gainers in a change back to the status quo. Since a total relaxation of immigration restrictions would almost certainly result in substantial distributional changes, this formal problem may be a reason to reject the Kaldor–Hicks criterion in the immigration context. Given the current state of the art, this would leave welfare economists with essentially nothing to say about immigration.

4 Coleman and Harding's "good" of membership in a political community (see Chapter 2, this volume) could be an example of an excluded good that is substantially affected by immigration restriction; liberty interests are another. As a matter of practice, if not theory, empirical applications of welfare economics tend to exclude any goods that are not traded in conventional markets.

5 In Chapter 2 of this volume, Coleman and Harding make the same point about theories of distributive justice generally.

6 See, e.g., Sykes, Chapter 8, this volume.

7 There are also problems when social welfare is defined with respect to "original" residents. How do we count people who are immigrants for purposes of today's but original residents for the purposes of tomorrow's welfare assessment? Do we, in making today's assessment, ignore the fact that tomorrow the welfare of a person significantly affected by today's judgment will matter to "us"?

8 Immigration also increases aggregate demand for goods and services, which compensates for increased labor supply. Borjas surveys the empirical literature and concludes that "the methodological arsenal of modern econometrics cannot detect a single shred of evidence that immigrants have a sizable adverse impact on the earnings and employment opportunities of natives in the U.S." George J. Borjas, *Friends or Strangers: The Impact of Immigrants on the U.S. Economy* (New York: Basic Books, 1990), 22.

9 Robert J. Lalonde and Robert H. Topel, "Labor Market Adjustments to Increased Immigration," in John M. Abowd and Richard B. Freeman (eds.), *Immigration, Trade and the Labor Market* (Chicago: University of Chicago Press, 1991).

10 See, e.g., Sykes, Chapter 8, this volume.

11 See, e.g., Richard A. Posner, *The Economics of Justice* (Cambridge, Mass.: Harvard University Press, 1983). "The specific distribution of *wealth* is a mere by-product of the distribution of *rights* [to one's body, labor, etc.] that is itself derived from the wealth-maximization principle. A just distribution of wealth need not be posited" (81).

12 Kenneth J. Arrow, "Values and Collective Decision Making," in *Collected Papers of Kenneth J. Arrow*, Vol. 1: *Social Choice and Justice* (Cambridge, Mass.: Harvard University Press, 1983), 68–9.

13 Coleman and Harding also note this function in Chapter 2, this volume.

14 Some constraints on political participation could fall out of administrative considerations alone. But since I wish to emphasize the distributional and incentive reasons for limiting participation or not, I ignore this for now.

15 This follows from an assumption that only territorial, and not global, political jurisdiction is administratively feasible on a large scale.

16 Borjas, in *Friends or Strangers*, has noted the "strong positive correlation between the extent of income inequality in a particular country and the rate of return to schooling in that country" and argued that self-selection among immigrants will tend to cause a positive correlation between the skills of immigrants and relative income inequality.

10

Some caveats on the welfare economics of immigration law

SUSAN B. VROMAN

In Chapter 8 of this volume, Sykes sets out the basic economic argument that global welfare increases if people are free to migrate when the gains from migrating exceed the costs. With the usual caveats, which Sykes provides, this argument is generally accepted by economists. It is quite similar to the argument used in favor of free international trade. According to this argument, immigration should be restricted only if it is in some way counter to the national interest, that is, if immigrants gain at the expense of natives. Even this argument for restricting immigration can be debated if the social welfare function is allowed to include individuals outside the country. In addition to providing theoretical arguments for less restrictive immigration, Sykes presents a policy prescription that includes expanding the number of temporary visas for unskilled workers as a way to stem the recent increase in illegal immigration.

The purpose of this essay is not to argue that increased immigration is bad. Immigration has been the basis for the growth of the United States throughout its history. Rather, I argue that Sykes's policy proposal is flawed, and present some arguments for the use of caution in using the simple economic model Sykes describes to support policy changes that may lead to substantial increases in immigration.

In the first section, I discuss Sykes's policy proposal for increased immigration of temporary workers in the light of recent evidence from my area of expertise, labor economics. I argue that although the evidence indicates that immigration in the past has not harmed U.S. workers, increased immigration of workers who are less skilled than previous groups of immigrants may have harmful effects on low-skilled native workers. Thus caution should be used in instituting policies that would lead to a rapid influx of such immigrants even if they are granted only temporary status. In the second section, I discuss the standard theoretical model used by Sykes. I argue that the use of more realistic assumptions concerning market structure may call into question some of the conclusions of the model. Furthermore, I argue that in applying the standard model, economists are apt to ignore the political and social realities of immigration policy. In the United States, for example, the political structure makes it difficult to compensate the losers from increased immigration and so it is not possible to argue that a less restrictive immigration policy unambiguously increases economic welfare.

I. The labor market implications of increased immigration

Sykes's specific policy prescription has two components. First, he argues that U.S. policy with respect to permanent immigration is consistent with the national interest. The criteria for permanent immigrant status are primarily family reunification and the possession of a significant amount of human or financial capital. I generally agree with this policy. The current policy encourages the immigration of highly skilled and well-educated workers who are likely to contribute to the economy both in terms of their output and in terms of their taxes. They are unlikely to use more public services than the average American so that on net their entry will be a benefit to the United States. The emphasis on family reunification, however, which may have large intangible benefits, could encourage immigration of individuals who are less skilled and might use a relatively large share of government services. With this caveat, the current policy with respect to permanent immigrants seems to be consistent with the national interest, as Sykes argues.

Second, Sykes's policy prescription would allow a large increase in the number of visas for temporary workers. He believes that if an employer expresses a need for temporary workers, Labor Department certification is unnecessary. He argues that this type of policy would reduce the problem of illegal immigrants, since many are temporary workers and such a policy would make them more likely to leave at the completion of their visa period. This policy prescription seems flawed in several ways.

First, Borjas et al. provide evidence that the majority of undocumented Mexican-born workers are here with their families.[1] These illegal immigrants appear to be very much like permanent immigrants from Mexico in terms of family structure, but they are younger, less skilled, and less educated. A policy of granting them temporary visas would be unlikely to convince them to be truly temporary. In addition, as Sykes notes, a significant number of illegal immigrants are people who have overstayed their visas. There is no reason to believe that the temporary workers would be very different. Thus, at a minimum one would expect a significant proportion of them to be illegal immigrants after their visas expired.

Supposing that a large influx of immigrants resulted from such a policy, would they be immigrants who would be of net benefit to the United States? The arguments used for restrictive immigration are that (a) immigrants may use public transfer programs and be a drain on the U.S. government at a time when such programs are contributing to our budget deficit problem, (b) immigrants might cause congestion externalities with respect to public services or other national resources, and (c) immigrants would take jobs from native workers or cause the wages of native workers to be reduced. In his policy prescription, Sykes proposes that the policy for temporary workers not allow them access to public transfer programs. This would solve the first problem. (Authors such as Simon have argued that in fact this is not a problem, since immigrants are young and working and so contribute to taxes without using social service programs.)[2] Because of a lack of data, the congestion argument is exceedingly hard to analyze, so I will ignore it.

To address the issue of whether native workers will be harmed by a large influx of workers on temporary visas, one must first look at who is likely to enter the United States on such visas. Borjas indicates that the ''quality'' of immigrants since the early 1970s is below that of earlier waves of immigrants.[3] If we allow this influx of temporary workers, who are they likely to be? The undocumented Mexican workers already in the United States are less skilled than those who entered legally. Many of those interviewed by Borjas et al. had made several unsuccessful attempts to enter the country before finally succeeding.[4] These people obviously believe that the benefits outweigh the costs. If entry into the United States is made easier, it is likely that those who enter will be workers for whom the benefit is lower than for those who currently enter illegally. That is, the additional immigrants would probably be even less skilled and less well educated. In other words, if the cost of entry is reduced, the benefit necessary to make immigration worthwhile will also fall.

Will these workers displace native workers? The evidence to date seems to indicate that U.S. workers have not been harmed to any great extent by immigration. Altonji and Card look specifically at the effect of immigration on low-skilled workers and find only modest effects.[5] LaLonde and Topel note that immigrants are clustered in certain standard metropolitan statistical areas and that there is some evidence of a small effect on the workers who are close substitutes for the immigrants in these cities.[6] However, these studies, as well as others on this topic, are based on historical data. If the United States were to allow immigrant flows of low-skilled workers that are far greater than the recent historical experience, native workers or permanent immigrants could well be harmed. They could either be displaced by less costly temporary workers or they might have their earnings eroded by competition with the temporary workers.

In economics, much is made of the fact that perfect competition is efficient and that workers should be paid on the basis of their productivity (marginal product). It should be noted, however, that in many of the industries where temporary immigrants might work, firms have market power both in their product markets and in their labor markets; that is, the perfectly competitive market model does not apply. This means that firms have the ability to use their market power to pay workers less than the value of their marginal product. In such markets (e.g., much of manufacturing), employers could use the temporary immigrants to reduce their labor costs. If this cost reduction were not passed on to consumers through lower prices, there would not even be an improvement in welfare for consumers. There would simply be a different sharing of the rent generated by production in the industry; that is, the employers would gain at the expense of the workers. Since shareholders of U.S. corporations are on average better off financially than workers, this represents a redistribution toward the more affluent.

Dropping Labor Department certification and relying on employers to establish the need for temporary workers, as Sykes suggests, is based on a very altruistic view of employers. As someone who has worked in labor relations for a long time, I do not believe this view is supported by the evidence. We have been in an environment since 1980 in which some employers have used illegal labor practices to break unions and generally have gained power with respect to their workers. This has given employers increased bargaining power. If employers are free to solicit temporary workers visas without any restraints by the Labor Department, they may use the temporary workers to further enhance their bargaining power with respect to native workers and permanent immigrants. This would mean that U.S. workers would be more likely to be harmed by Sykes's policy.

II. The theoretical case for less restrictive immigration: caveats

The basic economic argument that Sykes gives for less restrictive immigration policy is based on a simple general equilibrium model in which there are constant returns to scale and perfect competition. Sykes's essay presents the basic model and several variants of it. Even in these models, while the result that global welfare is improved by less restrictive immigration is maintained, the possibility of a negative effect on some natives in the country of immigration arises. In several versions of the model, returns to labor in the country of immigration fall while owners of capital are better off. Thus a less restrictive immigration policy has an effect on the distribution of national income that may entail a redistribution from less-well-off to better-off segments of the population. I will return to this issue in more detail later. In addition to the possible problem of income redistribution, there are other caveats to the use of the simple model that Sykes mentions. Some of these bear further discussion.

The simple model assumes that resources are fully utilized. If the economy suffers from involuntary unemployment, the conclusions in terms of welfare are unclear. The immigrants would contribute to aggregate demand and could help to improve the situation, but they could displace native workers, who would then be unemployed. The point is that, in this case, increased immigration might lower economic welfare.

As already noted, Sykes's simple model assumes constant returns to scale and perfect competition. Modern international trade theory has focused much attention on scale economies (increasing returns to scale) and imperfect competition, and has discovered that some conclusions of the simple competitive general equilibrium view of international trade do not necessarily hold when there are scale economies and market structures other than perfect competition.[7] Sykes mentions this new theory, but only briefly. Since I am not a trade economist, my aim is not to use modern trade theory to develop a new model of immigration, but rather to note that most U.S. industries are characterized by market structures that involve market power for firms, and so caution should be used in analyzing the effects of immigration based on a simple competitive model. As I noted earlier, labor market power for firms may enable the firms to use increased immigration to extract a greater share of the rent produced in an imperfectly competitive market and thus may hurt the firms' current work forces.

Thus relaxing some of the assumptions of the model casts doubt on the conclusion that less restrictive immigration improves global welfare and welfare in the country of immigration. Suppose, however, that this contention is correct. That is, suppose that even though the real world is more complicated than envisioned by the simple model, the net economic benefit of a less restrictive immigration policy for a country such as the United States is positive. Even if this were indeed the case, there are political and social considerations that should be raised in evaluating immigration policy.

When we argue that freer immigration increases economic welfare, we mean that the gains to the gainers exceed the losses to those hurt by immigration. Only if the losers are compensated is the change in policy unambiguously welfare-improving. Suppose that harm is done to some native workers as a result of an increased flow of immigrants. Sykes argues, as do most economists, that this can be dealt with most efficiently by redistributive transfers. In other words, the efficient immigration policy should be used, while redistribution should be addressed through the tax/transfer system. The problem with this approach is that in the United States we do not seem inclined to compensate the losers. Many blue-collar workers have lost their jobs and seen their wages fall as a result of the increase in international trade, but the Trade Adjustment Assistance Act has been inadequate to compensate for their losses. This is the main reason that unions and others who represent these workers lobby for protectionism even though free trade may be beneficial to the nation in the aggregate. These same groups lobby for a restrictive immigration policy. Perhaps they are not misinformed, as some economists believe, but are rather informed as to who will lose and whether they will be compensated for their losses.

In addition to these political considerations, one should also note the social costs of increased immigration. We are used to thinking of the United States as a land of immigrants, but in Europe, immigration is viewed quite differently and may entail costs that we ignore. We do not focus on whether immigrants will change our culture, since ours is an immigrant culture. Many Europeans, on the other hand, are very concerned with the cultural effects of immigration. Thus, in Europe the social disruption and the effect on culture dominate the policy debate. In some countries, such as Germany, the social disruption caused by the reaction to immigrants from different cultures has imposed social and political costs. In other countries, such as Sweden, where there is little social disruption, government programs to help immigrants assimilate into the Swedish culture have been enacted and impose direct economic costs. This may seem beyond the scope of a welfare economics discussion, but our welfare models purport to address social welfare and we should at least note that social costs may be involved, some of which may translate into direct economic costs.

III. Conclusions

First, a policy of greatly increasing the number of visas for temporary workers seems ill-advised. Such a policy would attract immigrants who were less skilled than the pool of permanent immigrants, and it would not be likely to reduce significantly the incentive for these workers to stay in the United States as illegal immigrants. Implementing such a policy without some controls would probably hurt U.S. workers and they would most likely not be compensated for the harm they suffered. At a minimum, if we expand the number of such visas, the increase should be gradual and well monitored.

This conclusion is reinforced by the fact that the theoretical arguments for less restrictive immigration are based on a simple model that is itself subject to many criticisms. It assumes full employment and perfect competition. The presence of unemployment and market power shed some doubt on the model's implication that free immigration necessarily enhances global welfare. Furthermore, even if increased immigration creates net benefit for the country of immigration, it is important to take into account that we have often been unwilling to compensate the losers from such policy changes. If the losers are not well off and have suffered losses from other policy changes, the typical economist's argument that efficient policies should be used and redistribution should be taken care of by other means seems inadequate. The other means are too often not implemented. Finally, in discussing immigration policy, we in the United States often ignore social costs that are more important in societies that have not previously had large immigrant communities.

Notes

1 George J. Borjas, B. Richard Freeman, and Kevin Lang, "Undocumented Mexican-Born Workers in the United States: How Many, How Permanent?" in J. M. Abowd, and R. B. Freeman (eds.), *Immigration, Trade, and the Labor Market* (Chicago: University of Chicago Press, 1991), 77–100.
2 Julian Simon, *The Economic Consequences of Immigration* (Oxford: Basil Blackwell, 1990).
3 George J. Borjas, "Immigration and Self-Selection," in Abowd and Freeman (eds.), *Immigration, Trade, and the Labor Market*, 29–76.
4 Borjas et al., "Undocumented Mexican-Born Workers."
5 Joseph G. Altonji and David Card, "The Effects of Immigration on the Labor Market Outcomes of Less-Skilled Natives," in Abowd and Freeman (eds.), *Immigration, Trade, and the Labor Market*, 201–34.
6 Robert J. LaLonde and Robert H. Topel, "Labor Market Adjustments to Increased Immigration," in Abowd and Freeman (eds.), *Immigration, Trade, and the Labor Market*, 169–99.
7 For a discussion of this theory, see Elhanan Helpman and Paul Krugman, *Market Structure and Foreign Trade* (Cambridge, Mass.: MIT Press, 1985), and idem, *Trade Policy and Market Structure* (Cambridge, Mass.: MIT Press, 1989).

11

The case for a liberal immigration policy

MICHAEL J. TREBILCOCK

I. Introduction

Classical free-trade theory assumed that goods could often readily be traded across national borders but that the factors of production employed to produce those goods (land, capital, and labor) were fixed and immobile. In the contemporary world, largely due to technological changes, this has become dramatically untrue of capital, and much less true of labor. However, the frequent resistance to international mobility of goods is often greatly intensified in the case of the international mobility of people. Here we move from the domain of international trade policy to the domain of immigration policy.

This essay addresses a question that has confronted all individuals and groups of individuals who, throughout history, have chosen to live in a state of civil society with one another and for whom social, political, and economic relationships are integral to the self-definition of each individual in the community of which they are a part. How does one define and justify the conditions of membership in the community? In the context of the modern nation-state, this directs our attention primarily to the substance and procedures of our immigration policies: who may become citizens and who must remain strangers, for nations imply boundaries and boundaries at some point imply closure. Current intense public debates in Canada, the United States, and Western Europe over central features of domestic immigration policies reflect the deep conflicts that immigration issues have always provoked. As of the late 1980s, approximately 100 million people were resident outside their nations of current citizenship. Roughly 35 million were in sub-Sahara Africa alone, and approximately 13 to 15 million each in the prosperous regions of Western Europe and North America. Another 15 million or so were in the Middle East and Asia.[1] Of the total number of immigrants, about 18 million were refugees, most of whom were located in Africa and Asia, unlike earlier post–World War II refugee movements, which originated mostly in Europe.[2]

II. The values

A. *Liberty*

At the heart of debates in all Western democracies over immigration policy now, and in the past, lie two core values that stand to some irreducible degree in opposition to each other: liberty and community. Though there are almost endless variations of these theories, for our purposes their essence in the context of immigration policy can be fairly readily captured. As Carens points out:

[All liberal] theories begin with some kind of assumption about the equal moral worth of individuals. In one way or another, all treat the individual as prior to the community. Such foundations provide little basis for drawing fundamental distinctions between citizens and aliens who seek to become citizens.[3]

Carens goes on to review three contemporary approaches to liberal theory: libertarianism, social contractarianism, and utilitarianism. From the libertarian perspective, exemplified by scholars such as Nozick, individual property rights play a central role.[4] In a state of nature, individuals have rights to acquire and use property and to alienate it voluntarily. The existence of the state is justified only to the extent that it is required to protect property rights and facilitate their voluntary transfer. On this view, if persons wish to move to Germany, Canada, or the United States, they should be free to do so, provided they do not violate anyone else's rights by imposing involuntary burdens on them. To the extent that citizens choose to enter into contracts of employment with them or sell them land, homes, or businesses, the rights of both citizens and aliens would be violated by externally imposed constraints thereon. From a social contractarian perspective, as exemplified most prominently by the writings of John Rawls,[5] an ideal social constitution would be constructed behind a veil of ignorance, where individuals knew nothing about their own personal situations, class, race, sex, natural talents, religious beliefs, individual goals, values, talents, and so on. The purpose of the veil of ignorance is "to nullify the effect of specific contingencies which put men at odds," because natural and social contingencies are "arbitrary from a moral point of view" and therefore are factors that ought not to influence the choice of principles of justice.

As Carens points out, whether one is a citizen of a rich nation or a poor nation, and whether one is already a citizen of a particular state or an alien who wishes to become a citizen, are the kinds of specific contingencies that could set people at odds. A fair procedure for choosing principles of justice should therefore exclude knowledge of these circumstances, just as it excludes knowledge of one's race, sex, or social class. We should therefore take a global, not a national, view of the original position (the "universal brotherhood of man'').[6] Behind this global veil of ignorance, and considering possible restrictions on freedom, we should adopt the perspective of those who would be most disadvantaged by the restrictions, in this case often that of the alien who wants to immigrate. From this perspective, very few restrictions on immigration can be morally justified. Rawls would recognize that liberty may be restricted for the sake of liberty, in the sense that all liberties depend on the existence of public order and security. To cite a metaphor used by Carens, it does no one any good to take so many people into a lifeboat that it is swamped and everyone drowns.[7] But short of a reasonable, as opposed to a hypothetical, expectation of this prospect, largely unconstrained immigration would seem implied by Rawls's social contract theory. Galloway, however, has recently challenged Carens's implication that a Rawlsian social contract version of liberal theory requires open borders in the sense of a recognition that each person in the world has a right to choose his or her country of residence. Just as within a given liberal society individuals cannot be viewed as having a duty to facilitate or promote the life plans of others where this would completely undermine the ability of the former to pursue their own life plans, so members of one society do not have a duty to make every sacrifice required in order to promote the autonomy of individuals in other societies where this would undermine the autonomy of members of the former society.[8]

From a utilitarian perspective, the utilities or disutilities experienced by both aliens and citizens would be entered in the utilitarian calculus.[9] Some citizens would gain from being able to enter into contractual relationships with immigrants; others might lose if jobs were displaced or wages depressed through the additional competition immigrants might bring to labor markets, while yet other citizens as consumers might benefit from access to cheaper goods or services. Against these costs and benefits accruing to citizens must be set whatever costs and benefits accrue to aliens by being permitted entry: in most cases one assumes that the benefits substantially outweigh the costs; otherwise, the aliens would presumably not have chosen to resettle in another land. Moreover, to the extent that many aliens will have made the wrenching decision to resettle because of economic privation or religious or political oppression or persecution in their homelands, the gains to them from being permitted to join a new and more congenial community may be very substantial. Thus a utilitarian perspective, while perhaps providing more scope for restrictions on immigration than either the libertarian or social contractarian perspective, would dictate relatively open borders.

B. *Community*

In opposition to these liberal values stand the core values of community. Here it is asserted, in the context of immigration policy, that the prerogative of determining which strangers might enter a country is a powerful expression of a nation's identity and autonomy – in other words its sovereignty. Sovereignty entails the unlimited power of a nation, like that of a free individual, to decide whether, under what conditions, and with what effect it will consent to enter into a relationship with a stranger.[10] The most prominent contemporary proponent of this view is Michael Walzer.[11] In justifying this view, he draws analogies between neighborhoods, clubs, and families. While it is true that in the case of neighborhoods, people are free, in general, to enter and exit as they please, he argues that to draw an analogy between nations and neighborhoods, permitting unconstrained entry by aliens from anywhere in the world, would destroy the concept of neighborhood. He argues that it is only the nationalization of welfare (or the nationalization of culture and politics) that opens neighborhood communities to whoever chooses to come in. Neighborhoods can be open only if countries are at least potentially closed. Only if the state makes a selection among would-be members and guarantees the loyalty, security, and welfare of the individuals it selects can local communities take shape as "different" associations determined solely by personal preference and market capacity. Walzer claims that if states ever became large neighborhoods, it is likely that neighborhoods would become little states. Their members would organize to defend the local politics and culture against strangers. Historically, it is claimed, neighborhoods have turned into closed or parochial communities whenever the state was open. Thus Walzer rejects the analogy between states and neighborhoods and instead draws one between states and clubs or families, where members are free to determine the conditions of membership. Walzer concludes:

The distribution of membership is not pervasively subject to the constraints of justice. Across a considerable range of the decisions that are made, states are simply free to take in strangers (or not) – much as they are free, leaving aside the claims of the needy, to share their wealth with foreign friends, to honor the achievements of foreign artists, scholars, and scientists, to choose their trading partners, and to enter into collective security arrangements with foreign states. But the right to choose an admissions policy is more basic than any of these, for it is not merely a matter of acting in the world, exercising sovereignty, and pursuing national interests. At stake here is the shape of the community that acts in the world, exercises sovereignty, and so on. Admission and exclusion are at the core of communal independence. They suggest the deepest meaning of self-determination. Without them, there could not be *communities of character*, historically stable, ongoing associations of men and women with some special commitment to one another and some special sense of their common life.[12]

Unlike the liberal theories, which imply no or few limitations on entry, Walzer's theory, at least without further qualification, appears to permit almost any limitations on entry that a state might choose to impose, including overtly racist admission policies. Two controversial features of his theory are the notion that political sovereignty is a nearly absolute value – a view increasingly challenged by the evolution of international human rights norms – and that the only communities of character are those that reflect ethnic, religious, or ideological commonalties – a view many liberals would challenge on the grounds that common commitments to liberal civic institutions and mutual tolerance of intermediate subcommunities of interest can sustain communities of character. In any event, these two core values of liberty and community clearly frame the major issues that must be confronted in the design of any country's immigration policies.

III. The issues

A. *The size of the intake*

The issue of the size of the intake of immigrants cannot readily be separated from the composition of the intake, in terms of deducing what kinds of demands the immigrants are likely to make upon our community. However, to the extent that the two issues can be separated, obviously whatever the composition of the intake, the notion that no country could accept and absorb millions of immigrants a year without critical features of its physical and social infrastructure collapsing and congestion externalities being created on all sides is likely to be readily accepted. One might, of course, argue that a natural equilibrium will probably establish itself before this happens – if the intake threatens these conditions, some would-be immigrants will abandon an interest in resettling. However, collective action problems may prevent such an equilibrium from emerging at all or, in any event, quickly or smoothly, and it is not obvious that Rawls's "public order" qualification on the right of entry tells us anything very helpful about when congestion externalities have reached the point where the lifeboat metaphor can appropriately be invoked. This concern is somewhat reminiscent of the concerns raised by Thomas Malthus in 1798 in his famous essay, *Principle of Population as It Affects the Future Improvement of Society*. As Heilbroner states the Malthusian thesis:

[The essay on population claimed] that there was a tendency in nature for population to outstrip all possible means of subsistence. Far from ascending to an ever higher level, society was caught in a hopeless trap in which the human reproductive urge would inevitably shove humanity to the sheer brink of the precipice of existence. Instead of being headed for Utopia, the human lot was forever condemned to a losing struggle between ravenous and multiplying mouths and the eternally insufficient stock of Nature's cupboard, however diligently that cupboard might be searched.[13]

In Malthus's view, land, unlike people, cannot be multiplied – land does not breed. While Malthus's fears were subsequently proven to be greatly exaggerated, and most dramatically refuted by the settlement of the New World, where increased population through immigration, in terms of increased labor and capital on the supply side and increased aggregate demand on the demand side, made possible the realization of enormous economies of scale and the technological advances that accompanied them. However, as birthrates and destitution levels in many impoverished Third World countries exemplify today, Mathus's concerns were not entirely without foundation, and a totally unrestricted immigration policy may legitimately implicate those concerns. Once some restriction on total intake is recognized as necessary, the composition of that restricted intake must be addressed.

B. The composition of the intake

A host of complex and morally sensitive issues arise here. With respect to many of them, the core values of liberty and community are likely to yield quite different implications.

1. A market in entitlements. A method of allocating scarce entitlements to entry that appeals to a number of economists is one in which the state auctions off these entitlements on a periodic basis and allocates them to the highest bidders.[14] It could presumably be claimed on behalf of this allocative mechanism that the successful bidders are those who most value the right of entry, because the opportunities for them following entry are likely to be the greatest, presumably reflecting the greater value that present citizens undoubtedly place on whatever economic activities these successful bidders intend to engage in. On the other hand, it could be cogently argued that this method offends notions of distributive justice by rewarding ability to pay, by disregarding claims that other noncitizens might be able to make for entry, on the grounds of, say, economic deprivation, religious or ethnic persecution, political oppression in their home countries, or family reunification, as well as by failing to take into account the fact that, despite their lack of material resources, the opportunity for such noncitizens to emigrate may dramatically enhance their individual autonomy and welfare, perhaps to the point of making the difference between life and death.

2. Lotteries. One could also employ the mechanism of a lottery. All aspiring entrants register their applications, and names of individuals in the applicant pool are drawn on a periodic basis until the total intake for the period is met. This method of allocation would obviously neutralize the role of wealth in the allocation of entitlements to entry, although it would be entirely insensitive to relative claims of merit or desert that individual members of the applicant pool, and existing citizens, might feel should be vindicated.

3. Queues (first come, first served). Scarce entitlements to entry could be allocated on a first-come, first-served basis, where the order of registration or filing of applications is recorded, and applicants are simply selected from the top of the queue until the total, collectively agreed upon intake for the period in question is met. Like a lottery, this method of allocation is wealth-neutral, but it is vulnerable to all the same objections in that it is entirely insensitive to relative claims of merit or desert that might be asserted by or on behalf of individual applicants.

Once these three methods of allocation are rejected, either in whole or in part, as the primary allocative mechanisms, administrative (merit) allocation is left as the only major alternative. In formulating the criteria for evaluating relative claims of merit or desert in legislative or administrative policies, the normative considerations surrounding the claims of the following categories of applicants have to be addressed.

4. Applicants who pose a national security risk. Obviously, no normative theory of immigration recognizes that an invading country is entitled to un-opposed entry on the grounds of free movement of people. Similarly, no theory would recognize an obligation to admit subversives committed to over-throwing the state by force. A more difficult question arises with respect to significant influxes of people who come from nonliberal societies, even if they do not come with any subversive intent. In other words, how tolerant must we be of the intolerant? Carens argues that there may be a case, even from a liberty perspective, for excluding such people if the cumulative effect of their presence might be to undermine the maintenance of liberal institu-tions. From a communitarian perspective, given that the state, with certain qualifications, can set any conditions of entry that it pleases, exclusion here would be viewed as unproblematic.

5. Refugee or asylum claimants. Aliens who have found their way to our country or are displaced in third countries and seek refugee or asylum status because of the threat of political, religious, or ethnic persecution in their homelands present a morally compelling claim for admission on most theories of immigration. Liberal theories would readily recognize such claims, given the premise of the recognition of the equal moral worth of all individ-uals and given the special concern in Rawlsian social contract theory with the plight of the most disadvantaged. Even on communitarian theories of im-migration, at least as articulated by Walzer, the mutual-aid or Good Samaritan principle applies where positive assistance is urgently needed by one of the parties and the risks and costs of giving it are relatively low for the other party. Historically, with some exceptions, refugee or asylum claims have tended to involve a relatively small number of people at any given time, so that Walzer's conditions were often readily satisfied. However, in the contemporary world, approximately 18 million individuals have been displaced from their homelands by war, civil unrest, or religious or ethnic persecution – up from 8 million in 1980 and 2.5 million in 1970; in addition, another 24 million are displaced within their own countries.[15] Now, with ready means of international mobility available to them, it is not clear how far the principle of mutual aid extends. Walzer states, ''I assume that there are limits on our collective liability, but I do not know how to specify them.''[16]

6. Economically necessitous aliens. This category of claimant embraces aliens who because of simple economic impoverishment in their homelands wish to resettle in our country (sometimes referred to as economic refugees). From a liberal perspective, their claims would be viewed as having different strengths, depending on which strand of liberal theory one espoused. Within a domestic libertarian framework, provided their entry did not interfere with rights of others, we should admit them. Within a utilitarian framework, much would depend on what they could contribute to our society relative to the costs they would impose on it, although a global utilitarian framework would also weigh the benefits to them. Within a social contractarian framework they would engage our special concern to the extent that they could properly be characterized as among the least advantaged but, according to Galloway, not beyond the point where promoting their autonomy might undermine ours. In contrast, from a communitarian perspective, Walzer claims that we have very limited obligations to such persons, or at least we are free collectively to take that view.[17] Perhaps we have an obligation to provide foreign aid, or, as he argues in his criticism of the White Australia policy, when a country has large empty land masses it may have an obligation to share these spaces with necessitous aliens. In his view, to recognize a more general claim would be to invite the prospect of a country being overrun by an almost unlimited number of disadvantaged aliens from around the globe who had very little in common with existing members of the community and who would thus threaten to undermine its sense of community.

7. Family members. Both Carens and Walzer recognize that aliens who have family relationships with citizens can make an especially salient normative claim for admission, in Walzer's[18] case because community bonds and affinities are readily embraced by such relatives and, in Carens's case,[19] presumably because to exclude them would be to deny their equal moral worth, although curiously Carens suggests that more distant relatives would not have as strong a claim. A libertarian perspective on family reunification claimants would readily countenance their admission, provided they imposed no costs involuntarily on others. The social contractarian perspective might be ambivalent to the extent that family members do not fall within the category of the least advantaged. A domestic utilitarian perspective might again be somewhat ambivalent, particularly in the case of older or infirm family members who might in some cases be expected to contribute little to our society and conceivably make significant demands on us, although a global utilitarian perspective would also weigh the benefits to them.

8. *Culturally homogeneous aliens.* A complex and sensitive issue arises as to whether a state can morally attach conditions of entry for aliens that are designed to maintain the community's cultural homogeneity. On most versions of liberal theory, such discriminatory conditions are likely to be suspect, in the sense that they do not treat all individuals as being of equal moral worth. From a communitarian perspective, the foundational premise is that the community is free to set any terms of entry that it wishes, particularly where the conditions are designed to reinforce shared, common values. Both core values here encounter difficulties. From a liberal perspective, it is necessary to accommodate the aspirations for national self-determination that independence movements around the world, particularly in the postwar years, have strongly evinced. In the contemporary world, the transformation of Eastern Europe, and the claims for independence or greater autonomy by many subparts of these countries, all reflect, to some degree, a claim to an entitlement to recognition and reinforcement of culturally, religiously, or politically distinct communities. Within Canada, Quebec's claim to being a distinct society and a potential claim to political independence, with a corollary claim in both cases to being entitled to control the characteristics of its immigrants, rests in large part on the claim to cultural distinctiveness, which may entail exclusionary implications. The claim of native North American Indian or Aboriginal people to self-government, at least on reserves, also rests on a claim to an entitlement to protect and preserve cultural distinctiveness, even where this entails exclusionary elements. Carens, within the liberal egalitarian framework that he adopts, is also prepared to concede that a country or society – one with a long tradition of close cultural homogeneity – might be entitled to maintain a restrictive immigration society, provided that it were applied more or less equally to all aliens.[20]

This proviso is important to him, because he does not want to countenance (as most liberals would not) policies like the White Australia policy[21] (formally abandoned in 1972), which he readily sees as having been motivated by racist sentiments (Canadian immigration policy until 1962 was not substantially different; U.S. immigration policy for most of this century has imposed quotas by country of origin, reflecting the country's ethnic composition in the 1920s). On the other hand, an Australian minister of immigration once defended that policy in terms that, on the surface, appear to apply to many of the other situations instanced earlier in which exclusionary policies may be justified: "We seek to create a homogeneous nation. Can anyone reasonably object to that? Is this not the elementary right of every government, to decide the composition of the nation? It is just the same prerogative as the head of the family exercises as to who is to live in his own house." Or as one Australian political leader once put the point, with less finesse: "Two Wongs don't make a White."

Carens argues that "difference does not always entail domination. One has to consider what a particular case of exclusion means, taking historical, social, and political context into account. For example, the White Australia policy cannot be separated from British imperialism and European racism. That is why it was never a defensible form of exclusion."[22] On the other hand, "Japan's exclusionary policy seems quite different. First it is universal i.e. it applies to all non-Japanese. It is not aimed at some particular racial or ethnic group that is presumed to be inferior, and it is not tied to a history of domination of the excluded,"[23] although Carens acknowledges that it is difficult to reconcile Japan's treatment of Korean immigrants with this rationalization. For Walzer, the White Australia policy presents even more serious problems, given his analogy between states and families and clubs, an analogy explicitly drawn by the Australian minister of immigration.[24] Walzer is driven to reliance on what appears to be a frivolous qualification of the generally unconstrained right he concedes to states to set the terms of entry by aliens into national communities by suggesting that a country with large unoccupied land masses may have an obligation to share the land even with culturally diverse aliens (a sort of South African "homelands" policy). First, most of the unoccupied land in Australia is unoccupied for a reason – it is desert and largely uninhabitable – and sharing this land with, for example, Asians or Africans would be to discharge no moral obligation at all to them. In the terms of the Lockean proviso, "as much and as good" has not remotely been left behind for them. Second, in countries without large unoccupied land masses it would appear to follow from Walzer's position that racially discriminatory admission conditions can be justified in terms of protecting long-established community values and characteristics.

9. Better-endowed and less well endowed aliens. Can a country in settling the terms of admission to the community it represents morally justify discriminating in favor of better-endowed and against less well endowed aliens (in terms of skills or material resources)? The different versions of liberal theory might respond to this question in different ways. Within a libertarian framework, it is more likely that better-endowed immigrants, in terms of skills or capital, will be able to establish mutually beneficial contractual relationships with existing members of the admitting community; less well endowed aliens presumably pose a greater risk of becoming a public burden – for example, in terms of health and education costs, unemployment and social welfare costs – and all of these programs involve coercive forms of redistribution, which libertarians traditionally object to. Within a domestic utilitarian framework, obviously the more an alien can contribute to the admitting society in terms of skills or capital, and the fewer demands he or she makes on that society, the more likely it is that the utilitarian calculus will be met, although from a global utilitarian perspective the calculus may go the other way, with special recognition being accorded to the benefits likely to be derived from immigration by less well endowed immigrants.

Within a Rawlsian social contract framework, the least well endowed aliens should engage our special moral concern. Moreover, it might be argued that by adopting a preference for the better-endowed aliens we encourage their exit from their homelands and promote a "brain drain" or capital drain that reduces the welfare of their communities of origin, which often face severe scarcities of human and financial capital. Carens believes that we cannot justify encroaching on the rights of such individuals on this account. Moreover, the effects of emigration on the welfare of citizens in the sending country are far from clear.[25] Arguably, owners of capital receive a reduced return if wage rates among workers who remain increase (and these workers are correspondingly better off). Some negative externalities from population density may be reduced, but some advantages from population density and size (e.g., ease of communication and transportation) may also be reduced. While the brain drain has often elicited concern, the assumption is that highly skilled professionals, businesspeople, or workers are not capturing in their earnings the full value of their marginal product, but are creating positive externalities that will be lost when they leave (e.g., imparting skills or knowledge to younger individuals). To the extent that their education has been financed by their home governments, their departure may entail a loss of this investment, but on the other hand taxes paid by parents may, on average, reflect these costs. To the extent that emigrants are younger and more productive than the home population on average, the sending country loses their taxes with which to finance social programs for older citizens and children. Finally, the substantial remittances sent home by immigrants (about U.S.$66 billion worldwide in 1989) largely mitigate or even offset many of these costs to sending countries.[26]

10. Guest workers. We are familiar with the contemporary phenomenon of "guest workers" in many countries in Western Europe. These workers are admitted on a temporary basis for confined categories of tasks and without most of the legal incidents of citizenship[27] and with no formal assurance of ever being able to qualify for citizenship. Programs for domestic workers and farm workers in North America possess similar features. However, the phenomenon has long-standing historical antecedents – in the past we called such people indentured workers or, more bluntly, coolie labor. In most versions of liberal theory, such arrangements are offensive, simply because they do not treat all individuals as of equal moral worth. This would be particularly so within the libertarian and social contractarian frameworks. A domestic utilitarian framework might be more ambiguous, to the extent that guest-worker arrangements are intended to confine aliens to sectors of the economy where indigenous labor is not available and to prevent competition with, and thus the imposition of costs on, indigenous workers in other sectors. However, on a global utilitarian calculus, given the typical circumstances of most guest workers, net utility would presumably be maximized by enlarging their rights to encompass full citizenship. From his communitarian perspective, Walzer argues that to admit guest workers as residents in one's community and permit them to develop personal, social, and occupational ties as members of that community, but to treat them as a community apart, or as "second-class citizens," undermines communal values.[28]

11. Illegal immigrants. This category of immigrants embraces those who have taken up residence in a host country without satisfying whatever substantive criteria of permanent admission have been prescribed by law with respect to the various characteristics of claimants already described, or at least without following the procedures that govern those determinations – for example, they are visitors or temporary workers who have outstayed their visas. On the one hand, it can be argued from a liberal perspective that to give priority or preference to immigrants, simply because they are here, over aliens with claims of similar substance who seek admission from outside our boundaries and in accordance with prescribed procedures is to violate the precepts of equal treatment of similarly situated individuals. On the other hand, it might be argued from a communitarian perspective that, where illegal immigrants have been resident in the host country for some significant period of time and have established ties and relationships with existing members of the community, perhaps procreated and reared children in the host community, and contributed positively to the community in productive ways through employment or other activities, we have no right to expel them, and indeed perhaps an obligation at some point retrospectively to validate their status by according them citizenship (through, e.g., amnesty policies), even though at the expense of according recognition to a class of intentional lawbreakers and queue jumpers.

IV. The historical experience

From about 1880 to 1920 the Canadian government, by means of various legal strategies, successively excluded almost all Chinese (through head taxes, i.e., tariffs, and quantitative restrictions), Japanese (through a voluntary immigration restraint agreement with the Japanese government), and East Indian (through continuous journey restrictions) immigrants from Canada. The preamble to a statute of the British Columbia legislature in 1886 captures much public sentiment of the times:

Whereas the incoming of Chinese to British Columbia exceeds that of any other immigrant, and the population so introduced are fast becoming superior in number to our own race, are not disposed to be governed by our laws, are dissimilar in habits, are useless in case of emergency, habitually desecrate graveyards by removal of bodies therefrom, and generally the laws governing the whites are found to be inapplicable to the Chinese, and such Chinese are inclined to habits subversive to the comfort and well being of the community.[29]

Prime Minister John A. Macdonald in the same year expressed the following view:

There is a great deal in the objection taken to unrestricted immigration into British Columbia of people from China. These people are not of our people. They are not of our race. They do not even become settlers. They come to British Columbia and work for a little time, make a little money, and then return to their own country, taking the money with them. Then there are moral reasons, which one need not discuss here, which render the presence of the Mongolian race very undesirable.[30]

Prime Minister Mackenzie King in 1922 said:

If I am correct – and I believe I am – in the assertion that it is a great economic law that the lower civilization will, if permitted to compete with the higher, tend to drive the higher out of existence, or drag it down to the lower level, then we see the magnitude of the question viewed as a great national problem.[31]

King reiterated the then-familiar contention that "it is impossible to ever hope to assimilate a white population with the races of the Orient''; indeed, even to contemplate assimilation would be to bring Canadians "face to face with the loss of that homogeneity which ought to characterize the people of this country if we are to be a great nation.''[32] The massive internment of Japanese Canadians during World War II and the refusal to accept Jewish refugees from Europe before and during World War II (''None Is Too Many''),[33] consigning many to the Holocaust, along with the long-standing policy of Asian exclusion reflected a community's collective resolve to define its communal values and characteristics. While communitarianism need not *necessarily* imply these policies, a moral license to exclude, expel, or intern individuals who are "not like us" carries a much higher risk than liberal values that majoritarian passions and prejudices will override the individual freedoms central to the commitment of all liberal theories to the equal moral worth of all individuals. Emphasizing commonalties rather than differences is a natural corollary of liberal values. The atrocities committed over the course of history as a result of tribalism, ethnocentrism, "ethnic cleansing," religious fanaticism, and ideological collectivism (e.g., Stalinism) are a tragic testament to this risk. The ethnic and religious conflicts that are currently manifesting themselves in the fragmenting countries of Eastern Europe and the former Soviet Union, the Middle East, Northern Ireland, Africa, India, and other parts of Asia suggest that the lessons of history have not been fully learned.[34]

V. Empirical evidence on the welfare effects of immigration

While the welfare effects of immigration policy have not traditionally received anything like the attention that has been devoted to other aspects of international economics, fortunately recent theoretical and empirical work[35] has begun to yield a fairly clear consensus on the effects of immigration, despite the fact that this consensus is sharply at variance, in many respects with widely held popular perceptions.

First, as with the analysis of international trade, it is crucial to distinguish the national from the cosmopolitan (or global) perspective. From a global economic perspective, I take it that it is largely beyond dispute that open immigration is the optimal global strategy, with some well-defined qualifications. The argument for this is quite straightforward: open immigration encourages human resources to move to their most productive uses, whatever the localized distributional impact in countries of emigration or immigration. Hamilton and Whalley, for example, provide estimates for 1977 that the gain from removing all restrictions on international immigration could exceed worldwide GNP in that year.[36] More qualified estimates would still yield gains constituting a significant proportion of world GNP and exceeding gains from removing all trade restrictions.[37] As Alan Sykes stresses in Chapter 8 of this volume, the most important qualification of this proposition is fiscally induced migration driven by a desire to access entitlement systems, such as social welfare, social security, and public health care systems in other countries. Obviously, migration undertaken for these reasons may not entail a redeployment or relocation of human resources to more productive uses. While both the open global immigration base case and its principal qualification are obvious enough, it is important not to lose sight of either, because from an economic perspective the base case suggests that domestic debates about immigration policy almost by definition pertain to distributional issues, about which economics as a discipline has a limited amount to say, beyond clarifying the actual distributional impacts of alternative policies.[38] The qualification is also important because it suggests economic, as opposed to distributional, reasons for adopting particular selection mechanisms for admitting new immigrants, or alternatively attaching limitations on their access to noncontributory public services.

The three most recent and comprehensive reviews of the empirical evidence on the effects of immigration – by Borjas, Simon, and the Economic Council of Canada – establish a fairly clear consensus on certain propositions and some differences on others. First, despite recurrent debates over Canada's history and that of other countries as to their "absorptive capacity" and vacillations between catastrophic Malthusian scenarios and scenarios where immigration is perceived as the central driving force in opening up the New World,[39] recent evidence now appears to establish that immigrants as a whole raise the average income of natives, principally in two ways: by a scale effect and by a dependency effect. The scale effect simply means that countries with a larger and more rapidly growing population will be able to sustain some industries and some social infrastructure activities that would not be economically viable at smaller population sizes. There is some difference of opinion among analysts on the magnitude of the scale effects. The Economic Council of Canada estimates these effects to be quite modest, finding that for every additional 1 million persons – a figure that could be attained through a net immigration rate of say 100,000 per year over a decade – GDP per capita in Canada would be increased by somewhere between 0.1 and 0.3 percent (about $71 per present resident). The council estimates that on the basis of today's production technology and capital investment, a population of approximately 100 million people in Canada (compared with the present 26 million) would maximize income per person as measured by GDP per capita. At that population size, the average income of Canadians would be roughly 7 percent higher than that of today's population.[40] However, long-term projections of this kind, entailing a population increase of this order of magnitude, seem highly unlikely to capture a number of intervening variables that may completely undermine the welfare judgment. While not assigning specific numeric weights to the gains from scale associated with a larger population, Simon argues that apart from scale effects per se, dynamic effects, such as broader diffusion of technological and other ideas and greater possibilities for learning by doing, may generate quite significant positive effects on average native incomes from a larger population.[41] I do not find Simon's arguments especially convincing, particularly in a country the size of the

United States, and particularly in an international environment where scale effects, most notably in capital- rather than labor-intensive industries, can often be captured by trading into foreign markets and do not require a large local employment or consumer base.

The dependency effect means simply that because immigrants on average tend to be disproportionately represented in the wage-earning age group, and relatively underrepresented in the younger and older age groups, the dependency ratio for immigrants will typically be lower than that for natives.[42] This implies that on average immigrants will contribute more through taxes and take out less in public expenditures than natives.[43] The Economic Council of Canada estimated that the net gain per capita from a doubling of the recently prevailing annual immigration to Canada from 0.4 to 0.8 percent of the present population – that is, going from about 160,000 immigrants a year to 340,000 by the year 2015, would be $78 per capita.[44] Adding the council's estimated scale gains to the gross savings in tax costs of dependency and subtracting the expenses associated with processing the extra immigrants yield an estimate that, by 2015, a doubling in the immigration rate would raise per capita incomes by $350 – approximately 1 percent of expected annual income at that time.[45] This increase in average incomes of residents is still quite modest and, because it entails an aggregation function, may obscure quite uneven distributional impacts on different subsets of the resident population. Some of these are mentioned later.

Beyond these general effects of immigration on average native incomes, other propositions are also reasonably well settled. First, taking immigrants as a group, including refugees, labor force participation rates, unemployment rates, and participation in welfare assistance programs, both in the United States and in Canada, seem comparable, and in some cases superior, to the performance of the native population on average. Second, the bulk of the evidence, both for the United States and internationally, suggests that while immigrants, following entry, start off earning less on average than their native counterparts, this gap closes in 10 to 15 years, and indeed after that point immigrants may earn more on average than their native counterparts. Third, the evidence suggests that immigrants exert no or minimal job displacement effects on natives' jobs, including the jobs of those from less skilled and minority subgroups, and cause no or minimal depression of the latter's incomes. Fourth, the evidence suggests that immigrants on average are better educated than is the native population on average. Fifth, residents' discriminatory attitudes toward immigrants of different racial, ethnic, or cultural backgrounds seem to decline markedly with increased contact.[46]

All of this is to suggest that not only do natives gain, perhaps modestly, from immigration, but that immigrants themselves, presumably reflecting a rational calculus favoring moving in the first place, also substantially improve their lot in life and, on most performance measures, do at least as well as the native population. Thus the Economic Council of Canada concludes:

Immigration offers a rare chance for a policy change where everyone can gain. Those already here gain a little more real income, a more excitingly diverse society, and the satisfaction of opening up to others the great opportunities that living in Canada gives. Among those who come, some gain safety from persecution, some gain freedom from want, some gain a secure future for their children, and nearly all become economically better off.[47]

In other words, a liberal immigration policy seems to represent a Pareto-superior policy, relative to alternative policy scenarios involving highly restrictive immigration policies. However, if all of this is true, and a liberal immigration policy has this attractive Pareto quality – unlike almost any other major public policy one can identify – we must then confront a major puzzle: why is immigration policy one of the most politically sensitive and divisive issues on the national agenda in Canada, the United States, and many other countries? This seems to me a question worth focusing on, because it may suggest that some important dimensions are missing from the recent economic analysis.

One line of explanation is that the empirical findings summarized here obviously largely reflect historical experience and are only weak indicators of the possible effects of immigration at much higher levels or with sharply different compositions in the future than in the past. Another line of explanation is that the findings are generally accurate, but they mask effects that can be uncovered only by disaggregating the data. In effect, this is the position taken by Borjas.[48] While accepting most of the findings summarized here, he argues that the most recent immigrants (e.g., from about 1975 onward) performed markedly less well than prior immigrants in the early post–World War II decades, and indeed in some cases worse than the average native population. He cites empirical data that would suggest that labor market participation rates for recent immigrants are significantly lower, unemployment rates significantly higher, education levels lower, and participation in welfare assistance programs higher than those for immigrants who came to the United States in the 1950s and 1960s and, in some cases, worse than the native performance rates.[49] Borjas argues that because of the dominant role played by family class immigration and refugees, only 4 percent of legal immigrants qualified to enter the United States in 1987 on account of their own skills,[50] although puzzlingly he also claims that the empirical evidence shows that family class immigrants outperform independent immigrants and that successive members in the family immigration chain outperform earlier members.[51]

These changes in the economic performance of immigrants, of course, parallel a dramatic shift in the composition of the immigrant flow, with immigrants to the United States from Europe declining from 52.7 percent between 1951 and 1960 to 11.1 percent between 1981 and 1986, while Asian immigration increased from 6.1 to 47.4 percent over these time periods.[52] Canada has also experienced a similarly dramatic change in its immigration demographics: over the period 1956–62, 84 percent of immigrants came from Europe and 3 percent from Asia. In the period 1977–90, 20 percent came from Europe and 42 percent from Asia.[53] While Borjas claims that Canada is beginning to experience the same deterioration in the performance of recent immigrants as the United States,[54] the Economic Council of Canada is much more cautious in its assessment.[55] The proportion of persons with only elementary education has slightly increased among recent immigrants, but the latter also include a higher proportion of university-educated persons than the native population. Knowledge of the English language has also declined with recent waves of immigrants. The council found no evidence that immigrants from the new source countries have consistently lower labor force participation rates than those from traditional source countries, although there was a decline in the participation rate for immigrants arriving in the 1980s. While unemployment rates are generally lower for immigrants than natives (8.2 percent compared with 10.8 percent), for immigrants arriving between 1978 and 1983 the rate has been slightly higher – 11.2 percent compared with 10.8 percent for natives – and for immigrants arriving in the period 1983–6 the unemployment rate was 16 percent. However, the council was unable to find any significant changes in the characteristics of the most recent immigrants relative to those who had arrived, for example, between 1978 and 1982, and was therefore not prepared to attribute changes in labor force participation rates to changing immigrant characteristics. With respect to participation in welfare programs, 12.5 percent of immigrants who came during the period 1981–6 received welfare compared with 1.7 percent of immigrants who came between 1976 and 1980, and 13.8 percent of the native-born population. Again these statistics are not suggestive of a dramatic decline in the economic performance of immigrants, especially when one bears in mind that the recent arrivals, being most weakly integrated into the labor force, were likely to be affected more severely by the recessionary environment of the late 1980s than longer-standing residents.

Whatever the correct interpretation of the data on the economic performance of recent immigrants, it is not clear what policy implications flow from the more adverse of the possible interpretations. Obviously, the world of the 1950s and early 1960s cannot be re-created, and neither Canada nor the United States has the ability to coerce more skilled immigrants from more traditional countries of origin to migrate to North America. Nor does it make any more sense to bribe such immigrants to come through collective inducement. If employers require their services, it would seem a sufficient response for immigration policy to put as few impediments as possible in the way of such employment decisions, but otherwise resurrecting assisted passage programs, or similar programs, would seem a misallocation of resources. Moreover, while recent immigrants may on average be doing worse than their predecessors, in many cases their performance does not seem substantially inferior to that of the native-born population, or to large segments of it, recognizing, on the one hand, the difficult recessionary environment in which they have had to cope in the late 1980s and early 1990s and, on the other hand, the more substantial challenge of integration that they face, given their typically very different ethnic, linguistic, and cultural backgrounds. Before concluding that drastic changes in our current immigration policy, or more specifically major restrictions on the current flow of immigrants, are warranted, it would seem prudent to wait and see how the second generation of these immigrant families performs. Indeed, in a five-year immigration plan tabled by the Canadian government in Parliament in 1990, an increase in the annual immigrant intake from about 190,000 to 250,000 over the five-year period is planned (about 1 percent of the total population) – an increase endorsed by all of the major political parties at the time and reaffirmed by most major political parties in the 1993 federal elections, despite the severe recessionary environment. When the plan is fully phased in, it contemplates family class admissions of 85,000 (34 percent), a refugee class of 53,000 (21 percent), independent immigrants and their dependents of 62,000 (25 percent), assisted relatives and their dependents of 30,000 (12 percent), and business immigrants and their dependents of 19,000 (8 percent).

VI. The choice of optimal immigration policies

As noted earlier, many economists see virtues in an auction system for quotas, assuming entry is to be limited. The appeal of auctioned quotas or visas to economists is obvious: one would assume that the immigrants who purchase these visas will be those who value the opportunity to immigrate most highly, principally because they are confident that the employment or business opportunities available to them in the country of immigration will warrant the investment in the quota, reflecting the higher value that residents place on their potential contributions. One can also view an auction system as a means of extracting monopsony rents from immigrants, analogous to the optimal tariff in trade theory.[56] The proponents of an auctioned quota system seem to accept that whatever its economic virtues, the system is politically untenable at this time, although none bothers to explore in great detail why this may be so. However, there seem compelling reasons in principle why an auction quota system cannot be assigned a central role in allocating entry

positions to immigrants. Assuming there are good humanitarian and compassionate reasons for preserving a central role for family reunification policies, there would seem to be no role here for an auction quota system, and
immigrants entering under this category account for the bulk of all immigrants. Equally, humanitarian and compassionate reasons, as well as international treaty obligations under the Geneva Convention on Refugees, make
it untenable to screen refugees on this basis. In Canada as of 1992, about 70
percent of all immigrants were family class, assisted relatives, or refugees.
Thus the auction quota system could apply only to independent immigrants
and business-class applicants (entrepreneurs, self-employed persons, or investors) – about 27 percent of all applicants, including their accompanying
spouses and dependents. The numbers cited by Sykes (Chapter 8, this volume) as to the distribution of visas by applicant category under the 1990
U.S. Immigration Act suggest a somewhat similar breakdown. With respect
to independent immigrants, typically seeking skilled employment, an auction
system seems both inefficient and unfair: inefficient, because given the well-
known difficulties of borrowing money against future employment income
or human capital (which is the rationale for, e.g., most student assistance
programs), many efficient relocation decisions may not be made; and unfair
simply because it penalizes those with few present resources, whatever the
future contributions they may make to the country of immigration – a premise
that is obviously central to the family reunification program and to a lesser
extent the refugee program. This would leave only the business immigrant
category, which, with spouses and dependents, accounts for only 11 percent
of all immigrants entering Canada, where the scheme could easily be oper-
ationalized and where it may well have some virtues, although even here I
have some misgivings about imposing an entry tax on small-scale entrepreneurs and self-employed individuals.

If we are not prepared to allocate scarce entry entitlements through the
market, what are we left with? First, I think we should be prepared to challenge more squarely the notion that entry places should be nearly as limited
as they are. As Simon points out, with much tighter ceilings than those con-
templated under the 1990 U.S. Immigration Act, in 1981 there were only a
million people on the U.S. waiting list for admission.[57] Admittedly, the costs,
uncertainties, and delays associated with queuing presumably discourage
many more potential immigrants from applying, but nevertheless one should
not assume that with a much more permissive system, North America would
be likely to be overrun by immigrants, and even if substantial increases were
to be permitted over time, the empirical findings summarized earlier provide
little basis for concerns over the likely effects of a higher level of immigration.

In addition to the restrictions on the total volume of immigration, I am deeply bothered by current policy in Canada, the United States, and elsewhere of placing caps or semibinding constraints on particular subclasses of applicants. Simon comments, ''As someone put in the 1960s, the desire for zero population growth is simply a nonrational preference for round numbers.''[58] Similarly, total intake numbers or caps on categories of immigrants typically seem to reflect round numbers largely plucked out of the air. If the input criteria have been appropriately specified, it is not clear why one needs output criteria as well. For example, if we collectively support the admission of close relatives of existing citizens or permanent residents, we should simply let them in, with minimum requirements pertaining to health and security checks, and so on, particularly if, through family sponsorship, newly admitted family members must look for a substantial period of time principally to their families for assistance, and not to noncontributory public assistance programs; similarly, with the category of assisted relatives under the Canadian Immigration Act, where more distant relatives may be admitted subject to their satisfying a more relaxed form of the points system that applies to independent applicants. If a family already established here is prepared to make a credible and enforceable commitment to accepting financial responsibility for more distant relatives, they should be admitted. If such commitments cannot credibly be offered, more distant relatives should be processed through the independent applicant stream and be required to satisfy immigration officials that they are capable of sustaining themselves.

The independent-applicant category is that to which the points system adopted by Canada in 1967, and subsequently adopted with modifications elsewhere, applies. I am concerned about the degree of bureaucratic arbitrariness and discretion entailed in the application of this system. In Canada, a list of occupations is prepared by immigration officials, in consultation with other departments of government and the private sector, and various points are allocated to different job categories, reflecting alleged demand for workers in each category. This list is revised at frequent intervals, with occupations being added to or deleted from the list, and the point weightings being varied. For occupations not on this list, only prearranged job offers from a Canadian employer will attract sufficient points to make it possible to qualify, and then only if the employer is able to satisfy immigration authorities that there is not an appropriately qualified Canadian available to undertake the job.[59] Recent amendments to the Canadian Immigration Act would fine-tune the system by giving preference to immigrants prepared to locate in specified geographic areas of the country with labor shortages, for minimum periods of time.

Much of this bureaucratic effort strikes me as unnecessary, and indeed perverse. Manpower forecasting or manpower planning is notoriously among the least successful branches of economics, and making immigration decisions on the basis of perceived short-run labor market shortages or surpluses seems something that bureaucrats are least likely to do well. A much simpler points system that focuses on a few key variables, such as age, health, language facility, level of education and/or degree of any job experience and/or level of financial assets and/or prearranged job offers would seem the only kind of screens that could economically be justified.[60] Moreover, in the case of nonlisted or undesignated occupations, to require an employer to justify to the bureaucracy that he, she, or it is unable to find a suitably qualified Canadian strikes me as highly inefficient and invidious: obviously, an employer has all kinds of reasons to hire someone close at hand, if appropriately qualified, rather than hire someone (often sight unseen) from across the world. The present restrictions are really a transparent form of protectionism, and unfortunately they have been applied to one set of institutions where their impacts may be quite serious – the Canadian university system. If there is one set of employers that should be scouring the world for the best talent in particular fields, it is surely our institutions of higher learning, which are, par excellence, part of an international market in ideas, whether they like it or not.

I should add that I see no role at all for variables relating to applicants' ethnic or cultural backgrounds, despite efforts by Walzer and others to justify exclusions on grounds of preserving cultural homogeneity – "they are not like us."[61] This form of communitarianism has been invoked in the past to justify some of the most egregious forms of racial and religious discrimination in the history of Canada and the United States.

This leaves something to be said about the remaining categories of immigrants. First, there is the case of refugees, who in 1992 in Canada accounted for about 20 percent (50,000) of all immigrants admitted[62] – a dramatic increase from levels prevailing before the early 1980s.[63] While this is not the place to pursue in detail the design or reform of the refugee determination process, in Canada and, I sense, elsewhere this has become a costly and protracted process, with decisions made after full hearings on an individual basis and very few actual deportations occurring for unfounded claims at the end of this process. Here the legal system, driven in part by constitutional considerations, has not been especially helpful in requiring this highly individualized determination process. It is not clear why it would not be in everyone's interests to settle on a list of countries where irrebuttable or at least rebuttable presumptions apply to the effect that individuals making refugee claims from those countries have well-founded claims, and alternatively a list of countries where the opposite presumptions apply, biasing the presumptions in all cases of doubt in favor of claimants. By a substantial streamlining of the refugee determination process, refugees with well-founded claims can begin the process of social and economic integration more quickly, while deportation in some cases of unmeritorous claimants is facilitated. This is not to suggest that positive and negative presumptions can entirely eliminate the need for individual determinations of claims – for example, there may be suspicions that undocumented refugee claimants are misrepresenting their country of origin or that claimants are carrying forged documents that misrepresent their country of origin, or there may be cases where only certain groups or regions within a country can reasonably claim persecution and there is no reason to extend refugee status to other groups or regions within such a country. But even with these caveats a more generic approach to refugee determinations seems to have many virtues.

In addition, as the recent Dublin Convention agreed to by a number of members of the European Community suggests, an international agreement is needed on the identification of countries where asylum claims are to be made and evaluated in order to prevent either forum shopping by claimants or dumping of claimants by one country on another. This is an important issue for Canada, given that one-third of all refugee claims are made along the Canada–U.S. border. Agreement that the country of first asylum, if a safe third country, should make the refugee determination would drastically simplify the process, subject perhaps to some agreement on subsequent burden sharing. Recent amendments to the Canadian Immigration Act move in this direction. Again, the issues should not be oversimplified. Where a legitimate refugee claimant has no relatives, or no close linguistic, cultural, or religious affinities with citizens in the country of first asylum, international arrangements need to be sufficiently flexible to allow subsequent transfers to more congenial settings, while still avoiding multiple refugee determination processes or opportunistic forum shopping. The lack of uniformity in the application of the Geneva Convention refugee criteria and sharply different success rates by claimants overall and by different religious and racial groups from one signatory to another presently exacerbate these problems and suggest the need for further international collaboration in these respects if the safe-third-country principle is to be rendered both practicable and humane.

This leaves only the category of temporary workers for brief comment. Here I find compelling Simon's argument that foreign students in the United States or Canada on student visas, on successful completion of their studies, should be entitled to apply for permanent residence status, fairly much as of right.[64] This would clearly seem to be in the national interest. Whether it is welfare-enhancing from a global perspective entails somewhat indeterminate debates about the effect of the so-called brain drain on developing countries.[65] But given that this is also entailed in a number of the other long-established immigrant categories, it is not clear why this is a particular objection to providing successful students with the opportunity to become permanent residents. To the extent that they have received financial assistance with their studies from their countries of origin, presumably these countries can demand bonds or security from the student or his or her family to ensure reimbursement of this assistance.

Finally, as to other temporary workers, I am not as sanguine as Sykes (Chapter 8, this volume) that programs providing for legal, unskilled temporary immigrants, which he advocates, would be easy to design and administer. While it is true that temporary workers often contribute positively to the dependency ratio, partly because of their age and partly because they are not entitled to noncontributory forms of public assistance, the European experience suggests that it is very difficult to send these people home if they have been temporary workers for a number of years and they and their families have established roots in the community. Simon suggests various financial bonding arrangements to ensure departure on the expiration of temporary work visas,[66] and Sykes sees such a program as a strong substitute for illegal or undocumented immigration. However, many temporary workers may simply go "underground" upon the expiration of their visas and become illegal or undocumented aliens. With a transient population such as is presumably often involved with unskilled guest-worker programs, it is not clear how easy it would be to design and enforce the bonding arrangements that Simon has in mind. In any event, both efficiency and humanitarian considerations seem to dictate that if a guest worker has worked productively in the country of immigration for any significant period of time, he or she should be entitled to apply for permanent residence status, perhaps applying the points system (without caps) referred to earlier and treating his or her work experience as a substitute for other forms of education, training, or financial assets. In this respect, the recent withdrawal of the right of temporary domestic workers to apply for landed immigrant status from within Canada after two years of service seems a retrograde and repressive step.[67]

I reemphasize my opposition to arbitrary caps on the total immigrant intake or on categories of applicants within the total intake. If input criteria are designed and applied sensibly, we should live with whatever numeric outcomes emerge in administering these input criteria. Moreover, attempts to fine-tune the specification and application of the selection criteria seem misplaced.

VII. Conclusion

The enormous volume of refugees or otherwise necessitous persons currently seeking resettlement in developed countries of the world, often from cultural, linguistic, religious, and racial backgrounds that are in many respects quite different from those of refugee claimants of previous periods and sharply different from those of the majority of the indigenous population of developed countries, places extreme strains on domestic immigration policies in developed countries and the social and political consensus surrounding the appropriate form of these policies. In moderating these strains, it is crucial to identify key linkages between immigration policies and other classes of international and domestic policies and in so doing not to impose on immigration policy more weight than it can reasonably bear.

In this respect, it is clear that the level of demand for resettlement would be substantially diminished if developed countries, through appropriate forms of international cooperation, took stronger and more effective policy stances toward human rights violations and political or religious oppression in many countries of origin. In addition, much more liberal trade policies toward developing-country exports, the provision of more generous forms of foreign aid in cases of natural disasters, and more effective forms of developmental aid in forms, or with conditions attached, designed to address and (if necessary) discipline governmental incompetence and corruption that is often pervasive in many developing and former command economies, are clearly important substitutes for immigration. For foreign aid to be fully effective, developing and former command economies must be encouraged to adopt domestic policies that promote high levels of economic growth at home. A key element of such policies is outward-looking trade policies that assign substantial weight to export-led growth and a concomitant reduction in reliance on trade and currency restrictions designed to foster often inefficient import-substituting domestic industries. Unfortunately, in this respect, reflecting the massive hypocrisy of many Western countries, the costs of protectionist policies imposed by developed countries on developing countries currently exceed the entire value of foreign aid provided to these countries.[68]

In short, all other things being equal, it seems clear that most refugees or displaced persons would prefer to return to their homelands, but the policies of most developed countries do not reflect this priority. Instead, the consequences of displacement are seen primarily as an immigration problem, where effective policy responses are highly circumscribed or in any event intensely controversial. It must be added that while growth-oriented development policies are likely to reduce migration rates over the long term, evidence suggests that in the shorter term the disruptive impacts of rapid development on traditional social and economic structures in developing countries (e.g., rural–urban migration and saturated urban labor markets) may actually increase international migration.[69] This said, however, the insights from recent empirical work on immigration tell us that perhaps within some broad parameters that we presently seem well inside, we could benefit modestly, and potential immigrants very substantially, from a much higher level of immigration than most developed countries are presently committed to and that a few basic proxies (simple decision rules) for determining the probable success in the country of immigration, or refugee status, are all that can be justified. The facts (as opposed to the prejudices) suggest that national and cosmopolitan perspectives on immigration policy do not sharply diverge.

Notes

Portions of this essay are reprinted with permission of the publishers from *The Limits of Freedom of Contract* by Michael J. Trebilcock, Harvard University Press, Cambridge, Mass.; copyright © 1993 by the President and Fellows of Harvard College.

1 See Sharon Russell and Michael Teitelbaum, *International Migration and International Trade* (Washington, D.C.: World Bank Discussion Paper no. 160, 1992), 1, 9.
2 *The Economist*, December 23, 1989, 17 et. seq.; *The Economist*, November 13, 1993, 45.
3 Joseph Carens, "Aliens and Citizens: The Case for Open Borders," *Review of Politics* 47 (1987): 251.
4 Robert Nozick, *Anarchy, State and Utopia* (Oxford: Basil Blackwell, 1974).
5 John Rawls, *A Theory of Justice* (Cambridge, Mass.: Harvard University Press, 1971).
6 Carens, "Aliens and Citizens," 256.
7 Joseph Carens, "Membership and Morality: Admission to Membership in Liberal Democratic States," in William Rogers Brubaker (ed.), *Immigration and the Politics of Citizenship in Europe and North America* (New York: University Press of America, 1989).
8 Donald Galloway, "Liberalism, Globalism and Immigration," *Queen's Law Journal* 18 (1993): 266.
9 Carens, "Aliens and Citizens." 263.
10 Peter H. Schuck, "The Transformation of Immigration Law," *Columbia Law Review* 84 (1984): 1 at 6.
11 Michael Walzer, *Spheres of Justice* (New York: Basic Books, 1983), chap. 2.
12 Ibid., 61–2.
13 Robert L. Heilbroner, *The Worldly Philosophers: The Lives, Times, and Ideas of the Great Economic Thinkers*, 5th ed. (New York: Simon & Schuster, 1980), 76.
14 See, e.g., Julian L. Simon, *The Economic Consequences of Immigration* (Oxford: Basil Blackwell, 1989), 329–35; George J. Borjas, *Friends or Strangers: The Impact of Immigrants on the U.S. Economy* (New York: Basic Books, 1990), 225–7.
15 *The Economist*, March 3, 1990, 18; November 13, 1993, 45.
16 Walzer, *Spheres of Justice,* 51.
17 Ibid., 4.
18 Ibid.
19 Carens, "Membership and Morality."
20 Joseph Carens, "Migration and Morality: A Liberal Egalitarian Perspective," in

Brian Barry and Robert Gordin (eds.), *Free Movement* (London: Harvester-Wheatsheaf, 1992), 25 at 36–40.

21 Ibid., 38.
22 Ibid.
23 Ibid.
24 Walzer, *Spheres of Justice,* 46.
25 For an excellent discussion of the somewhat indeterminate debates on the effects of emigration on developing countries, see Simon, *Economic Consequences,* chap. 14; see also Jagdish Bhagwati, *Political Economy and Economics* (Cambridge, Mass: MIT Press, 1991), chaps. 18–20.
26 See Russell and Teitelbaum, *International Migration,* 28–32.
27 Carens, "Aliens and Citizens," 268.
28 Walzer, *Spheres of Influence,* 60.
29 Audrey Macklin, "The History of Asian Immigration," mimeo, University of Toronto Law School, 1987, 69.
30 *The Colonist,* April 13, 1884, 2.
31 House of Commons Debates; Official Report, 1922 (Ottawa: Queen's Printer), 1555.
32 Ibid., 1555–6.
33 Irving Abella and Harold Troper, *None Is Too Many: Canada and the Jews of Europe, 1933–1948* (Toronto: Lester & Orphan Dennys, 1982).
34 See Arthur Schlesinger, Jr., *The Disuniting of America: Reflections on a Multicultural Society* (New York: Norton, 1992), 10, 11.
35 See Simon, *Economic Consequences*; Borjas, *Friends or Strangers*; Economic Council of Canada, *Economic and Social Impacts of Immigration* (Ottawa: Supply and Services, 1991).
36 Bob Hamilton and John Whalley, "Efficiency and Distributional Implications of Global Restrictions on Labour Mobility: Calculations and Policy Implications," *Journal of Development Economics* 14 (1984): 61.
37 Ibid., 73–5.
38 See W. L. Marr and M. B. Percy, "Immigration Policy and Canadian Economic Growth," in John Whalley (ed.), *Domestic Policies and the International Economic Environment* (Research Vol. 12 for the Macdonald Royal Commission on the Economic Union and Development Prospects for Canada, Supply and Services Ottawa, 1985), 71 et. seq.
39 See Alan G. Green, *Immigration and the Post-War Canadian Economy* (Toronto: Macmillan, 1976), chap. 1; David Corbett, *Canada's Immigration Policy* (Toronto: University of Toronto Press, 1957), 103 et. seq.
40 Economic Council of Canada, *Economic and Social Impacts,* 25.
41 Simon, *Economic Consequences,* chap. 8.
42 Ibid., chap. 5.
43 This implication is strongly contested by Donald Huddle in a recent study, "The Costs of Immigration" (Rice University, Department of Economics, June 4, 1993), in which he claims that over the 1993–2002 period the net cost to U.S. taxpayers of all immigrants will total more than $450 billion.

44 Economic Council of Canada, *Economic and Social Impacts,* 50.
45 Ibid., 51.
46 Ibid., chap. 9.
47 Ibid., 141.
48 Borjas, *Friends or Strangers.*
49 Ibid., chaps. 8 and 9.
50 Ibid., 32.
51 Ibid., chap. 11.
52 Ibid., 36.
53 Economic Council of Canada, *Economic and Social Impacts,* 11.
54 Borjas, *Friends or Strangers,* chap. 12.
55 Economic Council of Canada, *Economic and Social Impacts,* chap. 7.
56 See Chapter 8 by Sykes, this volume.
57 Simon, *Economic Consequences,* 49.
58 Ibid., 30.
59 See Gary L. Segal, *Immigrating to Canada,* 9th ed. (Vancouver: Self-Counsel Press, 1990), chap. 9.
60 See *Royal Commission on the Economic Union and Development Prospects for Canada* (Macdonald Commission) (Ottawa: Supply and Services, 1985), 2: 668.
61 Walzer, *Spheres of Justice.*
62 See Immigration Canada, Annual Report to Parliament, Immigration Plan for 1991–5, November 1991.
63 For data on the dramatic increase in refugee claims in Canada, see Economic Council of Canada, *Economic and Social Impacts,* 97; more generally, on the dramatic increase in the number of refugees in the world, see *The Economist,* December 23, 1989, "The Year of the Refugee," 17 et. seq.
64 Simon, *Economic Consequences,* 315–18.
65 Ibid., chap 14.
66 Simon, *Economic Consequences,* 302.
67 See Audrey Macklin, "Foreign Domestic Worker: Surrogate Housewife or Mail Order Servant?" *McGill Law Journal* 37 (1992): 681.
68 See John Whalley, "The North–South Debate and the Terms of Trade: An Applied Equilibrium Approach" *Review of Economics and Statistics* 66 (1984): 224, 231–323.
69 See Russell and Teitelbaum, *International Migration,* 33, 34.